THE GREEKS AT WAR

FROM ATHENS TO ALEXANDER

**Philip de Souza,
Waldemar Heckel
& Lloyd Llewellyn-Jones**

Foreword by **Victor Davis Hanson**

First published in Great Britain in 2004 by Osprey Publishing,
Elms Court, Chapel Way, Botley, Oxford OX2 9LP, UK
Email: info@ospreypublishing.com

Previously published as Essential Histories 36: *The Greek
and Persian Wars 499–386 BC*, Essential Histories 27: *The
Peloponnesian War 431–404 BC*, and Essential Histories 26: *The
Wars of Alexander the Great*

ISBN 1 84176 856 1

Editor: Anita Hitchings
Design: Ken Vail Graphic Design, Cambridge, UK
Cartography by The Map Studio
Index by Glyn Sutcliffe
Originated by Grasmere Digital Imaging, Leeds, UK
Printed and bound in China by L. Rex Printing Company Ltd.

04 05 06 07 08   10 9 8 7 6 5 4 3 2 1

For a catalogue of all books published by Osprey Publishing
please contact:

Osprey Direct UK, PO Box 140,
Wellingborough, Northants, NN8 2FA, UK.
Email: info@ospreydirect.co.uk

Osprey Direct USA, c/o MBI Publishing,
PO Box 1, 729 Prospect Ave,
Osceola, WI 54020, USA.
Email: info@ospreydirectusa.com

www.ospreypublishing.com

Contents

Foreword
by Victor Davis Hanson

What we know about the Greek city-states at war mostly begins with their desperate struggle to hold off the Persians between 490 BC and 479 BC – the dramatic Hellenic victories at Marathon, Salamis and Plataea, the historic but failed defence of Thermopylae, and the final pursuit of the Persians across the Aegean at Mycale. From our exciting ancient accounts of these battles, there emerges a peculiar – and especially lethal – way of fighting embraced by these small Greek communities. War making based on shock tactics, group discipline, superior technology, and an audit of military operations by civilian governments trumps numbers and, in fact, presages the Western way of war as it evolved centuries hence.

Phalanxes of heavily-armed infantrymen (hoplites) proved unbeatable on level ground against the far more numerous but lighter-armed and less-disciplined Persians. At sea, victorious Greek triremes reflected not merely the excellence of Greek naval technology, but the empowerment of the lower classes who, from their brilliant seamanship at Salamis, won full participation in radical Athenian democracy.

However, the miracle of the Greek victory over Xerxes' Persians also soon led to an uneasy partnership between the land power Sparta and the maritime Athenians. True, their respective preeminent armies and navies kept Persia on its side of the Aegean for the next half-century, but the growing rivalry between them also turned fifth-century Greece into a bipolar world of Athenian democratic imperialism set against Sparta's coalition of rural oligarchic states.

Civil war broke out in 431 and then raged for the next 27 years. Sparta proved to be as incapable of drawing the Athenians into a hoplite battle as the Athenian fleet was in conquering the Laconian homeland.

The results of the subsequent three-decade-long war of attrition were the great plague at Athens that killed off over a quarter of the population, the Athenian catastrophe at Syracuse where 40,000 of Athens' imperial troops never returned home from Sicily, and a terrible last decade of naval warfare in which over 400 Spartan and Athenian triremes were lost in the eastern Aegean.

The defeat of Athens in 404 did not lead to a permanent Spartan empire, but instead to near constant fighting in the subsequent fourth century. Thebes, Sparta and Athens all learned the military lessons of the Peloponnesian War and increasingly broadened their armed forces to include mercenaries, light-armed and missile troops, and integrated cavalry forces. To the north King Philip II of Macedon was watching these developments eagerly, as he radically modified the old Greek phalanx of citizen soldiers into pike-yielding phalangites – hired professionals who, along with a crack heavy cavalry of landed aristocrats, formed the core of a new national Macedonian army. Along with such a novel and potent military, Philip and his young son Alexander also promoted a new propaganda: only Greek unification under Macedonian leadership could avenge Persia's invasion of Greece nearly 150 years earlier.

After the final defeat of the free Greek states at Chaeronea, and despite the murder of Philip himself, in 334 the 23-year-old Alexander led a small army of 40,000 into Asia Minor in a grand effort to 'liberate' the Greek city-states of Ionia and dismantle the Persian Empire. After three great battles at Granicus, Issus and Gaugamela, by 331 the empire of Dareios III was in Alexander's hands. But the 20-something prince kept pressing eastward, defeating an Indian royal army at the Hydaspes river, before meeting near mutiny on the borders of India and then subsequently almost ruining his army in a disastrous trek back to Babylon through the unforgiving Gedrosian desert. Exhausted, sick and increasingly paranoid, Alexander died in 333, leaving his vast newly acquired, but hardly pacified empire to be fought over and divided by his surviving Macedonian marshals.

The small amateur armies that had once stopped Xerxes at Thermopylae had now come full circle, as Greek-speaking soldiers found themselves 3,500 miles to the east on the borders of India. If an empire of a million square miles and over 50 million subjects once threatened to make a tiny and squabbling Greece its westernmost satrapy, a century-and-a-half later it lay in ruins thanks to the rampage of Alexander and his lethal Macedonians.

These Persian and Peloponnesian Wars, and the conquest of Alexander the Great, are the themes of a new Osprey offering in its welcomed Essential Histories Specials series. The work of Philip de Souza and Waldemar Heckel offers far more than a narrative history but rather analyses how the Greeks fought on land and sea, in making sense of the seemingly impossible Greek achievement. Yet because it is often difficult to learn of Greek military practice from ancient historians alone, the authors also offer a variety of critical aids to enhance their scholarly analysis, itself based on an array of archaeological, epigraphical, and artistic evidence.

Coloured maps, plentiful photographs, and drawings augment time-lines, glossaries, mini-biographies, and excerpts from ancient historians. Of particular interest is the occasional focus on individual Greeks – Aristodemos and Demaratos, Hipparete, or Callisthenes – whose own private stories help us understand the radical events of the times. These biographical sketches remind us that history is made by real people.

More importantly, the Osprey history is not the usual bland retelling of events so often found in surveys of ancient military practice. Philip de Souza, for example, notes the irony that Sparta's victory over Athens did not liberate the Greeks, but instead substituted an arrogant and poorly run hegemony in place of a coercive but perhaps enlightened empire, leading to a peace imposed by Persia – the original common enemy that had earlier brought the two Greek powers together in the first place. And Waldemar Heckel ends his account of Alexander's startling conquest by emphasising the young conqueror's lack of foresight in establishing a clear succession, a lapse that meant his successor Generals would kill more of each other's armies than were lost to the Persians during Alexander's initial conquest.

The Osprey survey of classical military history is accessible, reliable, and a joy to read. These wars are really not so ancient after all, and will remind us that besides culture and politics, military dynamism is also part of our Hellenic heritage from those most remarkable ancient Greeks.

Chronology

559	Kyros the Great becomes king of Anshan in Persia	**492**	Persians remove tyrants from Ionian Greek states
550	Kyros takes control of the Median Empire	**491**	Dareios demands that all Greek states submit to Persian rule
547	Kyros conquers Lydia and captures Kroisos	**490**	Aigina defeats Athens in sea battle; Persians capture Naxos;
539	Kyros conquers Babylon		Persians defeated in the battle of Marathon
530	Death of Kyros and accession of Kambyses	**486**	Death of Dareios; Xerxes becomes king of Persia
527	Death of Peisistratos; Hippias becomes ruling tyrant of Athens	**484**	Birth of Herodotus
525	Kambyses invades Egypt	**483/82**	Ostracism of Aristeides; Athenians begin building fleet of 200 triremes
522	Death of Kambyses; assassination of Bardiya; Dareios becomes king of Persia; death of Polykrates, tyrant of Samos	**481**	Xerxes gathers forces at Sardis; Persian envoys sent to Greece; Hellenic League formed at Sparta; Athens and Aigina make peace
520/19	Dareios campaigns against the Skythians	**480**	Xerxes invades Greece; battles of Artemision and Thermopylai; Xerxes captures Athens; battle of Salamis; Xerxes returns to Asia Minor
519–18	Dareios extends Persian control over Ionians		
510	Hippias expelled from Athens		
508/07	Reforms of Kleisthenes; popular democracy established in Athens	**479**	Battles of Plataia and Mykale; some Ionians join Hellenic League
499	Persians attack island of Naxos; Aristagoras visits Athens and Sparta	**478**	Greek expeditions to Cyprus and Byzantion; recall of Pausanias to Sparta
498	Ionians, Eretrians and Athenians attack and burn Sardis	**478/77**	Formation of the Delian League
		465–64	Earthquake at Sparta; (Messenian) Helots revolt
497	Unsuccessful attempt by Ionians to aid Greeks of Cyprus against Persians	**462**	Spartans appeal for Athenian help against Messenians; Kimon's forces sent away by Spartans; reforms of Ephialtes; Athenians form alliance with Megara, Argos and Thessaly
497–96	Persian counter-offensive against Greeks in Asia Minor; death of Aristagoras		
494	Persians defeat Ionians in the battle of Lade	**461**	Ostracism of Kimon
493	Persian rule restored in Ionia and eastern Aegean; Themistokles elected archon at Athens	**459–54**	Athenian expedition to Cyprus and Egypt
		459	Athenians begin building their Long Walls

457	Battles of Tanagra and Oinophyta
456	Defeat of Messenians at Mt Ithome; Tolmides' expedition around the Peloponnese
c. 455	Thucydides the historian born
454	Delian League Treasury transferred to Athens (Tribute Lists begin)
451	Perikles' law on Athenian citizenship; five-year truce between Athens and Sparta; 50 year peace treaty between Sparta and Argos
c. 450	Alkibiades born
449	Peace of Kallias between Athens and Persia
447	Building of the Parthenon begun
446	Athenians defeated at battle of Koroneia and driven out of Boiotia; Thirty Years' Peace agreed between Athens and Sparta
c. 443	Athenians make treaties with Sicilian cities of Leontini and Rhegion
441–440	Revolt of Samos
c. 440	Hipparete born
439	Surrender of Samos
438	Dedication of the Parthenon
437/436	Foundation of Amphipolis
435	Conflict between Corinth and Corcyra over Epidamnos begins
433	Alliance of Athens and Corcyra; sea battle of Sybota; Athens renews treaties of alliance with Leontini and Rhegion
432	Revolt of Poteidaia; Megarian decrees
431–404	Peloponnesian War
431	Thebans attack Plataia; Peloponnesians invade Attika
430	Plague reaches Athens; Perikles' expedition to Peloponnese; Perikles is deposed as general and fined; Poteidaia surrenders to Athenians; Phormio's expedition to Naupaktos
429–27	Siege of Plataia

429	Death of Perikles
428–27	Revolt of Mytilene; *eisphora* tax levied in Athens
427–24	First Athenian expedition to Sicily
425	Athenians fortify Pylos; Spartans captured on island of Sphakteria; Spartan peace offer refused by Athenians
424	Athenians take Kythera and launch raids on Lakonian coast; Boiotians defeat Athenians at the battle of Delion; Brasidas captures Amphipolis; Thucydides the historian exiled
423	One year armistice between Athens and Sparta; revolts of Skione and Mende; Dareios II (Ochos) becomes king of Persia
422	Kleon and Brasidas killed at Amphipolis
421	Peace of Nikias; 50-year alliance concluded between Athens and Sparta
418	Battle of Mantinea
416	Athenians invade and capture Melos
415	Egesta appeals to Athens for help against Selinous; Second Athenian expedition to Sicily; Alkibiades recalled
414	Siege of Syracuse; death of Lamachos; Spartans send Gylippos to Syracuse
413	Athenians send reinforcements to Sicily; Spartans capture and fortify Dekeleia; defeat and surrender of Athenians in Sicily
412–11	Spartans and Persian king negotiate treaty; revolts of Athenian allies
411	Oligarchic revolution installs government of 400 in Athens; army and fleet at Samos remain loyal to democracy; Alkibiades takes command
410	Spartans defeated at Kyzikos; restoration of full democracy in Athens

409	Messenians driven out of Pylos; Spartans take control of Chios
408–407	Kyros the Younger sent to take control of Persia's western satrapies
407	Lysander takes control of Spartan fleet
406	Athenians defeated at Notion; Alkibiades goes into exile; Spartans defeated at battle of Arginousai; trial of Athenian generals
405	Athenians defeated at battle of Aigospotamoi
405–404	Siege of Athens; Death of Dareios II; Artaxerxes II becomes king of Persia
404	Peace between Athens and Sparta; Athenian Long Walls partially destroyed
404–403	Rule of Thirty Tyrants in Athens
401	Revolt of Kyros the Younger; Battle of Cunaxa; March of the ten Thousand
396–394	Agesilaus in Asia Minor
394–387/386	The Corinthian War
387/6	The King's Peace
371	Battle of Leuctra
360/359	Perdiccas killed in battle with Illyrians; accession of Philip II
359–336	Reign of Philip II of Macedon
356	Birth of Alexander the Great
353	Philip II's victory over the Phocians in the 'Crocus Field'
346	Peace of Philocrates; Philip becomes master of northern Greece
338	Battle of Chaeronea; Philip becomes undisputed military leader (hegemon) of Greece
337	Formation of the League of Corinth
336	Death of Philip; accession of Alexander the Great
335	Alexander campaigns in Illyria; destruction of Thebes
334	Beginning of the Asiatic expedition; battle of Granicus

	river; major coastal cities of Asia Minor fall to Alexander
333	Alexander cuts the Gordian knot; defeats Dareios III at Issus
332	Capture of Phoenician coastal cities; siege of Tyre and Gaza
332/331	Alexander in Egypt; founding of Alexandria at the mouth of the Nile
331	Dareios III defeated for the second time at Gaugamela in northern Mesopotamia
331/330	Capture of Babylon, Susa, Persepolis and Ekbatana
330	Death of Dareios and end of the official 'Panhellenic' War; Alexander moves into Afghanistan; execution of Philotas and Parmenion
329–327	War in Central Asia between the Amu-darya and Syr-darya (the Oxus and Iaxartes rivers)
328	Death of Kleitus; Alexander's political marriage to Roxane
327	Failed attempt to introduce proskynesis at the court; conspiracy of the pages; Alexander invades India
326	Battle of the Hydaspes (Jhelum) river; the Macedonian army refuses to cross the Hyphasis (Beas) river
325	Alexander at the mouth of the Indus
324	Alexander returns to Susa and punishes those guilty of maladministration in his absence
323	Death of Alexander in Babylon Distribution of power and satrapies at Babylon; Philip III and Alexander IV recognized as 'Kings'
323-320	First War of the Successors; Perdiccas' bid for supreme power
320	Deaths of Craterus and Perdiccas; Settlement of Triparadeisus; Antipater becomes guardian of the 'Kings'

319	Death of Antipater
319–317/6	Antigonus the One-Eyed at war with Eumenes in Asia; Cassander opposes Polyperchon and Olympias (the mother of Alexander)
317	Battle of Gabiene; Death of Eumenes; Murder of Philip III in Europe.
316	Capture of Pydna; Death of Olympias
315	Cassander refounds the city of Thebes, which Alexander had destroyed 20 years earlier;
312	Demetrius the Besieger's first battle; He is defeated by Ptolemy's general at Gaza
310	Murder of Alexander IV and his mother Rhoxane at Amphipolis
307–301	Demetrius controls Athens
306	Demetrius wins the battle of Salamis; Demetrius and Antigonus are declared 'kings' by their men; Other successors follow suit (Lysimachus, Ptolemy, Cassander and Seleucus)
301	Battle of Ipsus; Death of Antigonus
297	Cassander dies of illness
283	Death of Demetrius the Besieger
281	Battle of Corupedium. Lysimachus dies on the battlefield; Shortly afterward, Seleucus is murdered by Ptolemy Ceraunus
280–30	The era of the Hellenistic Kingdoms, concluding with the death of Cleopatra VII in 30 BC

NOTE ON DATES: All dates are BC. The official Athenian year, which was often used by Greek historians as a dating device, began and ended in midsummer. As a result some of the dates in this book are given in the form 478/77, which indicates the Athenian year that began in the summer of 478 and ended in the summer of 477.

Part 1
The Greek and Persian Wars
499 – 386 BC

Introduction

Herodotus and the invention of history

Part of the fascination of the Greek and Persian Wars lies in the fact that they had a great influence on the history of the western world. By preventing the Persians from conquering Greece, the Athenians, the Spartans and other Greeks made it possible for their own unique and highly influential culture to develop independently of Persian dominance. Equally important, however, is the fact that the events of the Persian Wars are recounted in one of the most important and influential works of Classical Greek literature, *The Histories* of Herodotus. Herodotus was born in the first half of the fifth century BC, in the Greek city

of Halikarnassos, which was on the edge of the Persian Empire. He travelled extensively, collecting information from people about themselves and their ancestors. He was able to talk to many who had experienced the events themselves, or who had heard first-hand accounts from others who were involved. The Persian Wars are, therefore, the first wars for which there exists a detailed historical narrative written by someone who was able to obtain detailed and reliable information. Herodotus' account can to some extent be supplemented by some other sources, including later Greek and Latin writers and the official documents of Athens and Persia, but he is the most significant source.

The idea of recording great achievements for posterity was not in itself a new one. Egyptian, Babylonian and Assyrian rulers had long been accustomed to setting up memorials to their own greatness, inscribing them with official versions of events. What makes Herodotus' work so special is that he sought to go beyond the mere collection of these records and to enquire into their origins and causes. He was consciously looking for explanations of the events. In this respect Herodotus can be seen as part of a much wider intellectual and cultural tradition of philosophical and scientific speculation and enquiry. There is also an element of learning from the events. Herodotus offers his readers his investigations into the origins and causes of the events he narrates, as well as his interpretations of their wider significance. He invites his readers to learn from his *Histories*, although some of his lessons can seem strange to a modern audience. This is how he introduces his account:

> *These are the enquiries* (the Greek word is 'histories') *of Herodotus of Halikarnassos, which he sets down so that he can preserve the memory of what these men have done, and ensure that the wondrous achievements of the Greeks and Persians* (he uses the Greek word *barbaroi*, meaning foreigners) *do not lose their deserved fame, and also to record why they went to war with each other.*

This relief sculpture from the Treasury section of the Achaemenid royal place at Persepolis was originally placed in the centre of the ceremonial staircase leading to the magnificent *Apadana* or audience hall. It shows an aristocrat in Median dress paying ritual homage to the king, probably Dareios. In front of the king are two incense-burners. Behind the throne stand his son, Xerxes, a eunuch attendant (he has no beard) and soldiers of the élite regiment of the King's Spearcarriers, who were all members of the Persian aristocracy. (Ancient Art and Architecture)

The tomb of Kyros the Great, the founder of the Persian
Empire (d. 530 BC). Alexander had Poulamachos,
a Macedonian, impaled for desecrating the tomb. (TRIP)

The coming of the Persians

The enquiries of the Greek historian Herodotus into the wars between the Greeks and the Persians led him to conclude that their origins lay in the rise to power of the Persian Empire under the first of the Achaemenid kings, Kyros the Great. It was Kyros who conquered the kingdom of Lydia in 547. The king of Lydia, Kroisos, had tried to take advantage of the turmoil caused by Kyros' seizure of the Median Empire by invading its western territories. Kyros met the Lydian king in battle in Kappadokia and forced him to withdraw. Kroisos stood his army down, thinking that there would be no further fighting, but Kyros pressed on to Sardis, the Lydian capital and laid siege to the city, which he captured after only two weeks. Kroisos had brought the prosperous Greek cities of Ionia on the western coast of Asia Minor under his rule and made them pay tribute to him. After his defeat they acknowledged the rule of Kyros, but many of them participated in a revolt of the Lydians and had to be brought back under Persian control by force. Some of the Greeks chose to flee overseas rather than submit to the Persians. Half the people of Phokaia emigrated to the western Mediterranean, where many Greek cities were already flourishing, and most of the inhabitants of Teos founded a new city at Abdera on the Thracian coast. The larger islands off the coast of Ionia retained their independence for some time, but by 518 the Persians controlled all of Asia Minor and most of the eastern Aegean islands, including Lesbos, Chios and Samos. In keeping with their practice elsewhere in the territories under their control the Persian kings installed or sponsored local aristocrats as rulers of the Greek cities of Asia Minor and the nearby islands. These men were called 'tyrants', a Lydian word used by the Greeks to describe an individual ruler who was not necessarily an hereditary monarch, but who had not been elected or put in power by overwhelming popular support. These local rulers were answerable to a Persian governor, called a 'satrap' – an Old Persian word meaning 'guardian of the land' – who normally resided in Sardis. The Persians also exacted tribute from the Ionians, probably at the same level as the Lydian kings before them.

The Ionian revolt

In 499 the Persians launched a major naval expedition against Naxos, the largest and most prosperous of the Cycladic islands. Herodotus presents this expedition as the result of an appeal by some exiled Naxian aristocrats to Aristagoras, the ruling tyrant of Miletos, to help them force their compatriots to accept them back and return them to power. Miletos was one of the largest and most important Ionian cities. It had enjoyed privileged, semi-independent status in relation to the Lydian kings, which the Persians allowed to continue. According to Herodotus' account Aristagoras said that he did not have sufficient resources to attack Naxos, but he persuaded Artaphernes, the Persian satrap of Lydia, to help. Artaphernes then obtained King Dareios' consent to assemble a fleet of 200 ships and a substantial Persian army to invade Naxos. It is unlikely that such a large force would have been authorised by the king unless he expected to conquer the island, paving the way for further Persian expansion across the Aegean. From Naxos it is only a short sail to the islands of Paros and Andros and thence

The Persian empire

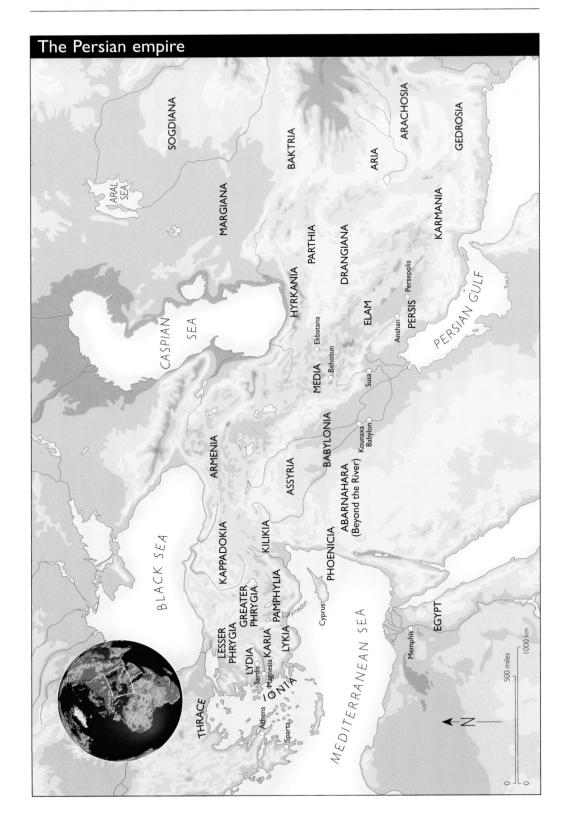

SOGDIANA

ARAL
SEA

MARGIANA

BAKTRIA

ARIA

ARACHOSIA

GEDROSIA

KARMANIA

PARTHIA

HYRKANIA

DRANGIANA

PERSIS ○ Persepolis

PERSIAN GULF

CASPIAN SEA

MEDIA ○ Ekbatana
○ Behistun

ELAM

Anshan ○

Susa ○

ARMENIA

ASSYRIA

BABYLONIA

Kounaxa ○ ○
Babylon

ABARNAHARA
(Beyond the River)

KAPPADOKIA

KILIKIA

PHOENICIA

BLACK SEA

LESSER
PHRYGIA

GREATER
PHRYGIA

LYDIA
○ Sardis
Magnesia KARIA

PAMPHYLIA
Eurymedon

LYKIA

Cyprus ○

EGYPT

Memphis ○

THRACE

IONIA

Athens ○

Sparta ○

MEDITERRANEAN SEA

N ←

500 miles

1000 km

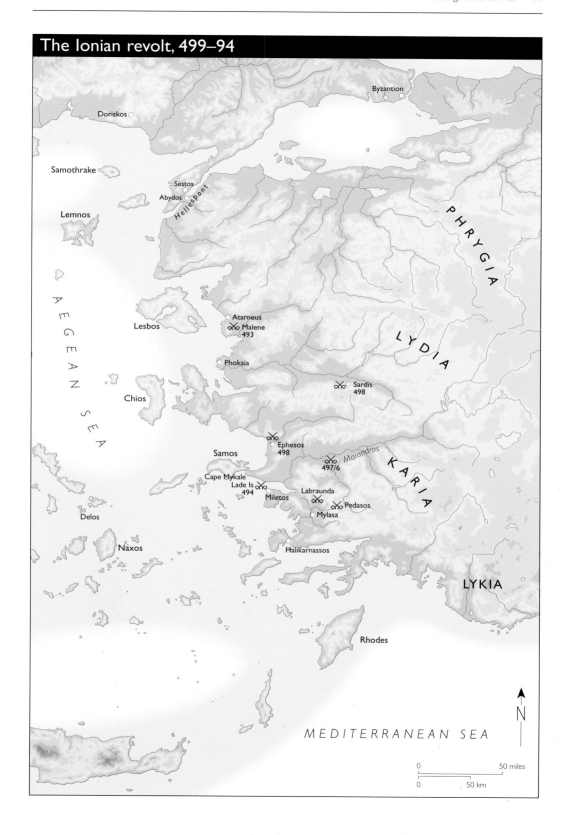

The Ionian revolt, 499–94

to Euboia and the mainland of Greece. It seems probable, therefore, that the initiative for the whole expedition came from the Persians, and that the exiled Naxian aristocrats' appeal to Aristagoras provided a pretext for the attack. Aristagoras also seems to have undertaken to pay a major part of the costs of the expedition, possibly on the understanding that he could recoup his outlay from the plunder of Naxos. The manpower for the fleet of 200 trireme warships was mostly drawn from the Greek cities of Asia Minor, but the army included a substantial contingent of Persian troops and was under the command of Megabates, a cousin of the Great King. When the invasion force arrived at Naxos, however, the inhabitants were ready for them. They had probably heard of the extensive preparations, particularly the assembly of the fleet, from maritime traders who sailed between the Cyclades and the mainland. They gathered their population and a stock of supplies into the main city of Naxos, which had strong defensive walls, and withstood a siege of four months. After their own supplies had been exhausted the Persians gave up and their forces returned to the city of Myous on the mainland.

At this point Aristagoras decided to precipitate a full-scale revolt of the Ionian Greeks against the Persians. His own motivations are difficult to determine. He seems to have quarrelled with Megabates, the Persian commander, although the trivial reason for their falling out given by Herodotus, namely that Megabates had mistreated an Ionian naval captain called Skylax, is unlikely to be the whole truth. Aristagoras had underwritten the cost of the failed expedition and now he, or rather the city of Miletos, could not afford to pay up. It also seems that his own city of Miletos was, like many other Greek cities at this time, becoming a hotbed of political discontent. The Persian-sponsored tyrants were unpopular with the majority of the citizens, who wanted a far greater say in the way their cities were governed. Aristagoras decided to offer himself as the leader of a revolutionary

reforming movement in Ionia that would throw off the burden of Persian rule, remove the tyrants and install governments based on the principal of *isonomia* (equal rights) for all citizens. Aristagoras declared that he was giving up his position as tyrant of Miletos, although he continued to be the dominant political figure there. The tyrants of the main Ionian cities and islands, including Erythrai, Teos, Samos, and Chios, were rounded up and expelled. Most of them went to Sardis, where they joined the entourage of the satrap Artaphernes in the hope that they would be reinstated by their Persian patrons. The newly liberated Ionian citizens proceeded to elect their own generals for the imminent military confrontation with the Persians.

The enthusiasm with which the Ionians responded to Aristagoras' call for a revolt was partly due to the autocratic nature of Persian rule. That is not to say that the tyrants or the Persian satraps who appointed them were excessively harsh in the way that they governed the Greeks, but the Ionians clearly resented having to obey tyrants who were appointed from among their fellow countrymen at the whim of a king whose court was far away and whose priorities rarely coincided with their own. Some of the Ionian cities and islands had been developing a form of democratic government when they came under Persian influence. Such developments continued in mainland Greece, especially in Athens, but the move to widespread popular participation in government was prematurely halted in Ionia. King Dareios, whom the Greeks referred to as 'the tradesman', demanded manpower for military expeditions and money, in the form of a regular tribute, paid in silver at a higher level than previously. The campaigns were against people like the Skythians, whom the Greeks could not possibly see as a threat to their own lands, and the silver was hoarded in distant Persia, or spent on gifts and wages for other foreigners. The Ionians got little in return for their annexation by the Persians. Archaeological studies have indicated that their share in the maritime trade of the

Mediterranean was declining towards the end of the sixth century. They may have felt that the cities of mainland Greece, Italy and Sicily, as well as the Phoenicians were doing well at their expense, and that they needed to be free of Persian control in order to recover their economic prosperity.

The Ionians were not so foolish as to believe that they could throw off the yoke of Persian rule unaided and they immediately sought assistance from their kinsmen in mainland Greece. Aristagoras travelled to Sparta to ask the strongest of the Greek states for aid, but he was unsuccessful. The Spartans were too preoccupied with their own problems, including a long-standing rivalry with the city of Argos, to send an army overseas. The Argives had recently received a dire oracular warning from the sanctuary of the god Apollo in Delphi which prophesied their own impending doom along with that of Miletos, so they were unwilling to help. It is probable that Aristagoras approached several other leading Greek states with similar results, but he did manage to persuade Athens and the Euboian city of Eretria to send some warships.

Why did the Athenians and Eretrians agree to help the Ionians, when the Spartans and others refused? A greater feeling of kinship with the Ionians may have been one reason. They spoke more or less the same dialect of Greek, their religious festivals were very similar, and they believed that they shared a common ancestry. Athens was thought to be the place from which the Greeks who settled in Ionia had first sailed across the Aegean. They had also had close diplomatic and economic ties before the coming of the Persians and they now had a common interest in democratic government. The Athenians had previously made an alliance with the Persian satrap Artaphernes, seeking to obtain his backing in their disputes with other Greek states, but they no longer respected this treaty because the Persians were sheltering Hippias, the former tyrant of Athens, at Sigeion. Hippias entertained hopes of being restored to power in Athens with Persian assistance. Aristagoras painted a

Oracles

Oracles were taken very seriously by the Greeks, especially those that were issued by the priestess of Apollo at Delphi, although they were not always given in terms which were easy to understand. The historian Herodotus quotes several Delphic oracles which he says were later seen to have been accurate prophesies concerning the triumphs and failures of the Greeks and the Persians.

The oracle concerning Miletos was as follows:

Then shall you, Miletos, the contriver of many evil deeds,
Yourself become a banquet and a splendid prize for many,
Your wives shall bathe the feet of many long-haired men;
And my temple at Didyma will be cared for by others.

It is clear that the oracle is a warning of impending doom for Miletos. The description of Miletos as 'the contriver of many evil deeds' indicates that there was a widespread prejudice among the people of mainland Greece against this rich and powerful city. Herodotus explains that this prophecy referred to the capture and sack of Miletos by the Persians, who wore their hair and beards long. They killed most of the men and enslaved the women and children. Didyma was a sanctuary of Apollo in Milesian territory, which also housed an oracle. It was plundered and burnt by the Persians.

picture for the assembly of Athenian citizens of the Persians as militarily weak and ripe for plundering by a combined Greek force. The Athenians voted to send a military expedition in 20 ships under the command of Melanthios to aid the Ionians against the Persians. Herodotus, looking ahead to the

ABOVE A fifth-century Athenian tetradachm, a silver coin of high value. The Athenians had a good supply of silver which they mined intensively during the fifth and fourth centuries. They also gained a great deal of silver coinage from their subject allies, who paid tribute to the Athenians at a similar rate to that which many of them had paid it to the Persians before 478. (Ancient Art and Architecture)

RIGHT A gold plaque from a large fourth-century treasure hoard found near the Oxus river in the north-eastern region of the Persian Empire. The figure is of a priest in the typical dress of the Medes, comprising a belted tunic, trousers and boots. He wears a soft cap that has flaps to cover the ears and chin to protect them from the wind. Persian and Median religious rituals emphasised the power of natural phenomena like fire, water and the fertile earth. (Ancient Art and Architecture)

battles of Marathon, Thermopylai, Salamis and Plataia, comments that these ships were the origin of troubles for both Greeks and Persians. By encouraging and assisting the rebels, the Athenians, and the Eretrians, who sent five warships to help in the revolt, might have hoped to dissuade the Persians from further expansion westwards. They must have been keenly aware of how vulnerable they were to attack if a Persian conquest of the Cyclades were achieved.

In 498 the Athenian and Eretrian contingents joined a mainly Milesian army at Ephesos. From there the combined force marched inland to attack the Persian provincial capital at Sardis. They took the satrap Artaphernes by surprise. He abandoned the lower part of the city and took refuge in the citadel. He held off the Ionians and their allies and waited for reinforcements to arrive. Even the accidental burning of much of the

This bronze hoplite's helmet of the Corinthian type is inscribed with
the name Dendas, perhaps the person who dedicated it in a
sanctuary around the year 500. Such helmets afforded good protection
to the wearer, but they severely restricted vision and hearing, causing
the hoplites' reliance on the coherence of their formation.
(Ancient Art and Architecture)

city, including the temple of Cybele, the Great Mother Goddess, did not break the resolve of Artaphernes and his Lydian and Persian troops. When a strong Persian cavalry force approached, the attackers withdrew but they were overtaken near Ephesos and heavily defeated. Aristagoras' prediction of easy pickings had proved to be wrong. The Athenians and Eretrians embarked on their ships and returned home with stories of the Persians' determination and the superiority of their cavalry. The Ionians were left to face the wrath of the Persian king on their own.

The Ionians decided to take the initiative once more by sending ships north and south to the Hellespont and Karia, to encourage wider rebellion among King Dareios' subjects. They also supported a revolt among the Greek cities of Cyprus, but this was short-lived. In 497 a large Persian army was despatched to Cyprus on a fleet drawn from the cities of Phoenicia. The tyrants whom the Persians had established as rulers in the cities of Salamis and Kourion deserted to the Persian side at a vital moment and, in spite of naval assistance from the Ionians, the Cypriots were defeated.

Also in 497 Dareios sent more Persian armies to regain control of the Hellespontine region and Karia, but one of them, under the command of his son-in-law Daurises, was ambushed by the Karians at Pedasos and almost completely destroyed. Although his other commanders enjoyed more success to the north, this defeat was such a major setback that Dareios had to wait until 494 to launch a strong land and sea offensive against the main seat of the revolt, Miletos. By this time, Aristagoras had been driven out of Miletos by his political rivals and killed. The loss of their main leader was to have a serious affect on the cohesion of the revolt, and distrust of those who tried to take his place hampered the co-ordination of the fight against the Persians. When Histiaios, the father-in-law and predecessor of Aristagoras as tyrant of Miletos returned to his city, ostensibly on a peace mission from Dareios, but actually to offer himself as the new leader of the revolt, he was driven off by the Milesians and had to take refuge in Mytilene on the island of Lesbos.

The nearest thing the Ionians had to a common political organisation was their *koinon*, a religious assembly which met annually at the Panionion, a sanctuary of Poseidon in the territory of Priene. This assembly was not meant to be a political one and it lacked the structures to produce a unified leadership. When they finally did manage to gather their naval forces at the island of Lade, off the coast of Miletos, there was a dispute over who should take command. The naval forces at the battle of Lade show the relative size, prosperity and power of the Ionians. There were 80 ships from Miletos, 12 from Priene, three from Myous, 17 from Teos, eight from Erythrai and three from Phokaia. The main islands furnished some of the largest contingents, 100 from Chios, 60 from Samos and 70 from the island of Lesbos, whose cities were not formally members of the Ionian League, but who nevertheless participated in the revolt. Eventually Dionysios of Phokaia, who led the smallest contingent, was put in charge, but although his appointment prevented arguments among the larger states, he lacked the authority to hold the different contingents together. In any case the combined Ionian fleet of 353 ships was only a little more than half the size of the Persian naval force of 600, which included ships from Egypt and Kilikia, but was mainly provided by the Phoenician cities. First the Samians deserted the cause, with the exception of 11 brave, but foolhardy, captains. Next the Lesbians followed suit and fled for their island homes. Without a major naval force to protect it Miletos was vulnerable to assault. The Persian commanders brought in expert military engineers from Phoenicia who forced their way into the city with the help of mines and battering rams. The rest of the cities and islands were gradually reduced to submission and punished for their revolt. Herodotus tells a grim tale of cities and their principal sanctuaries being burnt down, men killed, girls taken off to harems, with castrated boys as their eunuch attendants, while the remaining women and children were sold as slaves.

This fifth-century Athenian red-figure painted cup by the artist Epiktetos shows an archer wearing the typical tunic, trousers and hood of Iranian mercenary units in the Persian armies that invaded Greece. Although the Greeks did use archers and other missile troops in warfare, they did not form a substantial proportion of their armies, whereas the Persians and other Near-Eastern peoples often relied heavily on them in battle. (Ashmolean)

There were eventually some positive outcomes of the revolt for the Ionian Greeks. In 493 the satrap Artaphernes required representatives of the Greek states to come to Sardis and swear oaths that they would submit all inter-city disputes to arbitration. This implies that their individual governments were functioning well enough for envoys to be selected; the arbitrators were probably chosen by the Ionian *koinon*. Artaphernes also reassessed the amounts of annual tribute that each city and island had to pay to the king, making this burden more acceptable and less likely to provoke rebellion in the future. The following year King Dareios sent another son-in-law, Mardonios, to take charge of the region. He removed the remaining tyrants and allowed the Greeks under his control to establish democratic governments, according to the principal of *isonomia* which had been one of the rallying cries of the revolt. Mardonios' appointment had another purpose, however: to begin the next stage of the Persian advance into the Aegean. He took his fleet and army across the Hellespont into Thrace and he received the surrender of the island of Thasos, along with its fleet of triremes. From there he moved along the northern coastline of the Aegean towards Macedon. A fierce storm claimed 300 ships off the promontory of Mount Athos, but Mardonios had prepared the way for a possible invasion of the Greek mainland.

Persia, Sparta and Athens

Kyros the Great and the Persian Empire

The Persians were part of a group of ancient peoples who spoke languages similar to modern Iranian. They probably originated in central Asia as nomadic cattle-herders, but by the end of the tenth century they had settled in the region known as Persia (modern Fars), on the south-eastern end of the Zagros mountains. Assyrian documents from the ninth century onwards mention them alongside the Medes, who occupied an area to the north and west. The powerful kingdom of Elam had controlled Persia until the mid-seventh century, but after Elamite power was weakened by the Assyrian king, Ashurbanipal, in 646 the Persians seem to have become increasingly autonomous, developing a small state of their own under the rule of a royal family whose seat of power was the Elamite city of Anshan. The fourth ruler of this fledgling kingdom, Kyros II, known as 'Kyros the Great', came to the throne in 559. His kingdom was attacked in 550 by the Median king, Astyages. Kyros persuaded Astyages' army to rebel against their king and they handed him over to Kyros as a prisoner. Kyros then marched into the Median city of Ekbatana and was recognised as the new ruler of the Medes. During the next 20 years Kyros used the combined strength of the Persians and the Medes to conquer Lydia, Assyria and Babylonia and increased his empire to the east by bringing Baktria and Sogdiana under his control. In 530 he was killed fighting to subdue a revolt among some of the Baktrian tribes and his son Kambyses succeeded him.

Kambyses directed his main efforts towards the conquest of Egypt. The Egyptian pharaoh, Amasis, had created a powerful navy and sought alliances with several states in the Mediterranean region, including the Greeks of Sparta and Samos, in an effort to resist the Persian advance. Kambyses had to create his own navy, manned by his maritime subjects in Ionia, Phoenicia and Kilikia. He launched his assault on Egypt in 525 and captured the new pharaoh, Psammetikos, after a 10-day siege at Memphis. He spent the next three years consolidating his control of Egypt.

In 522 Kambyses was on his way back to Persia when he fell from his horse and died. The circumstances of his death are mysterious and there is a suggestion that it was not an accident. He did not have a son, so he should have been succeeded by his brother, Bardiya, but an ambitious aristocrat called Dareios led a palace coup which resulted in the assassination of Bardiya and the installation of Dareios, a distant relative of the royal family, as the new king. These dramatic events plunged the Persian Empire into chaos and civil war which lasted for over a year. Dareios was able to count on the support of several leading Persians whose armies remained loyal to him in spite of his unorthodox seizure of power. Eventually he subdued all the rival aristocrats and several local dynasts who seized on the internal unrest as an opportunity to throw off the yoke of Persian rule. Dareios inaugurated a new Persian dynasty, known as the Achaemenids, because they traced their line back to the Persian Achaemenes, an ancestor of Kyros the Great. Dareios added parts of central Asia and most of north-west India to the Persian Empire, he campaigned unsuccessfully against the Skythians of the western Black Sea region and he extended the territory under his rule into Europe by conquering the parts of Thrace which lay along the northern coastline of the Aegean.

Dareios the Great King

The Persian king Dareios was a usurper who came to the throne as the result of a coup and the assassination of the rightful king. Nevertheless, in his official version of events, inscribed on a high rockface at Behistun in northern Iran, beside the royal road from Ekbatana to Babylon, he proclaimed that he was the legitimate successor of Kambyses and that his kingship was sanctified by Ahuramazda, the patron god of the Achaemenid rulers. The following extracts from the inscription show how Dareios wanted to be thought of and how he regarded the empire over which he ruled.

I am Dareios the Great King, the king of kings, the King of Persia, the king of all lands … So says Dareios the King: Eight times were my family kings and I am the ninth king in succession from my family. So says Dareios the King: I am king by the grace of Ahuramazda. Ahuramazda gave me the kingship. The following lands belong to me. I am their king by the grace of Ahuramazda: Persia, Elam, Babylonia, Assyria, Arabia, Egypt, the Peoples on the Sea (Phoenicia), Lydia, Ionia, Media, Armenia, Kappadokia, Parthia, Drangiana, Aria, Arachosia and Makan, 23 lands in all … So says Dareios the king: In these lands anyone who was loyal I treated well, anyone who was faithless I punished severely. By the grace of Ahuramazda these lands obeyed my rule. Whatever I told them to do, was done …

The inscription was written in three languages, Elamite, the *lingua franca* of much of the empire, Akkadian, the language of the kings of Babylon, and Old High Persian, the official language of the Persian kings. Because this language had never been written before, a new cuneiform script had to be devised for it.

Although the Persian king was known officially as the 'Great King, the king of kings, the king of all lands', his power was not absolute. In practice he relied on the support and co-operation of a large Persian aristocracy whom he was obliged to provide with positions of wealth and power in the newly conquered lands. Hence these lands were divided into provinces and each province was administered by a Persian aristocrat, a satrap. One way to explain the dramatic rise of the Persian Empire is in terms of the ambitions of its aristocracy. The need to satisfy the ambitions of these men was a major reason why Kyros and his successors embarked on campaigns of imperial expansion.

Persian nobles had a long tradition of being fierce warriors and independent aristocrats, so they did not accept a minor role in the hierarchy of the empire. Individuals who were closely related to the king were often made the satraps of large or strategically important provinces, while others were given command over armies or other positions of responsibility. They lived in magnificent palaces and enjoyed the use of large estates in the provinces. The public distribution of prestigious gifts, particularly items of gold and silver, was a method used by the kings to indicate who were the most favoured nobles. The Persians maintained their cohesion and distinctiveness in several ways, including their dress, their use of the Persian language and the education of their sons. Persian boys spent the first five years of their lives away from their fathers in the company of their mothers and other women of the household, but thereafter were taught to be soldiers and rulers. It was said that the Persians expected three things above all from their sons, that they should ride a horse, use a bow and speak the truth.

The ruling Persian élite did not remain completely apart from the subject peoples of the empire. Intermarriage between Persians and non-Persians was encouraged, with the daughters of Persian nobles marrying local princes and the Persians taking local aristocratic women as wives or concubines.

Kyros had adopted a policy of respecting local traditions and retaining some local aristocrats and religious leaders in his administration of Media, Lydia and Babylonia, and Kambyses and Dareios followed this policy in Egypt and elsewhere. People from conquered lands who had been in positions of power were often granted high status and were accepted into the king's court with the honorary title of 'royal friend'. Similar treatment was sometimes granted to exiles from states outside the empire who sought the protection and assistance of the Great King.

A golden dagger with a pommel in the form of two lion heads. It was probably made in the fifth century as a present for someone in the court of the Persian king. Such gifts from the king to his nobles both symbolised that the recipient enjoyed royal favour and transferred some of the enormous wealth of the Achaemenid kings to their Persian aristocrats. (Ancient Art and Architecture)

The Persian kings exploited their huge empire in two main ways. They taxed the subject peoples with regular payments of tribute and they utilised their manpower in military expeditions to conquer new territories or to suppress revolts in those they already ruled. In several satrapies

lower-ranking Persians and Medians were granted small estates which provided them with modest revenues. In return they were expected to maintain themselves as cavalrymen, or charioteers, or to provide infantry soldiers for the king's armies. In years when such services were not demanded the estates were subject to taxes in silver or in kind, much like the rest of the land in the satrapy.

Surviving records show that the Persian Empire evolved a complex bureaucracy to administer the satrapies and dispose of their revenues according to the king's instructions. Members of the royal court and many other persons of importance were granted food and provisions from the royal storehouses. A system of roads linked together the major centres like Sardis, Ekbatana, Babylon, Susa and Persepolis. These roads were primarily for the use of soldiers and royal couriers,

This relief sculpture is from the royal palace at Persepolis, built in the late sixth and fifth centuries. It probably shows the two main builders of the palace, King Dareios I and his son and heir Xerxes. They have very long beards and wear square crowns. The flower-like objects carried by the king and his heir are probably bronze or golden lotus-blossom tokens. These would be handed out to members of the court as marks of favour at festivals. (Ancient Art and Architecture)

who were provided with way-stations, but the roads also facilitated the movement of trade and tribute across the empire. By the reign of Dareios, the Persian Empire was the largest the ancient world had ever seen. It stretched from the Balkans to the river Indus and its resources of wealth and manpower made the Great King the most powerful ruler in the ancient world.

The principal soldiers in all Persian armies were usually infantrymen who were Persians by birth and who carried large

shields, often made of leather and osier. They fought with a variety of weapons including long spears, axes, swords, and bows and arrows. Their armour was minimal, consisting at most of a padded cuirass of linen and perhaps a helmet, although most images show them wearing caps or hoods. The Persians were organised

A golden coin of the fifth century, known as a Daric, showing the king carrying a spear and a bow. This type of coin was introduced by King Dareios in the late sixth century. Coins were used throughout the ancient world to pay mercenaries. In the fifth and fourth centuries Persian gold played an increasingly important role in the political struggles of the Greeks, as the Persian kings used their enormous wealth to finance the wars of one Greek state against another. (Ancient Art and Architecture)

in regiments of 1,000 which could be grouped together in divisions of 10,000. The most important of these divisions was that of the 'Immortals', so called because casualties were always replaced to maintain the full complement of 10,000. The Immortals contained an élite regiment known as the King's Spearcarriers. This regiment was made up entirely of members of the Persian aristocracy. The conquest of Lydia in 547 demonstrated to Kyros the Great the need for a reliable corps of Persian cavalry, so he distributed conquered lands among the Persian nobles so that they could raise horses and fight as cavalry. The Persian kings also used Medes as cavalry and from the reign of Dareios onwards they recruited mercenary infantrymen and cavalrymen from the Saka tribes of central Asia. For major campaigns they levied troops from the subject peoples of the empire, gathering men from as far afield as Egypt and India, but the most reliable soldiers were always the Persians and the mercenaries from Iran and central Asia.

A gold bowl from Ekbatana. It is inscribed around the outside with the name of King Xerxes in three languages, Old High Persian, Akkadian and Elamite. Each of these is written in a cuneiform script, the style of writing developed in Mesopotamia in the fourth millennium. Akkadian was the language of the Babylonian kings. (Ancient Art and Architecture)

The rise of Sparta

The Greeks who confronted the might of the Persian Empire in the fifth century were mostly organised in small city-states. These communities varied in size, but they usually consisted of an urban centre, containing the major shrines and public buildings, surrounded by a rural territory, which was farmed by the male citizens, their families and slaves. The historical origins of these city-states are obscured by the layers of myths and legends with which later generations embellished the stories of their ancestors.

The Spartans were descended from a group of Greek-speaking tribes who had settled in a region called Lakonia, in the south-eastern Peloponnese, towards the end of the 11th century. About a hundred years later five villages in the broad plain of the river Eurotas amalgamated to form a single city, called Sparta. As part of the compromise involved in this arrangement it was decided that the new state would be ruled jointly by two royal families, the Agiadai and the Eurypontiai, each of which provided a king for the Spartans. These kings were advised by a council of elders, called the *gerousia*, whose membership was later restricted to 28.

The new city gradually exerted its influence over some of the surrounding communities and brought them under its control. Some were reduced to the status of slaves, but others retained a degree of autonomy. Their inhabitants were not fully integrated with the Spartans in social and political terms, but they fought alongside them in further campaigns of expansion and annexation. Their inhabitants became known as the *perioikoi*, meaning 'those who dwell around'. Towards the end of the eighth century the Spartans and their allies managed to defeat the inhabitants of Messenia, a wide, fertile region in the south-western Peloponnese, separated from the plain of Lakonia by the high ridges of Mount Taygetos. The Messenians proved to be difficult to dominate, however, and in the middle of the seventh century they rebelled

against the Spartans and engaged them in a long, hard war. This war eventually ended in total victory for the Spartans, who took possession of Messenia and forced the inhabitants to become slaves. The former lands of the Messenians were divided into estates of roughly equal size and allocated to individual Spartan citizens, who did not live on the estates themselves but received up to half of their agricultural output as a form of rent. The Messenians themselves became known, like the Spartans' Lakonian slaves, as 'helots'.

Possession of the human and agricultural resources of Lakonia and Messenia enabled the Spartans to organise their community in a unique manner. The helots provided a servile workforce who furnished them with food and basic necessities, while the *perioikoi* engaged in manufacturing crafts and trading with the world outside Lakonia. This division of labour allowed the Spartan citizens to form an élite social and political group, called the Equals (*homoioi*). They were still ruled by their two kings, who acted as military commanders when the Spartans went to war. The Equals met in an assembly to vote upon major issues, such as whether or not to go to war, or make alliances with other states, but on a day-to-day basis their community came to be governed by five elected officials called 'ephors'. By the end of the sixth century the ephors had achieved a considerable degree of authority, even over the kings. The Equals devoted themselves to military training and gradually evolved into the most effective army in the Greek world. They perfected the art of hoplite warfare, fighting on foot in close formations using a large, round shield and a long thrusting spear. The Spartans became renowned for their courage and discipline and, because of this, they began to intervene in the political affairs of neighbouring city-states, usually at the invitation of one or other faction within that state. (See 'Portrait of a soldier' for a description of the Spartan educational and social system.)

During the seventh and sixth centuries many of the Greek city-states experienced

A bronze figurine of a Spartan hoplite, made in Lakonia in the sixth century. Items like this were frequently dedicated to the gods in temples across Greece, but hoplite figures are one of the commonest forms of dedication from Lakonia. This one has the typical pointed beard and long hair of a Spartan citizen. (Ancient Art and Architecture)

periods of social and political instability. The hereditary aristocracies who ruled them came under increasing pressure to share power and resources, above all agricultural land, which was the main source of wealth. For a while this pressure was eased by encouraging people to migrate overseas, particularly to Sicily, southern Italy and the northern Aegean, where many prosperous Greek communities had been established in the eighth and seventh centuries. Eventually the demands for political and social reform produced violent conflicts and in many city-states charismatic individuals emerged as leaders of the discontented elements. They overthrew the ruling groups and set themselves up as sole rulers. The Greeks used *tyrannos*, a word of Near-Eastern origin, to describe such men. It is usually translated as 'tyrant' in modern histories of ancient Greece, but it did not necessarily carry the overtones of oppressive or unpopular rule that the modern use of the term 'tyranny' implies. During the sixth century the Spartans overthrew many of these tyrannies, including those at Corinth, Sikyon, Naxos and Athens. They also attempted to overthrow Polykrates, the tyrant of Samos.

Athens before the Persian Wars

Athens was one of the largest of the Greek city-states. The city of Athens itself was the religious and political centre of an extensive territory comprising all the peninsula of Attika. Tradition held that the region had been unified under the kingship of the mythical hero Theseus, but by the middle of the seventh century the Athenians were governed by nine annually appointed officials, called 'archons', who were chosen from the males of a small group of

Tyrtaios describes the ideal Spartan hoplite

In the middle of the seventh century, when Spartans were struggling to overcome the rebellious Messenians, the Spartan poet Tyrtaios composed songs to exhort his fellow citizens to fight well. In the following extract (lines 21–38 of fragment 11) he gives a vivid, contemporary description of Greek hoplite warfare, which relied on the bravery and determination of infantrymen armed with a large shield and spear.

Let each man stand firm with his feet set apart, facing up to the enemy and biting his lip, covering his thighs and shins, his chest and shoulders with the wide expanse of his shield.
Let him shake his spear bravely with his right hand, his helmet's crest nodding fiercely above his head.
Let him learn his warfare in the heat of battle and not stand back to shield himself from missiles, but let him move in close, using his spear, or sword, to strike his enemy down.
Place feet against the enemy's feet, press shield against shield, nod helmet against helmet, so that the crests are entangled, and then fight your man standing chest to chest, your long spear or your sword in your hand.
And you, the light-armed men, hiding behind the shields, launch your sling-stones and javelins at them, giving good support to the heavy infantry.

In later years these poems became compulsory listening for Spartan armies. Tyrtaios also provided some additional encouragement for the lightly armed troops, who were normally recruited from helots or the *perioikoi*. See 'Portrait of a soldier' for more extracts from the poems of Tyrtaios.

aristocratic families. Many of the ordinary people of Attika resented the aristocrats' monopoly on power and their discontent encouraged an Athenian aristocrat called Kylon to attempt to set himself up as tyrant in 632. Kylon had been the victor in a chariot race at the Olympic Games, which implies that he was very wealthy, and he was married to the daughter of Theagenes, the tyrant of Megara. With Theagenes' help Kylon gathered a small band of followers and seized the Acropolis of Athens. His coup failed to attract wide support among the Athenians, many of whom joined in besieging Kylon and his men. Although Kylon and some of his immediate family escaped, the rest were forced to surrender and were subsequently killed. The causes of discontent remained, however, including aristocratic control of land, high rents and excessive use of debt-bondage, as well as the exclusion of many of the wealthier citizens from participation in government.

In 594 an aristocrat called Solon was chosen to revise the social and political structures of Athens. He reduced the problems of debt-bondage and opened up the archonship to wealthy non-aristocrats. He also established a people's council of 400 to widen participation in government. His reforms did not go far enough for many of the Athenians and they continued to quarrel over the right to govern the Athenian state. In 546, after two earlier failures, an aristocrat called Peisistratos, who had won great popularity as a military leader against the neighbouring state of Megara, set himself up as tyrant. He managed to remain in power until his death in 528, mainly by ensuring that the archons for each year were dominated by his supporters. His eldest son, Hippias, tried to continue the dynasty, but after his younger brother Hipparchos was murdered in 514 his rule became oppressive and unpopular. A leading aristocratic family, the Alkmaionidai, who had been closely involved in the defeat of Kylon's attempt at tyranny, bribed the Delphic oracle to persuade the Spartans to intervene. In 510 the Spartan king, Kleomenes, led an army into Attika and deposed Hippias, who sought refuge with the Persian king, Dareios.

When he intervened in Athens, Kleomenes was following an established Spartan policy of deposing tyrants in other Greek states so that they could revert to the control of their aristocratic families and become allies of the Spartans. In the case of Athens, however, further quarrels among the leading families resulted in the creation of a different form of government. In 508/07 Kleisthenes of the Alkmaionidai was losing out in a power struggle with a rival aristocrat called Isagoras, but he attracted widespread support by promising radical reforms of the political system in Athens. In response Isagoras invited Kleomenes to lead a Spartan army into Attika and force Kleisthenes and his supporters into exile. The mass of Athenian citizens preferred the promised reforms to a continuation of aristocratic strife, so they eventually forced Kleomenes and his men to withdraw, taking Isagoras with them.

Kleisthenes was able to return to Athens and implement his programme of reform. He introduced a new organisational structure for the Athenians based on 140 local communities called 'demes'. All men over the age of 18 were registered as citizens through their deme and the demes were grouped into 10 newly created tribes, replacing the previous four tribes, which had been localised kinship units, dominated by certain aristocratic families. The demes offered an effective structure for local government. The tribes provided a mechanism for all citizens to become actively involved in running the state through a new council of 500 citizens who were appointed by selecting 50 men from each tribe by lot. This council discussed proposals for new laws and policies, but each proposal had to be put to a vote in the assembly before it could be implemented. All male citizens were entitled to attend this assembly and vote on the measures put before it, a principle of political equality, *isonomia*. One man from each tribe was elected to serve on a board of generals, who were both political and military leaders. To

prevent more internal political conflicts of the kind that had led to his reforms, Kleisthenes also instituted a procedure for the citizen assembly to have the opportunity to vote once a year to banish a leading political figure for a period of 10 years. The voting was done by inscribing the name of the person on a piece of broken pottery, the Greek word for which was *ostrakon*; hence the process was known as ostracism.

Their new-found political unity and military strength encouraged the Athenians to assert themselves against other Greek states. They defeated their northern neighbours, the Boiotians, and took some territory from the city of Chalkis on the island of Euboia. They also began a long war against the island of Aigina for domination of the Saronic Gulf, but they lacked a large navy with which to challenge the Aiginetans at sea. Attika was a prosperous region with a growing population and some of the more adventurous aristocrats led expeditions to the Hellespont and other parts of the Aegean, where new settlements had been established during the rule of Peisistratos and his son. Some of these groups returned to Athens in the early fifth century as the region came under Persian influence during the reign of King Dareios.

This *ostrakon*, or potsherd, is inscribed with the name of Aristeides, the son of Lysimachos. The Athenians could vote once a year to exile a politician for 10 years by inscribing his name in this way. Aristeides was 'ostracised' in the late 480s, but returned to assist in the defeat of Xerxes in 480/79. A famously honest man, it is said that during the voting he was asked by an illiterate citizen who did not recognise him to write the name 'Aristeides' on an *ostrakon*, which he did, asking why the man wanted to exile him. 'I'm tired of hearing him being called Aristeides "the Just",' was the man's reply. (Ancient Art and Architecture)

Dareios sends an expedition to Greece

In 491 King Dareios of Persia sent envoys to the leading states of mainland Greece demanding that they submit to his rule by offering him symbolic gifts of earth and water. Many of them conceded to this demand, including the large island state of Aigina, but among those states that refused to acknowledge his authority were Athens and Sparta. In Athens the king's envoys were executed by being thrown into a pit normally used for the punishment of criminals. The Athenians may have been partly motivated by their own ongoing conflict with Aigina, their main maritime rival in the Saronic Gulf. It is possible that they had also learned of Dareios' intention to re-establish Hippias the son of Peisistratos as tyrant of Athens.

Dareios assembled an army in Kilikia and ordered his maritime subjects, including the Ionian Greeks, to prepare a fleet of warships and horse transports. This involved supplying tens of thousands of oarsmen to row the ships and providing some soldiers for the expedition, but the bulk of his army probably came from the Iranian heartlands of the Persian Empire. The figures given by the ancient sources for the size of the army, which range from 90,000 to 600,000 men, are clearly exaggerated, but it may have comprised around 25,000 soldiers, including 1,000 cavalry, and a fleet of up to 600 ships. The commanders of the expedition were Datis, a Median aristocrat who had been involved in the Persian counter-offensive against the Ionians in 494, and Artaphernes, son of the satrap of Lydia and the king's nephew.

The aim of this expedition was not the complete conquest of mainland Greece, for which a far larger force would be needed, but rather the establishment of a bridgehead on the eastern coast of Greece, preferably at Athens. Once this base was secured larger forces could be amassed for a full-scale invasion. The first target for the expedition was the island of Naxos, whose people wisely decided not to attempt to resist the Persians this time, but fled into the mountains, abandoning their city and temples to the enemy. Other islands in the Cyclades also made their submission and some contributed ships to the fleet of the Great King. The inhabitants of Euboia put up determined resistance, forcing the Persians to besiege the cities of Karystos and Eretria. The latter had contributed five ships to the ill-fated Ionian raid on Sardis in 498 and appealed to Athens for help. The Athenians had recently confiscated some land from another Euboian city, Chalkis, and settled 4,000 of their own citizens there. These men were instructed to march to Eretria and help defend the city, but on their arrival they discovered that the Eretrians were divided on the wisdom of continuing to oppose the Persians. So the settlers crossed over to Athens and avoided being caught in Eretria when Datis and Artaphernes arrived with their fleet and army, having persuaded the Karystians to surrender after only a few days. The Persians laid siege to Eretria and pressed their attack vigorously, with severe casualties on both sides. On the seventh day of the siege the pro-Persian faction in Eretria opened the gates. The inhabitants were made to pay for their earlier assistance in the Ionian Revolt; their city and temple were burned down and most of them were enslaved.

Having successfully achieved its initial objectives the expedition set sail for the coast of Attika. Given the casualties they had suffered while subduing Euboia and the need to leave strong detachments behind with Artaphernes to maintain control of the island, it is likely that the force which Datis led to Attika numbered less than

20,000 men. Datis' mission was to effect a landing in Attika, capture the city of Athens and restore the deposed tyrant Hippias to power. Hippias, who accompanied the Persians as a guide, adviser and potential puppet ruler of Athens, advised Datis to take the fleet across the narrow Euboian Strait and land the army at the Bay of Marathon, on the eastern coast of Attika. It was the nearest suitable landing site to Eretria and could provide ample water and pasturage. The plain at Marathon was broad enough for the deployment of the whole Persian army,

An Athenian red-figure painted jar of the mid-fifth century. This unfortunate Persian soldier has used up all his arrows, as the empty quiver on his belt shows. His bow is now useless, although he hangs onto it in the hope that he may recover some arrows. His only other weapon is a curved sword, but it is insufficient against the large shield and long spear of the Spartan hoplite attacking him. (Ancient Art and Architecture)

including the cavalry, against any defending forces. Hippias may also have expected to receive a friendly welcome from the people of eastern Attika, who had been strong supporters of his father's tyranny.

The battle of Marathon

The Athenian generals decided to confront the Persians as soon they landed, rather than allow them to march on their city and then face a siege, as the Eretrians had done. They too may have been wary of the possibility of some of the citizens preferring to side with the invaders and the exiled tyrant Hippias, if they were allowed to establish themselves on Athenian territory. The Athenians assembled an army of about 9,000, mainly hoplite soldiers. They were joined by a further 600 or so men from the smaller city of Plataia, which lay north west of Attika and had been an ally of Athens for some 30 years. On hearing that the Persians had landed at Marathon they marched across the central plain of Attika and up the east coast to Marathon.

The Athenians and their Plataian allies took up a position on high ground, near to the road leading south from Marathon to Athens and awaited the Persians' next move. Herodotus says that there were protracted discussions among the Athenian commanders as to whether they should attack, but this may reflect embellishments made to the story of the battle in later years. It is more likely that the Greeks waited for the enemy to make a move. The Athenians and Plataians were heavily outnumbered and their generals will have been reluctant to move from their strong defensive position into the open plain of Marathon. To do so would have left them vulnerable to cavalry attacks and the possibility of being outmanoeuvred by the larger Persian force. It is also possible that the Athenians were waiting for the arrival of reinforcements from Sparta. Before they left Athens to march to Marathon the Athenians had sent their best runner, Philippides, to the Spartans with a request for aid. He covered the distance of approximately 140 miles in less than two days. The Spartans agreed to send a small army to help the Athenians, but their departure was delayed because they were in the middle of a major religious festival and had to wait until the full moon

signalled its completion. When they did set out, six days later, they marched with such great speed to Marathon that they arrived just three days later. Nevertheless, they were too late to participate in the battle, which had been fought on the previous day.

Herodotus' account describes a lengthy disagreement among the 10 Athenian generals, with half of them arguing that the size of the Persian force made it advisable to wait until they advanced, while the other half insisted that it was imperative to attack at once. According to Herodotus the impasse created by this equal division of opinions was broken by the intervention of Kallimachos, who held the office of *polemarchon*. In earlier times this official had been the commander of Athens' army, but under the new democratic constitution the army was commanded by a board of 10 elected generals, one from each of the 10 tribes. Kallimachos' position was more an honorary one, but he accompanied the army when it was engaged in fighting within the borders of Attika and he was entitled to a vote on major decisions. Herodotus says that one of the generals, Miltiades, persuaded Kallimachos to vote in favour of an attack by saying that further delay would mean victory for the Persians and slavery for the Athenians.

Herodotus also has Miltiades refer to the likelihood that continued inaction would breed dissension and fear among the Athenians, 'so that they will go over to the Medes'. This seems to be an indication that the decision to attack was taken in order to prevent treachery or defections. The presence among the Persians of Hippias, the former tyrant of Athens, provided one good reason to suspect that some of his supporters might choose to swap sides and

Persian infantrymen of the army division known as the Immortals. They wear long robes embroidered with regimental badges and are armed with a spear and a bow. This glazed brick relief of c.520 is from the palace of King Dareios at Susa, the original capital of the Median Empire. Dareios held his royal court there until his new palace in Persepolis became available. (Ancient Art and Architecture)

persuade others to follow them. The recent example of the betrayal of Eretria to the Persians was another. The longer the Athenians and Plataians were required to stand their ground and contemplate the strength of the enemy army, the easier it would be for them to believe that they could not defeat it and would be better off submitting to the rule of the Great King. It may also be that the Persian commander Datis had decided to wait for a sign that the enemy's resolve was weakening.

This tense stand-off lasted several days, during which no negotiations took place, nor was there even any skirmishing between the two sides. Eventually, the Athenian generals made the decision to attack the Persians. Several explanations have been offered for this bold decision. One possibility is that the Persians themselves formed up for battle and began to advance towards the Athenian position, with the intention of drawing them out onto the plain for a decisive battle. Certainly, if they wanted to march on Athens itself, the Persians had to remove the army, which was blocking the routes to the south and west. An alternative to this idea is the suggestion, made by a Byzantine scholar writing many centuries later, that the Athenians were informed by the Ionian Greeks among the enemy that parts of the Persian army, especially the cavalry, had begun to embark on their ships for a voyage around southern Attika to attack the city from the sea. Either way it seems probable that the Athenian advance was prompted by a change in the disposition of the Persian troops.

The Greeks attacked early in the day, perhaps while the Persian commanders were still getting their forces into position. Because the Persian army was spread out along a very wide front, the Athenians and their Plataian allies feared that they might be outflanked, so they extended the length of their own front, thinning out the ranks of their hoplites in the centre, but retaining a strong force on each wing. Datis positioned his best troops, a mixture of Persians and

TOP RIGHT The Persians landed on the beach in front of the marsh and made their camp to the north of the Kynosoura promontary. The Athenians and Plataians stationed themselves on high ground to the south, near the road to Athens. When Datis moved the Persians towards them and took up battle positions, the Greeks came down onto the plain and attacked. The Persians pushed back the centre of the Greek line, but their own wings were defeated and fled back towards their camp.

BOTTOM RIGHT Realising that their flanks were exposed, the Persian centre retreated, under attack on both sides from the victorious Greek wings. Most of the Persians forces reached the ships and escaped after fierce fighting at the ships, but many were hemmed in between the marsh and the beach and were killed.

Sakai, mercenaries from the regions north-east of Iran. His army included a large number of archers and slingers, as well as men equipped with javelins, whose function was to bombard the enemy from a distance with missiles before the other troops engaged them with spears, swords and axes.

As they faced each other on the plain the two armies were about a mile apart and the Greeks had to march across the open plain in order to engage the Persians. They completed most of this advance at a walking pace, but they ran the last 200 metres or so in order to reach the enemy before their own ranks were too heavily reduced by the arrows, javelins and slingstones. This decision to charge took the Persians by surprise. They seem to have underestimated their opponents' determination, which is not entirely surprising, given that they had recently overcome the Euboians and had been allowed to camp unchallenged on Athenian territory for several days. Nevertheless, they made ready to receive the charge, sending several volleys of missiles into the Greek ranks, with the aim of slowing or even halting the charge and then driving them back.

The Greeks closed the distance between the two armies as quickly as they could and they clashed across a broad front. In the centre, where the best Persian troops were concentrated, they pushed the Athenians back, pursuing them towards their original

The battle of Marathon, 490: Phase one

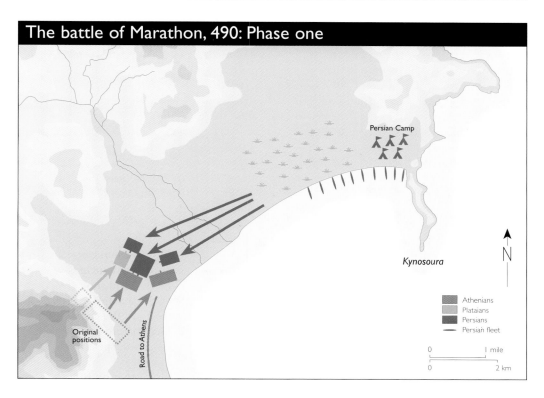

The battle of Marathon, 490: Phase two

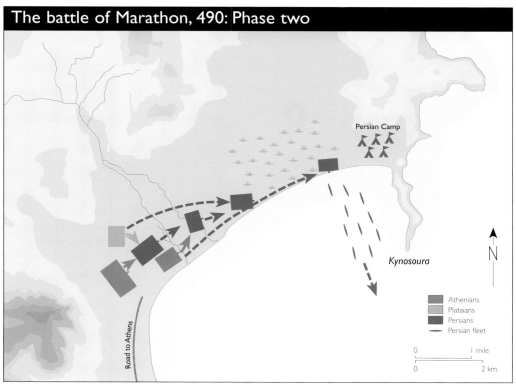

camp. On the wings, however, the Athenians and the Plataians, who were concentrated on the left wing, succeeded in driving the Persian forces back and disrupting the cohesion and discipline of Datis' army. Under the pressure of the Greek onslaught the two wings of the Persians broke and fled back to their own camp. Realising that their flanks were now exposed and in danger of being surrounded by the victorious elements of the Greek army and attacked at the rear, the Persians and Sakai retreated as well. The Athenian and Plataian commanders gathered their forces together and fell upon them as they made their way back to their camp. There was not a complete rout, thanks to the discipline and experience of the Persian officers, who organised a rearguard and managed to embark many of their men onto the ships which were moored in shallow water just beyond the camp. Their casualties were high, however, with 6,400 men killed, many of them cut down as they crowded together, trapped between the sea, the pursuing Greeks and a marshy area to the north of the Persian camp. The Athenians lost only 192 men, including the *polemarchon* Kallimachos; Plataian casualties were also light.

Some modern scholars have been puzzled by the apparent lack of participation in the battle by the Persian cavalry. Herodotus does not mention them at all in his narrative of the action, which is the main reason why the Byzantine phrase about the cavalry embarking on the ships is taken seriously. The Persian cavalry was made up of a variety of ethnic units, including native Persians and subjects from other parts of the empire. Their main weapons were swords and spears, but they also used bows and arrows and javelins for hit-and-run attacks. It may well be that those Athenians who had survived the raid on Sardis and the subsequent retreat to Ephesos in 498 had exaggerated the threat posed by such cavalrymen. When pursuing heavy infantry, light cavalry would certainly have a major advantage, but in a battle fought at close quarters, over a relatively small area, the infantry would

have been far less vulnerable. If, as was their normal practice, the Persian commanders stationed their cavalry on the flanks of the main infantry formation, then they will have been driven back by the determined charge of the Greek hoplites and, with the extra speed and mobility that their horses provided, they may have been among the first to flee back to the ships.

Despite his defeat on the plain of Marathon, Datis, probably on the advice of Hippias, still felt that there was a chance to reach Athens by sea and capture it before the Athenian army could return. Accordingly he took his remaining men by sea around Cape Sounion and up to the Bay of Phaleron. Realising that the Persians were sailing south and heading for the city, the Athenians marched back as fast as they could and arrived in time to dissuade them from launching an assault. Herodotus reports the story that the Persians set off for Athens because they had received a signal, a polished shield flashing in the sun, which some Athenians claimed was given by members of the Alkmaionid family, but Herodotus himself does not believe this story and modern scholars have been inclined to agree with him. Unable to make any further progress against the Athenians, Datis sailed back to Asia Minor to report the failure of the expedition to the king.

The Athenians who died at Marathon were cremated and their ashes were buried in a funeral mound on the site of the battle. This mound, known as the Soros, still stands and is the approximate location of the main clash between the two armies. A force of 2,000 Spartans arrived on the battlefield the day after the battle. They inspected the Persian dead and praised the Athenians for

This bronze helmet is inscribed along the rim with the words: 'The Athenians, to Zeus, having taken this from the Medes.' It was captured as part of the booty, perhaps at the battle of Marathon in 490, and dedicated in the sanctuary of the god Zeus at Olympia. Dedications of captured arms and armour were an essential part of warfare for the Greeks, for whom they symbolised that victory had been won with the support and approval of the gods. (Ancient Art and Architecture)

The exterior of a red-figure painted wine cup, produced in Athens around 480. It features a Greek hoplite fighting at close quarters with a Persian infantryman. Both carry spears and shields, but the shields are of very different types. The round, concave Greek shield is made of wood covered with bronze and held by a hand-grip on the rim and an arm-grip in the centre. The rectangular, flat Persian shield is made of wicker and osiers and held by a single hand-grip in the centre. The hoplite also wears bronze armour, whereas his opponent is dressed in cloth and leather. (Ashmolean)

their victory before returning to Sparta. Once they were sure that the Persian forces were no longer a threat the Athenians celebrated their unexpected victory. It was the first time a Greek army had successfully overcome a Persian one. For the Athenians in particular it also represented a considerable triumph for their democratic citizen body. The ordinary Athenian (and Plataian) hoplites had defeated a larger, more

experienced and probably better disciplined
army in a magnificent display of solidarity,
bravery and sheer determination to defend
their homeland. From the Persian kings'
point of view the defeat at Marathon was a
serious setback for his campaign to punish
the Athenians and to conquer the Greek
states, but Marathon was far from the end
of the matter as far as the Persians were
concerned.

Xerxes' invasion of Greece

According to Herodotus, Dareios vowed to get revenge for the defeat of his army by the Athenians. Shortly after the news of Marathon reached him he ordered the best and bravest men in Asia to be levied for another campaign. That this levy was conducted for the sole purpose of subduing the Greeks is, however, unlikely, as there were many parts of the Persian Empire that also needed to be kept in line by strong military action. In 486 Dareios was called upon to deal with a revolt in one of the most troublesome provinces of the Persian Empire, Egypt. This satrapy had been conquered by his predecessor Kambyses in 525/24 and had remained under Persian control thereafter, even during the revolts and civil wars that characterised the first few years of Dareios' reign. Eventually the burden of tribute imposed by the Great King became too much for the Egyptians to bear and they attempted to drive the Persians out. Egypt was one of the wealthiest and strategically most important satrapies, so its revolt constituted a far greater threat to Dareios' power than the stubborn resistance of a few Greek cities. While Dareios was in Persia preparing for an expedition to bring the Egyptians back into line, he died of natural causes and was succeeded by his eldest son, Xerxes. The new king lost no time in crushing the Egyptian rebellion and asserting his authority as the 'king of all lands' and the favoured one of Ahuramazda. By 484 the whole of Egypt was once more under Persian control. Xerxes left his brother Achaimenes in charge as satrap of Egypt and returned to Persia.

Xerxes prepares to invade Greece

The Egyptian revolt was one of several problems that Xerxes inherited from his father. Babylonia, one of the central satrapies, also revolted in 481. Because of its position across the main communication routes between the eastern and western halves of the empire this satrapy was of even greater strategic importance than Egypt. Xerxes put down the revolt with considerable force and divided Babylonia into two smaller satrapies in an effort to make it easier to control. Another major concern for the son of Dareios was what to do about the Athenians and those other Greeks who had defied his father's demand to submit themselves to his authority. Although it is uncertain how much of Xerxes' military preparations in the first few years of his reign were directed towards the goal of defeating the Greeks, we can be sure that avenging the defeat at Marathon remained a high priority, and in 481 he was ready to move his armies westwards into Greece.

There are two facts that indicate the great importance that Xerxes attached to his invasion of Greece. Firstly, there is his decision to lead the expedition in person. By doing this he was following the precedents set by Kyros, Kambyses and Dareios, who all led major campaigns of imperial expansion to the west, against the Lydians, Egyptians and Ionians respectively. And as a new king he probably felt the need to show his nobles that he was a worthy successor to the renowned Dareios. Secondly, the sheer size and diversity of the forces that Xerxes assembled from all parts of his empire show that he intended this to be a great military triumph. It was, of course, meant to be primarily a Persian achievement, but one that was contributed to and witnessed by all the peoples who were subject to Persian rule.

Xerxes left Persia in the spring of 481 and headed for Sardis, the former capital of the kingdom of Lydia and the main administrative centre for Persian rule in western Anatolia. He assembled the bulk of his army there and then marched north-west to the Hellespont, which he crossed in early summer between Abydos and Sestos. From there he moved his army to Doriskos, which lay at the mouth of the river Hebros and was a suitable place to rest his forces. There was also a garrison fort there, originally established by his father Dareios in 512 when he was campaigning against the Skythians. Here at Doriskos, Herodotus says Xerxes held a review of his army and his fleet, which had been ordered to rendezvous with the army. Herodotus uses the occasion of this review to describe the different contingents of the Persian army and their sizes. As well as the usual core of Iranian infantry and cavalry, the Persians themselves, the Medes, and the Sakai, Herodotus says that the army comprised substantial contingents from other parts of Asia, including Baktrians, Babylonians and Kappadokians. Among the more exotic, and therefore questionable, groups that Herodotus says were present he lists a detachment of camel-riding troops from Arabia and some primitive infantry from the depths of Ethiopia. The king's Ionian Greek subjects were also required to furnish men for the army, in the shape of hoplites, but their main contribution, like that of the Egyptians, Kilikians and Phoenicians was to the navy. In general Xerxes seems to have taken a high proportion of archers and other missile troops, as well as a great deal of cavalry.

The size of Xerxes' army presents historians with an awkward problem. According to Herodotus the army consisted of 1,800,000 troops levied in Asia, plus a further 300,000 from the parts of Europe that the army marched through on its way to Greece, giving a grand total of 2,100,000. In addition he claims that there were over 2,600,000 servants, attendants and other camp-followers, giving a combined force of over 4,700,000, without including the personnel of the fleet. The numbers that Herodotus gives are clearly an exaggeration, no doubt resulting from a contemporary historical tradition that magnified the success of the defence of Greece by multiplying the numbers of the enemy. The size of Xerxes' army is, therefore, very difficult to establish. Modern scholars disagree widely on how much to reduce the figure for the land army. Some put the number as low as 50,000, but a more generous estimate is 200,000. Possibly the true figure lies somewhere between these two, at around 100,000–150,000 fighting men, but a definitive answer to the question eludes us.

It is somewhat easier to believe the numbers offered by Herodotus for the size of the naval forces because ships were much easier to count than soldiers. Observers standing on a shoreline and watching a fleet sail past them would have a reasonable chance of accurately counting each individual vessel. Alternatively if, as some scholars maintain, Herodotus or his sources had access to official Persian records of the forces involved in the expedition, it is much more likely that the numbers for the various sections of the fleet were given precisely, whereas the contingents of the army may have been listed in general terms, rather than given as exact figures. Herodotus tells us that, at its greatest size, Xerxes' fleet numbered 1,207 trireme warships, and was accompanied by over 3,000 transport and supply ships. In spite of the comments made above, there are some difficulties posed by these numbers, which seem very large, even if they are assumed to represent the total capacity of the Persian navy. Herodotus claims there were over 250,000 oarsmen and sailors on these ships, but it may be that some of the vessels were manned by only skeleton crews, or even towed behind other ships to provide reserve vessels. Certainly it was a common procedure later in the fifth century for naval commanders to concentrate their manpower on their best and fastest warships prior to a battle.

The range and diversity of the peoples of the Persian Empire is indicated by this fifth-century black-figure painted vase from Athens. It shows two Negro soldiers with clubs and shields fighting a Greek hoplite. Ethiopian units were part of the army that Xerxes assembled for the invasion of Greece in 480. Many also fought on board the Egyptian ships of the Persian fleet. (Ancient Art and Architecture)

Whatever the numbers were, it is clear that Xerxes was anxious to ensure his expedition was successful, and he reasoned that mustering an overwhelming numerical superiority by land and sea was the best way to do it.

From Asia Minor to Greece

Xerxes ordered extensive preparations to be carried out along the route of the expedition, from western Asia Minor to northern Greece. In order for his army to cross the Hellespont from Asia into Europe two pontoon bridges were built. They spanned one of the narrowest sections of the straits, between the cities of Abydos and Sestos. To create each bridge several hundred warship hulls were anchored at right angles to the prevailing currents and linked together by six heavy cables. Between these cables planks of wood were laid to make a continuous platform, and then a causeway was constructed on top of the platform out of earth and brushwood. Finally a fence was built up on either side of the causeway, so that those animals crossing the bridges, horses, mules, oxen and camels, would not see the water and take fright. These bridges will have saved a great deal of time, for the process of embarking and disembarking such a huge army on transport ships would have taken many days, and unfavourable weather might have resulted in further loss of time. Even so the weather almost wrecked the whole scheme, as a storm blew up while the bridges were under construction and wrecked both of them. Xerxes' anger led him to execute the men supervising the work and, in what may seem to us a rather bizarre ritual, he had the waters

of the Hellespont symbolically whipped and branded, as though they were a recalcitrant slave.

From Doriskos, the army and navy progressed along the coast of Thrace towards Macedonia, meeting up at various pre-arranged points along the way. By co-ordinating the movements of the fleet and navy in this way Xerxes and his commanders sought to guard against the possibility of the Greeks making seaborne raids on his land forces and supply depots and also to ensure that safe havens were available for his fleet once it moved into hostile waters. Initially the paths of the fleet and army lay quite close together, but they separated near Akanthos in order to follow distinct routes. Xerxes was determined that his fleet would not fall victim to the dangerous north-Aegean storms that had wrecked the ships commanded by Mardonios in 492 as they attempted to sail round the headland of Mount Athos. He therefore ordered the cutting of a canal through the low-lying plain at the narrowest part of the peninsula, near the city of Akanthos. There are still some traces of this canal visible today.

The two elements were reunited at Therme, a small town at the head of the Thermaic Gulf. Xerxes then led the army southwards into northern Greece, passing through the lower reaches of the kingdom of Macedon and from there into the open plains of Thessaly. The Macedonians had enjoyed friendly relations with the Persians since the days of Dareios, whose campaigns against the Skythians had reduced the threat to Macedon from its northern neighbours. The Macedonian king, Alexander I, allowed Xerxes to prepare a supply depot on his territory and he contributed some infantry to the ever-growing ranks of the Persian army. The supply depot was part of a series of such bases established along the marching route through Thrace and Macedonia. One of the most impressive achievements of the whole march from Sardis to central Greece is that Xerxes' commanders managed to keep feeding and watering their men and animals. An army of over 100,000 men would have required many tons of food and water, as would their draught animals, horses and camels. It might be thought that the large Persian fleet was supposed to supply the army by carrying food and fodder from one staging point to the next, but the sheer size of the fleet would have made this an impractical idea. The 1,207 trireme warships alone would have carried at least 200,000 oarsmen and sailors, even if it is assumed that many of them were not fully crewed. The 3,000 or so other vessels that Herodotus says accompanied the warships would not have needed such large crews, and their purpose would have been to carry sufficient supplies to keep the fleet provisioned, but not the army.

Some food will have been transported with the army, using draught animals, including camels, as well as some human porters. Supplies of fresh water will have been collected and carried from one camp to the next, but only in small quantities. Ensuring a constant supply of water was always a very high priority for ancient armies. Herodotus claims that Xerxes' men and animals were so numerous they drank whole streams and rivers dry, but this is no doubt another picturesque exaggeration that we should not take too seriously. Nevertheless, finding and distributing adequate supplies of fresh water must have been one of the most difficult tasks faced by the men charged with keeping the army and navy going, especially in the latter stages of the campaign when they were passing through parts of northern and central Greece, where large rivers are rare and many

The 'Strangford Shield' is a Roman copy of the shield held by the statue of Athena that was housed in the Parthenon, the largest of the temples on the Athenian Acropolis. The statue was covered with ivory and gold that could be removed and used to pay wartime expenses. Although Athens was rich by the standards of the Greek states of the fifth century, her wealth was small in comparison with that of the Persian Empire. (Ancient Art and Architecture)

watercourses dry up naturally in the summer. In practice the details of the marching route will have been largely determined by the location of adequate sources of drinking water.

When it came to finding food a very heavy burden was laid upon the inhabitants of those territories through which the army and the fleet passed on their long journey. The Thracians and Macedonians in particular were expected to provide food for the army and to allow the animals to graze on their meadows. At each stage of the march the army camped around a huge tent erected for Xerxes and his closest followers, mainly Persian and Median nobles, who expected to be served from vessels of silver and gold. According to the accounts of the islanders of Thasos, whose possessions on the mainland obliged them to contribute, the combined cost of entertaining Xerxes and his court in the accustomed luxury as well as supplying the bread and meat needed for the soldiers and the grain for the animals for just one day came to the enormous sum of 400 talents of silver. Megakreon, one of the leading citizens of Abdera, is said to have remarked to his compatriots that they should be thankful Xerxes only took one main meal in the day, otherwise they would have been forced to abandon their city altogether rather than try to cater for his army twice in a day.

Even if their resources were not up to the task, these peoples will have had no alternative but to acknowledge their obligations to Xerxes as their overlord and supply as much as they could. Xerxes' forces were too large for the tribal and city leaders of the region to confront directly and the fact that he was clearly intent on passing

The inside of a red-figure painted wine cup, made in Athens around 480. The artist has portrayed a young man putting the finishing touches to a bronze helmet of the Corinthian type. The helmet was made from a single sheet of bronze, heated and beaten into the appropriate shape. Helmets of this type were commonly worn by Greek hoplites in the early fifth century, but they were gradually replaced by lighter helmets that allowed better vision and hearing.. (Ancient Art and Architecture)

through, rather than stopping to assert control over their territories will have encouraged them to do everything they could to speed the Persians on their way. The prospect of joining such a massive army of invasion for the sake of sharing in its plunder of the Greeks may also have contributed to the readiness with which the peoples of the northern coast of the Aegean submitted to the Great King. Xerxes made a point of gathering these additional forces under his command to emphasise that their homelands were part of his empire. Consequently there were no attempts to challenge the army or the fleet as they made their way towards Greece, although Herodotus does mention that some of the camels were attacked by lions as the army was passing through Macedonia.

The Greeks prepare to defend themselves

In Greece the reaction to the news that the Persian king was preparing a large invasion force was mixed. Many of the Greek city-states banded together into a league which modern historians have called the Hellenic League, because the ancient Greeks used the word *Hellenes* to describe themselves. One of the most significant aspects of the initial meeting of this league in 481 was that the member states agreed to end any conflicts with each other and swore an oath to be allies permanently. Hence Athens and Aigina, two of the members who had been at war with each other for over 20 years, now became firm allies in order to resist the Persians. The Spartans were appointed the commanders of the League forces, by both land and sea, in spite of a suggestion that the Athenians should head the naval contingents. Spies were sent to Asia Minor to find out more about Xerxes' preparations, and envoys were sent to some of the more powerful Greek states and confederations across the Mediterranean to ask for help.

It is clear that by no means all the major Greek city-states joined the League, but its precise membership is difficult to establish. Herodotus gives a list of those Greeks who 'medised', that is, they submitted to the Persian king and gave him symbolic presents of earth and water to acknowledge his authority over them, but he includes many states that were originally members of the Hellenic League, such as the Thessalians, the Thebans and the Phokians. These states only surrendered to Xerxes after his army overran their territory and they were abandoned by their allies, whereas Argos, a bitter enemy of Sparta simply refused to have anything to do with an alliance under Spartan leadership. Some of the other Greek states accused the Argives of already being committed to helping Xerxes. The Argives did not provide any actual assistance to the Persians, but it may be that they were awaiting the outcome of the conflict with the Hellenic League *before* committing themselves.

Another state that refused to help was Syracuse, whose ruler Gelon was leading a Sicilian confederation in a war to resist the increasing influence of the Carthaginians in Sicily. The association of Cretan cities also refused to send any assistance. The prosperous island state of Korkyra (modern Corfu) did dispatch a force of 60 ships in response to the Hellenic League's appeal, but they got no further than the southern coast of the Peloponnese and played no part in the actual fighting. It is possible that the Corcyreans, like the Argives, decided to play a waiting game and not get involved in the conflict until it was clear that one side was victorious.

In the early summer of 480, at about the time that Xerxes and his army were crossing the Hellespont, the principal ruling family of Thessaly, the Aleudai, were preparing to welcome him, having committed themselves to the Persians as early as 492. There were some dissident groups among the Thessalians who did not support this policy and they requested that the Hellenic League send a force to oppose the Persians at the border between Thessaly and Macedonia. An army of 10,000 League hoplites, under the command of Euainetos the Spartan, marched to the valley of the river Peneus at Tempe, the main pass into Thessaly from lower Macedonia. After only a few days they abandoned this position and left the Thessalians with no alternative but to submit to Xerxes. The League commander seems to have decided that there were too many alternative routes into Thessaly that Xerxes could use to outflank the pass at Tempe. It is noteworthy that the Hellenic League forces had been transported by sea as far as the Gulf of Pagasai, on the southern edge of Thessaly. The intention was probably to station their own fleet there against the possibility that the Persians might try to sail around and land forces at their rear.

Opinion in the Hellenic League was now divided between the Peloponnesian members, like Sparta and Corinth, who advocated retreating as far as the narrow Isthmus of Corinth, and the non-Peloponnesian states like Thebes and Athens, who argued that their territories should not be abandoned without a fight. It was decided to make a stand in central Greece at a very narrow passage of land between the mountains and the sea called Thermopylai, meaning 'hot gates', so called because of its hot sulphurous springs. It was virtually the only route from Thessaly into central Greece that could be used by Xerxes' huge army and it was chosen as the best defensive position available. A small army was sent to occupy the pass and a fleet was assembled to take up a position at Artemision on the northern end of the island of Euboia. The fleet would prevent the Persians from landing troops along the coastline at the rear of the Greek army at Thermopylai. The overall command of these forces was taken by Leonidas, one of the Spartan kings, and the naval contingent was placed under the direction of another Spartan called Eurybiades.

The army sent to Thermopylai was made up of about 8,000 hoplites, very few of whom were Spartans. The main Lakonian contingent of about 1,000 was probably drawn from the *perioikoi*. Leonidas was accompanied by a picked bodyguard of 300 Spartan citizens, chosen for their bravery and determination, and because they each had living sons whom they left behind in Sparta. As was usual they were accompanied by personal helot servants, who could also participate in the fighting as light-armed troops. There were 2,800 other Peloponnesians present, mainly from the cities of Arkadia, the region to the north of Lakonia, and the rest of the troops came from central Greece, principally the regions of Malis, Phokis, eastern Lokris and Boiotia. The reason Herodotus gives for the small number of Spartans is the same one that explained their delay in reaching Marathon ten years earlier. They were celebrating an important religious festival, the Karneia, and could not leave Sparta until it was finished. The limited number of other Peloponnesians is also accounted for by a religious commitment, although in their case it was the four-yearly Olympic festival which kept many of them away. Some scholars have suggested a less noble reason, however, which is that the Peloponnesian states were reluctant to commit their manpower to the defence of central Greece, preferring to keep their man strength closer to home.

Nevertheless, there were many other Greeks involved in the joint land and sea operation. Herodotus says that the Greek fleet at Artemision numbered 271 triremes. The principal naval resources of the Greeks were the trireme fleets of Athens, Corinth and Aigina. If, as in later years, each of these carried 170 oarsmen and 30 sailors and marines, there would have been around 54,000 men in the fleet, including at least 10 hoplites and four archers per ship, making a total of nearly 4,000 soldiers. The strong Athenian presence was the result of a very recent ship-building programme. In 488/87 the Athenians were

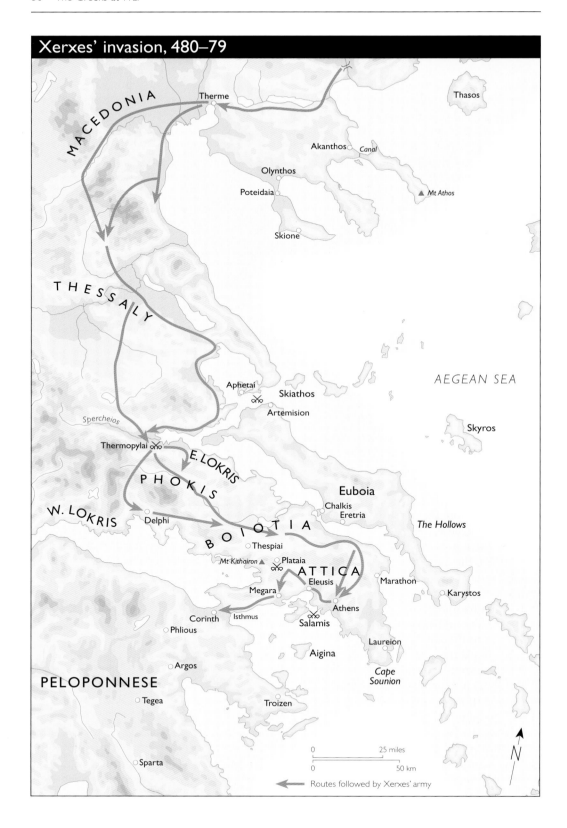

Xerxes' invasion, 480–79

MACEDONIA

Therme

Thasos

Akanthos   Canal

Olynthos

Poteidaia

▲ Mt Athos

Skione

THESSALY

Spercheios

Aphetai

Skiathos

Artemision

AEGEAN SEA

Skyros

Thermopylai

E. LOKRIS

PHOKIS

W. LOKRIS

Delphi

Euboia

Chalkis
Eretria

The Hollows

BOIOTIA

Thespiai

Mt Kithairon ▲   Plataia

ATTICA

Megara   Eleusis

Marathon

Karystos

Corinth   Isthmus

Athens

Phlious

Salamis

Laureion

Aigina

Cape
Sounion

PELOPONNESE

Argos

Tegea

Troizen

0   25 miles
0   50 km

Sparta

N

Routes followed by Xerxes' army

so short of vessels for their war against the island of Aigina that they had to buy some old warships from Corinth. In 483 the Athenians received a financial windfall from the discovery of a very rich silver vein in the public mines at Laureion. An ambitious politician called Themistokles persuaded them not to distribute the profits among the citizens, but to invest them in a new fleet of triremes. By 480 they had 200 warships, making them the largest naval contributors to the Hellenic League. They were keen that one of their generals should be appointed to command the Greek fleet, but Sparta's numerous allies insisted on a Spartan commander.

The Persians approach Thermopylai and Artemision

The pass of Thermopylai was, in ancient times, a narrow strip of land where the main route between Thessaly and central Greece is bordered by high mountains on one side and the sea on the other. It was barely 15 metres across in its central section, known as the Middle Gate, where there had been an old defensive wall built by the Phokians. Leonidas ordered some of his men to rebuild this to add to the strength of the position. He chose this point to make his main stand because, although the pass was even narrower at its two ends (the East and West Gates), the mountain slopes were much gentler at those points and could be scaled by large bodies of men. On his arrival he was told by some of the local Malians that there was a route through the mountains to the south of Thermopylai which rejoined the main route at the East Gate. It was known as the Anopaia path. As this pathway also branched off southwards into the territory of Phokis he placed the Phokian hoplites midway along it, preventing the Persians from using it to outflank his position and attack his army from the rear.

Xerxes' army crossed the river Spercheios and camped near the town of Trachis, to the

west of Thermopylai, at the end of August 480. It took several days for the entire army to assemble and for the Persians to scout the enemy positions and report back to the king and his commanders. On seeing the enormous size of the Persian army now marshalled against him, Leonidas sent an urgent message to the states of the Hellenic League asking for reinforcements. Rumours of the huge forces being prepared by Xerxes for his invasion of Greece must have been circulating for some time before the Persians reached Greece. Herodotus says that three Greek spies were sent to Asia Minor to gather information. They observed the marshalling of Xerxes' forces at Sardis, but were captured and were about to be executed when Xerxes himself intervened and ordered them to be taken around the camp and shown all the contingents of infantry and cavalry, in order to impress upon them the overwhelming superiority of his army. Like so many of the anecdotes passed on by Herodotus this one is not easy to believe, but even if the Greek spies were given a guided tour of the army at Sardis, it is unlikely that these reports and rumours would have been given full credence by the Greek leaders until they could confirm them with their own eyes. Despite the daunting size of the Persian army Leonidas seems to have been fairly confident that his force of 8,000 men was adequate for the task of holding the pass temporarily, but he felt the need for further troops to shore up the defence over a longer period. It was later said that Xerxes, in an attempt to avoid a battle, offered Leonidas the chance to join his army and become his satrap of Greece, but Leonidas refused, saying that it was better to die for the freedom of the Greeks than to live and rule them.

As the Persian army reached Thermopylai, the fleet made its way from Therme to Aphetai on the southern tip of the peninsula of Magnesia, encountering three advance scout ships from the Greek fleet and capturing two of them. Severe

A bronze statuette of a warrior, dedicated in the sanctuary of Zeus at Olympia in the western Peloponnese in the sixth century. By the time of Xerxes' invasion, Olympia was one of the most important sanctuaries in the Greek world and the famous Olympic festival, held every four years, attracted thousands of celebrants from across the Mediterranean. The athletic competitions at the festival included a race for men wearing bronze helmets and carrying hoplite shields. (Ancient Art and Architecture)

losses were incurred by the Persians when they put into the shore on the eastern side of Magnesia en route. A storm blew up and wrecked nearly a third of the Persian ships. Eventually the survivors made it to Aphetai and prepared to engage the Greeks at sea.

The size of the Persian fleet that gradually assembled at Aphetai after the storm must also have come as something of a shock to the Greeks. Before it was hit by the storm the Persian fleet numbered 1,207 triremes and about 3,000 other vessels. It will have taken a long time, possibly several days, to settle into its new anchorage. At this point the Greeks debated abandoning their position at Artemision and heading south. Herodotus claims that it was only through bribery that the principal Greek commanders, the Athenian, Themistokles, the Spartan, Eurybiades, and the Corinthian, Adeimantos, were persuaded to remain and continue with the co-ordinated strategy of stopping the Persian advance by land and sea. The Greeks had 271 triremes and about 50 other ships. They were later joined by 53 Athenian triremes, which seem to have been part of the Athenians' reserve forces, held back to guard Attika, but they were apparently sent north, perhaps in response to a plea for reinforcements similar to that which Leonidas sent after seeing the size of Xerxes' army. The Persians' advantage in numbers was potentially overwhelming, a fact that would have been obvious to the Greeks while they observed or received reports on the build-up of Persian forces at Aphetai.

The Persians were well informed about the size of their opponents' naval forces,

mainly as a result of their early success in capturing two Greek triremes and their crews. According to Herodotus the Persians expected the smaller Greek force to sail away under the cover of night, so, after the king's fleet had assembled at Aphetai, they held off from attacking the Greeks until a squadron of 200 ships, which had been dispatched southwards to circumnavigate Euboia and prevent the Greeks from escaping, signalled that it was in position. Although the basic idea seems credible enough, there are some problems in accepting all of what Herodotus says about this stratagem. He suggests that the ships took a route beyond the island of Skiathos in order to avoid being observed as they journeyed round Euboia, but this seems unlikely to have worked, since there were Greek observers on Euboia who would surely have spotted the Persians as they started out and could even have monitored their progress at several points en route. It is more likely that they would have separated from the main fleet before they reached Aphetai, although even then they could not have expected to avoid detection throughout their voyage, which, at a distance of over 400 kilometres, would probably have taken several days to complete. The move was presumably part of a plan to trap the Greek ships between the two elements of the Persian fleet and capture or destroy them. A further question arises as a result of these considerations, namely, how could the Persians co-ordinate the two sections of their fleet? Herodotus clearly says that the main force at Aphetai was not supposed to engage the Greeks until it had seen the signal that announced the approach of the 200 ships sent round Euboia. The plan was probably to allow a certain amount of time, perhaps three or four days, for the 200 ships to complete their voyage, after which the main fleet could assume that they were in position and begin to drive the Greeks away from Artemision and into the trap. The initial reluctance of the Persians to attack the Greeks at Artemision, at least for two days, is thus explained by the need to give their flanking force time to get into position. Given what Herodotus says about their expectation that the Greeks would flee, they may even have expected to be informed of the 200 ships' successful circumnavigation of Euboia by the enemy's panicked withdrawal.

While the Persians were assembling their main force at Aphetai, the Greeks captured 15 ships that had got detached from the rest of the fleet and sailed into the Greek base at Artemision by mistake. It was probably from the commanders of these ships that the Greeks learnt of the Persian plan to send a squadron round Euboia, although Herodotus recounts the story of Skyllias of Skione, a Greek diver employed by the Persians, who supposedly swam across the straits from Aphetai to Artemision to warn the Greeks of the Persian plan. Some of the Greek captains were in favour of avoiding battle until nightfall and then heading back to meet these 200 ships well to the south. Eventually Eurybiades decided that his forces were strong enough to challenge the Persian fleet, which was still recovering from the earlier storm damage. The Greeks sailed out to attack while the Persian land forces were beginning to engage their compatriots holding the pass at Thermopylai. The Persian fleet comfortably outnumbered the Greeks, and its commanders responded to the challenge. The two fleets met in relatively open water and the Persians immediately began to encircle the Greeks, hoping to close in on them and use boarding tactics to capture their ships. They carried far more fighting men than the Greek ships, including detachments of Persian, Median or Sakai soldiers. The Greek ships stayed close together in a circular formation to avoid being set upon one by one and overwhelmed, but they gradually crowded in on each other so much that they had to risk a mass breakout through the enemy lines. After some brief ramming action, in which the Greeks excelled because their less heavily manned ships were lighter and faster, 30 Persian vessels

were captured. A ship from the Greek island of Lemnos also defected from the Persian side. Eurybiades withdrew for the night and sent a message to Leonidas saying that he would hold his position for another day.

Overnight the Persian detachment of 200 ships that was making its way round Euboia was caught in yet another bad storm at a place called 'the Hollows' and was completely destroyed. Not only did this cancel out any chance of trapping the Greeks between two sections of the fleet, it also reduced the overall numerical advantage that the Persians enjoyed. The 53 Athenian ships that arrived at this point also helped to redress the balance a little. When the Greeks learnt of their good fortune they went on the offensive again and launched a swift attack on the Persians, who were still waiting for a sign that their detachment had completed its journey. Several Kilikian ships were sunk and Eurybiades again told Leonidas that he was could hold out another day.

The battle of Thermopylai

The Greek defence of the pass of Thermopylai lasted three days. Initially the Persians seem to have thought that they could overwhelm the Greeks by sheer weight of numbers, but the extreme narrowness of the central section of the pass made it impossible for them to make effective use of their superior numbers. Xerxes himself was particularly contemptuous of the small Greek army. He is said by Herodotus to have sent two Median divisions (about 20,000 men) forward with orders to capture the Greeks and bring them to the king. When the Medes retreated after losing many men he ordered Hydarnes, commander of the élite Persian division known as the Immortals to take up the battle. But even his best soldiers could not overcome the determined resistance of the Greeks. It seems likely that Leonidas and his small Spartan force

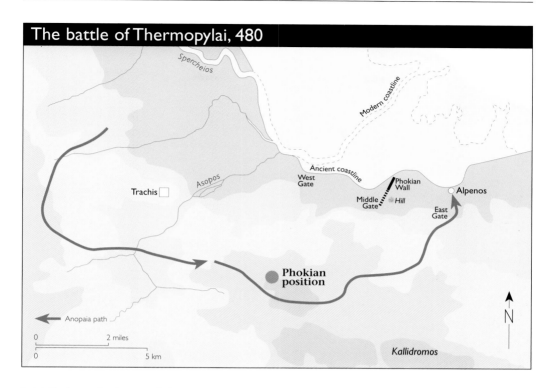

The battle of Thermopylai, 480

initially bore the brunt of the attack, but the Greeks rotated their forces so that they were able to rest many of their contingents and regularly deploy fresh men into the front line of the battle. The large, round shields and long thrusting spears of the Greek hoplites were very effective in this kind of close-quarter fighting and the Spartans had developed good tactics for drawing the enemy into the fight. They would feign a retreat and, as the enemy pressed forward, confident of victory, they would turn about and engage them face to face.

Towards the evening of the second day of fighting, Xerxes, impatient to remove the Greek forces and carry on into the heart of Greece, ordered Hydarnes to take the Immortals over the treacherous Anopaia path over the mountains and attack Leonidas and his men from the rear. The pathway through the mountains was a difficult one to traverse even in daytime, but at night there was increased danger. Fortunately for the Persians a local man from Trachis, Ephialtes, son of Eurydemos,

came forward in the hope of receiving a substantial reward from Xerxes. He offered to show them the path and guide them along it and back down to the eastern entrance of the pass. Hydarnes and his men set off at sundown and made their way along the mountain track towards the East Gate of the pass. As it was getting light the Persians encountered the 1,000 Phokians who had been positioned there to guard against just such a move. At first Hydarnes was afraid that they were more Spartans, but he was reassured by Ephialtes that they were not. The Phokians heard the Persians approaching but they had little time to prepare. Assuming that the Persians were intent on engaging them, as soon as the arrows started flying they retreated to a better defensive position on a nearby hilltop, ready to fight to the death. Hydarnes was too experienced a commander to let this opportunity slip by and he ordered his men to pay no further attention to the Phokians but to carry on towards the pass.

This dynamic bust of a Spartan warrior from the fifth century is thought by some to be a portrait of the heroic Spartan king, Leonidas, who died at the battle of Thermopylai. It certainly captures the sense of resolution that enabled Leonidas and his small force to continue to oppose the huge army of Xerxes after their position became hopeless. (Ancient Art and Architecture)

Leonidas had a few hours' warning of the approach of the Persians from some scouts who had been stationed with the Phokians to report any enemy movements. Leonidas now had to make a crucial decision whether to continue his defence of the pass, or to abandon it and retreat southwards. Some of Herodotus' informants claimed that many of the Greeks did not even wait for their commander to make up his mind, but fled as soon as they heard that the Persians were on their way. Herodotus is more inclined to believe that they were ordered to depart by Leonidas who realised that the Greek force was no longer capable of holding the pass now that the enemy could attack from two sides. In the event not all of the Greeks retreated because Leonidas and his 300 picked Spartans stayed behind, along with some of the Boiotians, namely 400 Thebans, whom some Greeks later claimed were kept there by Leonidas as hostages, and 700 hoplites from Thespiai.

Leonidas' decision to keep a small force in place is difficult to understand in strategic terms. The force was now too small to cause much delay to the progress of the Persians; though it might have been intended as a rearguard to cover the retreat of the rest of the Greeks. If so, it was a brave gesture to fight to the death against the invaders, belying the suggestion that the Spartans were not committed to the defence of the rest of the Greeks. Herodotus was told of an oracle given to the Spartans by the priestess of Apollo at Delphi at the start of the campaign, which said that the Spartans must lose either their city or their king to the Persians. Leonidas had become king rather unexpectedly, because he had two older brothers who both predeceased him. It may be that he felt he needed to do something brave and honourable to justify his position as king, or it may be that there really had been a prophecy suggesting that the death of a king would save the city of Sparta, but we cannot hope to know his reasons. The decision of the Boiotians to remain behind and fight to the death with Leonidas and his men shows that the Spartans were not the only Greek hoplites who could be brave in the face of overwhelming odds.

While the rest of the Greeks retreated and a messenger was sent by ship to the fleet at Artemision to tell Eurybiades that the defence of the pass was over, Leonidas led the remaining hoplites forward to engage the enemy. Xerxes' main army was urged on by the officers, some of whom used whips to drive their more reluctant soldiers into battle. The result was a fierce and bloody combat in which many Persians fell, some trampled by their own comrades. The hoplites initially fought with their spears, but when these were broken they used their short swords. Among the casualties were two of Xerxes' half-brothers, presumably fighting in the front ranks of the Persians. Finally Leonidas himself fell and his body then became a prize fought over by the Spartans and the Persians. When Hydarnes and the Immortals emerged from the Anopaia pathway and approached the rear of the Greeks, the Spartans, their surviving helots and Thespiaians moved to a small hill behind the Phokian wall and made a last stand there, fighting with swords, bare hands and even teeth, until the Persians drew back and slew the last of them with arrows. Some of the Thebans managed to separate themselves and surrender, but the Persian king was ill-tempered in victory. He enslaved the Thebans and branded them with his royal symbol; their city had submitted to him, but they had joined his enemies. He also had the body of Leonidas impaled and decapitated, so enraged was he with the Spartan king's defiance. According to Herodotus, Leonidas and his army had cost Xerxes 20,000 men.

The Greeks later honoured Leonidas and his fallen comrades with a monument and several verse epitaphs, one of which was for Megistias, a seer and diviner from Akarnania in western Greece who accompanied Leonidas. He was said to have predicted that disaster was about to happen when he examined the sacrificial animal that was slaughtered in the early hours of the morning, as Hydarnes and the Immortals were making their way through the mountains. Leonidas offered him the chance to join the retreat, but he refused, sending his son away instead. The epitaph was composed by his friend, the poet Simonides:

In remembrance of the renowned Megistias, slain by the Medes when they crossed the river Spercheios; although the seer saw clearly his impending fate, he did not choose to abandon the Spartan leader.

Ephialtes, the local man who had guided the Persians through the mountains and behind the Greeks fled to Thessaly, fearing that the Spartans would take their revenge upon him. A price was put on his head and although he was eventually killed in a private quarrel by another man from Trachis, the Spartans nevertheless rewarded his killer.

The evacuation and capture of Athens

At sea the Greeks had gained considerable confidence from their earlier successes and good luck, but a third day of fighting did not go so well for them. Their opponents had again managed to encircle them and in the ensuing struggle both sides suffered heavy casualties, which the Greeks could ill afford. After hearing the bad news from Thermopylai the Greek fleet headed for the island of Salamis, off the coast of Athens. They did this at the request of the Athenians, whose population was being evacuated to Troizen in the eastern

Peloponnese and the islands of Salamis and Aigina in an attempt to save them from the Persians. The decision to abandon Athens and Attika to the Persians and evacuate the population by sea was a brave one, made by a vote of the Athenian citizen assembly. It is a remarkable example of Athenian democracy in action, with the majority view prevailing after an impassioned debate, carried out under the shadow of the Persian invasion.

While the Persians were advancing through northern Greece the Athenians sent an official delegation to the famous oracle of the god Apollo at Delphi to ask for divine guidance. The usual procedure when consulting the oracle at Delphi was for the sacred envoys to the priestess of Apollo, called the Pythia, would then utter the god's words, which tended to be a stream of unintelligible phrases that the priests would have to 'interpret' for the suppliants. On this occasion, however, the envoys had scarcely taken their seats in the Pythia's sacred chamber before she screamed directly at them, saying, 'Wretched ones, why do you sit there? Leave your homes and your rocky citadel and flee to the ends of the earth!' This command was followed with dire warnings of impending doom not just for Athens, but for many other Greek cities at the hands of the Persians. Although they were taken aback by this outburst, the two Athenian envoys had a mission to complete, so they heeded the advice of a leading Delphic official and made another, humbler entreaty for Apollo's guidance. Their second approach yielded a somewhat more encouraging reply. As was usual, the oracle was delivered to the Athenians in poetic form:

It is not in the power of Pallas Athena to appease Olympian Zeus, although she entreats him with many words and subtle wisdom, but I will speak a second time to you, having become almost adamant.
When all the other places are seized that are bounded by Kekrops and the secret groves of divine Kithairon, heavenly Zeus gives to the

to Athena being unable to appease Zeus, and the seizure of places within boundaries of Kekrops (a mythical king of Athens) and the groves of Mount Kithairon (on the border with Boiotia) suggested that the whole of Attika would be overrun by the Persians. The reference to a wooden wall remaining intact seemed to some Athenians to be a command to defend one area, logically the Acropolis of Athens, with a wooden palisade, but Themistokles and his supporters argued for another meaning. They pointed to the mention of Salamis, an island in the Saronic Gulf to the west of Athens, and the mention of an army coming from the mainland, interpreting the oracle as an instruction to abandon the overrun territory of Attika and retreat to Salamis. On their interpretation the wooden wall was a figurative one and meant the wooden hulls of the Athenians' new fleet of warships. The reference to Demeter, goddess of the harvest, even gave a time of year for the promised victory. Their arguments carried the day and the Assembly passed a decree ordering the evacuation and the preparation of the fleet. A revised version of this decree was preserved at Troizen. The following are extracts from it:

children of Triton a wooden wall that alone remains intact, to the benefit of you and your sons.

Do not wait for the army of cavalry and infantry coming from the mainland, but retreat and turn your backs on them. You shall confront them again.

Divine Salamis, you shall destroy the sons of women, either when Demeter is scattered or gathered together.

As often happened when states got an official response from the Delphic oracle, there was a dispute back in Athens over the significance of these words. The references

Decided by the Council and the People: Themistokles, the son of Neokles, of the deme Phrearrhioi proposed: The city is to be entrusted to the protection of its patron Athena and to the protection of all the other gods, against the barbarians on behalf of the land. The whole of the Athenians and the foreigners who live in Athens shall move their wives and children to Troizen ... and their old folk and moveable property to Salamis ... All the rest of the Athenians and the resident foreigners who have reached manhood shall embark on the 200 ships prepared and fight against the barbarians for the sake of their own freedom and that of the other Greeks …

The decree was passed in the summer of 480, prior to the battle of Salamis. The Athenians were committing themselves to resisting the Persians and putting their trust in the co-operation of the other Greeks. An earlier decree had recalled all those Athenian citizens who were ostracised and required them to go to Salamis. Several of Themistokles' political opponents were among the exiles who assembled there.

In the end a few people did remain behind in the city, mainly the temple treasurers and priestesses of the cults on the Acropolis, which could not be abandoned entirely to the enemy. Some of the poorer Athenians persisted in the belief that a literal wooden wall would be proof against the Persians and they barricaded themselves on the Acropolis behind a wooden palisade. The Persians occupied Attika in early September of 480 and ransacked Athens. They took up a position on the Areopagos hill, opposite the entrance to the Acropolis, and fired flaming arrows into the palisade. Some Athenians descended from Peisistratos were with the Persians and they tried to persuade the defenders to give in, but eventually the Persians had to storm the citadel. They killed the remaining defenders then ransacked the temples and set fire to them.

Xerxes also sent some of his army into Phokis to ravage the countryside and loot the towns. The Phokians fled westwards, as did many of the citizens of Delphi, but the sanctuary of Apollo escaped plundering by the Persians. The story that Herodotus was told to explain this, by the officials at Delphi, held that as a Persian detachment was approaching the remaining priests asked the god what to do and he replied that he would protect his own. Then, as the Persian soldiers were coming up the narrow mountain path to the sanctuary,

there was a crack of thunder and two bolts of lightning struck the cliffs above them, sending two enormous rocks crashing down, killing some and putting the rest to flight. An alternative explanation is that Xerxes was well disposed towards the priests at Delphi, who had done their best to convince the Greeks that resistance was futile, so he specifically exempted the sanctuary from plunder. Respectful treatment of this kind was not unusual for major religious centres in the provinces of the Persian Empire.

The fleets prepare to do battle

Having assisted in the evacuation of the Athenians to Salamis the Greek fleet waited in the bay on the east side of the island while the commanders debated whether to withdraw to the more defensible land position at the Isthmus of Corinth. Many of the Peloponnesian states had already decided that this narrow strip of land offered them the best chance of resisting the Persian advance. When the news of the defeat at Thermopylai reached them, the Spartans and the other Peloponnesians, who had just finished celebrating the Olympic festival, immediately gathered at the Isthmus and began constructing a fortification wall across its narrowest point. The fleet commanders began discussing their options as the Persians were entering Attika. After a day of inconclusive arguments they broke up for the night. The following day the Persian fleet arrived and took up station in the waters beyond the Bay of Phaleron to the east of Salamis. Their numbers had been reduced by storms and battle, but they had picked up some reinforcements from Greeks who were forced to come over to the Persian side, so the effective strength was probably over 700 warships. The Greeks, who had only just over 300 ships, did not come out to fight. Instead they carried on with their deliberations which were interrupted by the news that the Persians had captured the

Acropolis. A large part of the Persian army also began to head for the Isthmus of Corinth. These developments only encouraged the majority of commanders to abandon Salamis before the Persian fleet closed in. Themistokles and the Athenians pleaded with Eurybiades, the Spartan who was still in overall command of the fleet, but he insisted that the Isthmus option was the best one. He ordered the ship's captains to prepare to depart under the cover of night. But later that night Eurybiades changed his mind and the following morning the Greek fleet was still at Salamis, ready to do battle with the Persians. What caused this change of plan?

Each fleet was aware of the other's position, although neither side had direct sight of their opponents and they were far enough apart to be able to carry out some manoeuvres undetected. The commanders needed to obtain further information before they made their next moves. From the Persians' point of view the information that mattered most was whether the Greek fleet was staying put at Salamis, or whether it was going to retreat westwards, via the Megarian Straits. To some extent this could be determined by observing the Greek position from the mainland opposite Salamis, although the small island of Hagios Georgios would have interfered with their view and, crucially, the Greeks could, if necessary, have slipped away under cover of darkness. From the Greek point of view the most important question was whether there was a realistic escape route available to them. The Persian army was moving along the coast of the Bay of Eleusis and would soon occupy the land immediately north of Salamis, as far as the Megarian Straits. If a section of the Persian fleet came around the south of Salamis and entered these straits from the west while the main fleet remained to the east, they would cut the Greeks off completely from the Peloponnese. A similar deployment had already been tried by the Persians against the Greeks when they were based at Artemision. But for the intervention of a

storm it might well have succeeded in trapping them on that occasion.

Herodotus says that this is precisely what the Persians did. He makes Themistokles responsible for prompting their deployment by saying that he sent a trusted slave, called Sikinnos, to Xerxes with a secret message, telling him that the Greeks were about to leave and urging him to seize his chance to attack them before they escaped. He claimed that Xerxes would catch them disunited and unprepared for battle and win an easy victory. Did Themistokles really send a message to the enemy and did they really believe that it was genuine? One reason for doubting the story is that Themistokles himself was later exiled by the Athenians and sought asylum with the Persians. His political enemies may have invented the message ploy to blacken his reputation. In any case, it is far from clear that the message would have made any difference. The Persians certainly began to move their ships into position that evening, but whether they did so on account of Themistokles' messenger, or because the king had independently decided to take the offensive that night is open to debate. They sent a squadron of 200 Egyptian ships round to the west side of Salamis to cut off the route to the Isthmus through the Megarian Straits. Another squadron was despatched with orders to cruise the southern and eastern approaches to the island while the rest of the fleet proceeded into the narrow straits between Salamis and the mainland towards the Greek positions. A small force of élite Persian infantry was landed on the tiny island of Psyttaleia to occupy it in anticipation of some ships being driven aground there during the fighting. It would have taken quite a long time for the Persian ships to move around from Phaleron to the opening of the straits, so even if they began to move at dusk, some of them may still have been taking up their stations towards midnight. Most of the captains were new to the waters around Salamis, and Herodotus adds the detail that these

movements were made 'silently', in order that the Greeks would be unaware of them. It seems reasonable to suppose that the Persians hoped to drive the Greeks out of the narrow channels around the eastern side of the island and into the more open waters of the Bay of Eleusis. The Greeks would not have been expected to attempt to defeat the main strength of Xerxes' navy, but rather to flee westwards and try to force their way past the smaller Egyptian detachment. Xerxes' commanders had to put his ships out to sea early, regardless of Themistokles' message, because he needed

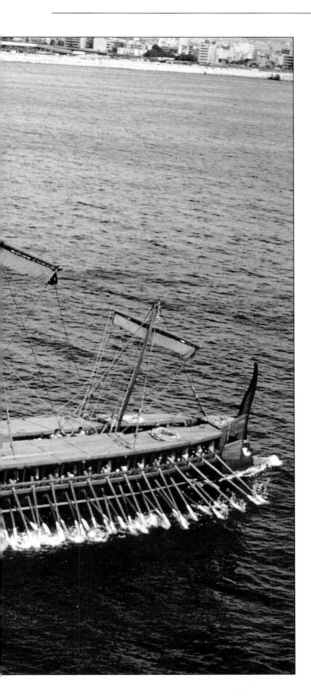

The Hellenic Navy's vessel *Olympias* is a reconstruction of a trireme warship of the type used by the Athenians in the fifth century. The ship is rowed by up to 170 oarsmen, sitting in banks of three along each side. Triremes used sails to make voyages over long distances, but the sails and masts were normally left on shore for battles. Both Greeks and Persians used triremes as the standard vessel in their navies, but the greater resources of the Persian Empire meant that the Great King could afford to man larger fleets. (Ancient Art and Architecture)

ships they may have had at sea, might not have been able to see the Greeks if they decided to escape under cover of darkness, or even dusk. By closing off the possible escape routes as darkness fell they ensured that this could not happen.

The Greeks received two reports of these movements. One came from the crew of another Greek ship that defected from the Persians, this time from the island of Tenos. They revealed the Persian plan to Eurybiades and his commanders, but their reliability was questioned. Late in the evening, however, one of the returned Athenian exiles, Aristeides, came back from a scouting voyage with the news that the Persians were surrounding the Greek position and that retreating to the Isthmus was no longer possible without a fight. Themistokles renewed his urging to engage the Persian fleet, arguing that the narrows on the eastern side of Salamis would be a better place to fight them than the Bay of Eleusis, or the more open waters around the Isthmus. A threat made by Themistokles and his fellow Athenians to abandon the rest of the Greeks entirely and take their families away to Italy may have carried particular weight in the discussions. The Athenian ships made up by far the largest contingent in the Greek fleet, so their presence was essential in any naval confrontation with the Persians. Under the circumstances it is hardly surprising that Eurybiades changed his mind and agreed to lead the Greek fleet into battle. Any hope of slipping away under the cover of darkness had been dashed by the Persians deploying their ships ahead of the Greek

to close his trap before darkness fell and the Greeks could more easily escape. It is, therefore, not necessarily the case that Sikinnos' message prompted Xerxes to act. The Persians would have needed to follow the same timetable without it, since their observers on the mainland, plus any scout

departure. The only course of action left was to sail out to battle and trust that the Persian ships would be unable to use their numerical superiority in the relatively narrow waters.

The battle of Salamis

In eager anticipation of a magnificent victory, King Xerxes had an observation point prepared so that he could watch the battle. It was positioned opposite the town of Salamis with a good view of Psyttaleia, the island where a detachment of Persian troops had landed during the night. But instead of witnessing his fleet's final triumph over the Greeks, Xerxes saw a naval disaster unfolding before his very eyes. The various ethnic contingents of the Persian fleet were lined up several rows deep across the narrow channel between the Phoenicians on the right wing, nearest to Xerxes' position, and the Ionians on the left, nearest to Salamis. As they moved further into the channel their ships became so compacted and confused that they found it impossible to keep in formation. The crews had been up all night and were tired and to make matters worse a strong swell developed which made it even harder for the ships to make headway. Themistokles, who knew the local sea conditions very well, had anticipated this and he seems to have persuaded the other Greek commanders to delay engaging the Persians until they were clearly in disorder. This would explain the apparent retreat of the Greeks that Herodotus says preceded the first clash, and which can be interpreted as a change from a passive formation of ships in a line to a more active one, with the Athenian and Aiginetan ships on the two Greek wings leading the Greek charge to break through the Persian lines and ram individual ships as they struggled to manoeuvre. From the Persians' point of view, it would have appeared that the Greek ships were turning away, and they would obviously assume that they were trying to

retreat, which was what their own commanders had anticipated. The tragic playwright Aischylos, in his play *The Persians*, mentions a signal given to the Greek fleet by a trumpet, which may well have been a pre-arranged one to tell the captains when to move forward and strike. Signals had also been used to co-ordinate the actions of the Greek fleet at Artemision. It would seem, therefore, that both sides had to some extent determined in advance how the battle would be fought. Like all battles, however, once the action had started it would be impossible to keep to a specific plan, even if there was one, and it was up to the captains of the individual ships to make decisions on the spot. The main decision that many of Xerxes' captains made was to turn away from the attacking Greeks, causing more confusion as they encountered their own ships trying to go forward and impress the Great King with their prowess. In the resulting chaos the captains of the Greek ships urged on their much fresher crews and pressed the attack with great success.

Herodotus' subsequent account of the battle is largely made up of anecdotes about the exploits of various individuals and groups. These anecdotes, like so many of the stories Herodotus recounts throughout his *Histories*, are versions of events given to him by particular groups or individuals, so they are often very biased and we therefore do not have a complete picture of the battle. Herodotus repeats the story that, at the last minute, the 70 Corinthian ships did turn and flee towards the Bay of Eleusis. It is likely that this supposed cowardly, northward retreat, which Herodotus presents as an Athenian slander against the Corinthians, may have been a deliberate move to engage the Egyptian squadron and prevent it from attacking the Greeks at the rear. The Corinthians maintained that their ships did not encounter the Egyptians but returned to the battle and acquitted themselves as well as any of the other Greeks.

One of the most colourful anecdotes concerns Artemisia, the ruler of Halikarnassos, Herodotus' home city, which was subject to the Persians. She was in command of her own ship and in the front line of the Persian fleet. When an Athenian trireme bore down on her she tried to escape but found her path blocked by other Persian ships. In desperation she ordered her helmsman to ram one of them, a ship that was commanded by the king of Kalydna in Lykia. This ship sank with the loss of the king and all his crew. The pursuing Athenian captain assumed that Artemisia's ship was on his side and changed course towards another Persian vessel. Xerxes and his advisers saw the incident and recognised Artemisia's ship by its ensign, but they assumed that she had sunk a Greek trireme, which earned her the king's admiration. Xerxes is also said to have remarked at this point, 'My men have acted like women and my women like men.'

Another story concerns the Persian soldiers on the island of Psyttaleia. They were placed there in anticipation of the bulk of the Greek fleet being driven north and westwards away from the island. Instead they were isolated from their own ships and left vulnerable to attack from the nearby shores of Salamis. Aristeides, who had been elected as one of the Athenian generals after his early return from exile, commandeered some small boats and led a group of Athenian hoplites over to the island. Right before Xerxes' eyes, his élite troops, who included three of his own nephews, were slaughtered by the Athenians. Along the coast of Salamis other Persians who managed to get ashore from their foundering ships were killed or captured.

Some of the Phoenician ships, which had been closest to the king's position, encountered less trouble in advancing on the Greeks and joined in the battle sooner than the Ionians on the opposite wing. Their principal opponents were the Athenians, who routed them and drove several of the Phoenician crews ashore,

right at the place where Xerxes was watching from his royal chariot. They proceeded to the king and tried to excuse their failure by complaining that they had been betrayed by the Ionians, whom they blamed for the confusion in the Persian fleet. Unfortunately for them, while they were in the presence of the king, one of the Ionian ships, from Samothrake, was seen to ram an Athenian trireme and then get rammed by an Aiginetan one. The marines on the Ionian ship immediately boarded and captured the Aiginetan vessel, proving to Xerxes both their loyalty and their valour. The king was now so angry at what he was seeing that he gave orders for the Phoenician complainers to be beheaded.

Towards the end of the day the Persian fleet retreated in confusion to the Bay of Phaleron, having lost more than 200 ships and having failed in its objective of forcing the Greeks away from Salamis. The Greeks had lost only about 40 ships and had sent the enemy back to their anchorage in disarray. The unexpected victory naturally led many to interpret it as an act of divine power, a fulfilment of the Delphic oracle given to the Athenians earlier in the year. Stories quickly began to circulate about divine apparitions during the fighting, a mysterious flash of light seen coming from Demeter's sanctuary at Eleusis and the sound of a holy chorus chanting prayers. The story also grew that King Xerxes immediately abandoned his army and fled back to Asia.

In fact, although it was getting late in the year and the weather was increasingly unhelpful, Xerxes seems to have attempted to carry on with the campaign for several more days. He attempted to build another bridge of boats across the straits to Salamis and ordered his fleet to prepare for further action. The Persians still had far more ships than the Greeks and the Egyptian squadron must have rejoined the main fleet intact after it became clear that the Greeks were not going to be driven into their part of the trap. The army had marched through the

The battle of Salamis, 480

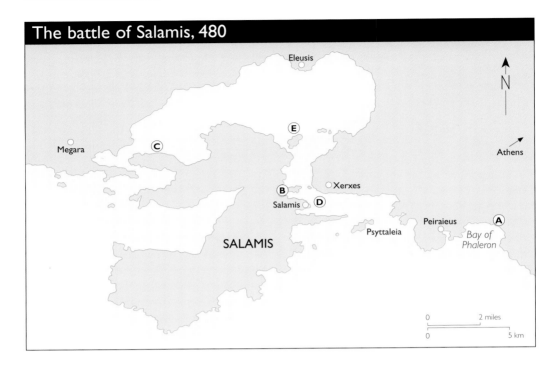

territory of Megara as far as the temple of Poseidon on the Isthmus, which was the headquarters of the Hellenic League. They ransacked and burned it, then moved up to, but did not challenge, the Greek defences further west. At this point Xerxes seems to have changed his mind and the Persian fleet departed for the shores of Asia Minor. The Greeks pursued them as far as Andros, but then gave up and returned to Salamis. Xerxes meanwhile took his army back through Boiotia and into Thessaly and Macedonia, where it could spend the winter in places with sufficient supplies of food and fodder. A portion of the army returned with the Great King himself to Persia.

The Greeks clearly thought that Xerxes had simply lost his nerve and run for home, but there were other reasons for his retreat and return to Persia. To some extent the campaign had been a success. While his fleet had not exactly covered itself with glory, his army had won the first major engagement, albeit with significant casualties. They had slain one of the principal enemy leaders and taken

ABOVE On the eve of the battle of the main Persian fleet left its station in the bay of Phaleron **(A)** and rowed quietly towards the position of the Greek fleet **(B)**. A detachment of 200 Egyptian ships was sent round the island of Salamis to the straits of Megara **(C)** to block off the route for a Greek retreat westwards. The Greeks rowed out at dawn and the main battle took place in the narrow channel **(D)** to the north of the tiny island of Psyttaleia, where Xerxes had stationed 400 elite troops. The Corinthian ships left the Greek fleet and sailed northwards towards the Egyptians, but after reaching approximately point **(E)** without coming into contact with the enemy they turned back and rejoined the main fleet. From his position on the headland opposite the town of Salamis Xerxes was able to see the entire battle.

RIGHT An archer wearing a Scythian-style pointed cap from the sculptures that decorated the temple at Aphaia on the island of Aigina. The Greeks used archers in warfare as support for their heavy infantrymen and in naval warfare. Archers were a standard part of the crews of triremes and were skilled at firing their bows from a kneeling or crouching stance to counteract the movement of the ship. (Ancient Art and Architecture)

possession of the city of the hated Athenians. Even after the move to Thessaly his empire had been substantially extended to the west and it might be argued that his presence was not essential to the rest of

the campaign, which could be resumed the following year. An eclipse of the sun occurred at the start of October. This may have been interpreted as an omen that Xerxes' patron god Ahuramazda was not favourably disposed towards further action for some time. There were also good political reasons for him not to stay out on the western extremities of his empire for too long, not least the danger of rebellion in some of the key satrapies. In 479 Xerxes suppressed another serious revolt in Babylonia and it is quite likely that news of the beginning of this unrest was what made him decide to leave Greece before the pacification of the new territories had been completed.

The battle of Plataia

The Persian commander left in Greece was Mardonios, a cousin of Xerxes and also his son-in-law; his second-in-command was Artabazos, who later became one of the satraps of Phrygia in western Asia Minor. Logistical requirements forced Mardonios to retire to Thessaly and Macedonia for the winter. His long-term objective was to crush the remaining Greek states and to do this he would clearly have to invade the Peloponnese. The defences at the Isthmus of Corinth were completed by early 479, making it a very strong position. It was necessary for Mardonios to prepare for the return of the Persian fleet, so in the spring of 479 he decided to try to break up the Hellenic League by inviting the Athenians to 'medise'. If he could remove their naval forces from the struggle, he would have a good chance of overcoming the remaining Greek ships and landing Persian troops behind the Isthmus defences. He used the king of Macedon, Alexander, to make the initial overtures because he was both a subject of the Great King and, partly as a result of supplying timber to build the Athenian fleet, he had been officially recognised as a friend and benefactor of the Athenian people. Mardonios offered to

get Xerxes' approval for the Athenians to retain their own territory, gain more at the expense of other Greeks and have their temples rebuilt at the king's expense.

On hearing of this development the Spartans hurriedly sent their own envoys to Athens to urge the Athenians not to leave the alliance. In spite of the attractions of Mardonios' offer the Athenians were resolute and insisted to Alexander that they would never make peace with Xerxes. At the same time they urged the Spartans to come out of the Peloponnese and fight to protect Attika, otherwise they might have to reconsider their position. This created a problem for the Spartans and the other Peloponnesian members of the Hellenic League, as there was no obvious place north of the Isthmus at which they could hope to bottle up the Persian army. They would have to risk a battle on more open ground against what was bound to be a larger army. The Spartans appointed Pausanias, a nephew of Leonidas, as regent for his young son, Pleistarchos, who was too young to command an army. Their other king, Leotychides, took command of the Hellenic fleet, which assembled at Aigina for the coming campaign.

In the summer Mardonios marched his army south, through Boiotia and towards Athens. Realising that help from the Peloponnese would not arrive in time, the Athenians staged another evacuation to Salamis. Mardonios refrained from ransacking Athens until the Athenians had been given another chance to accept his offer of peace. Herodotus says that when the offer was repeated to the Athenian council of 500, only one man suggested that it should be put to the citizen assembly for a vote, and he was stoned to death by his colleagues. They did send messengers to the Spartans to complain that they were being forced into a position where their only alternative was to join the Persians. This had the desired effect and a large army was assembled to challenge Mardonios. As well as several thousand *perioikoi* and thousands of other Peloponnesian hoplites, the army that marched with Pausanias out of the Peloponnese included 5,000 Spartan citizens, the largest Spartan force ever to do so.

From Mardonios' point of view the emergence of the Greeks from the Peloponnese was the next best thing to an Athenian defection. He moved his army to Thebes on the plains of Boiotia, which were flat enough for him to exploit his advantages in numbers and make good use of his cavalry. Pausanias was joined by a large Athenian force as well as several other groups of allies. The Greek army eventually settled into a strong position on the northern slopes of Mount Kithairon, facing the Persians, who established a fortified camp across the river Asopos on the open plain, which was more suited to their cavalry. The Spartans and Tegeans were on the right of the line, the rest of the Peloponnesians in the centre and the Athenians and Megarians on the left. The total number of Greek hoplites according to Herodotus was 38,700, more than four times as many as fought at Thermopylai. There were also tens of thousands of helots accompanying the Spartans and many light infantrymen from the other Greek states.

Mardonios probably had many more men than Pausanias, including several thousand soldiers from Thebes and the other Boiotian cities, although not the Plataians who fought on the Greek side. His army contained a lot more cavalry than the Greeks' and he used it to harass the supply lines of Pausanias and his men. On one occasion his cavalry captured a whole Greek supply column. They also succeeded in rendering unusable the main source of drinking water for the Greeks, a spring called Gargaphia. These cavalry raids continued for nearly two weeks, gradually reducing the Greek supply lines until Pausanias was left with no choice but to move his army closer to the city of Plataia, where there was water and a good supply of food.

Pausanias decided on a night-time withdrawal and sent messages to the various contingents of his army to retire under cover of darkness. The left wing of the Greek army retreated almost to the walls of Plataia, but there was confusion among some of the Spartan and Peloponnesian contingents. According to one story that Herodotus was told, a Spartan commander flatly refused to retreat and this delayed the movement of the rest, so they were still a long way from their destination when dawn broke and the Persian cavalry renewed their attacks. Mardonios was informed by his scouts that the Greeks were in retreat and he decided to attack them while they were not properly formed up for battle. Mardonios' Persian infantry engaged the Spartans and the Tegeans, who were nearest to them, while Pausanias sent a messenger to summon the rest of his army to his aid, but they were prevented from doing so by the Boiotians and other Greeks in Mardonios' army, who hurried across the river Asopos to attack the former left wing of Pausanias' army, including the Athenians. The Spartans and Tegeans had to fight Mardonios' main force on their own. The odds were against them, but the Greeks were better equipped for close-quarter combat and the Spartans excelled in disciplined fighting as a unit. After a hard struggle the Greeks forced their opponents back and Mardonios himself was killed. This caused a general panic in the Persian lines as men rushed back to the sanctuary of their camp. On the other side of the battlefield the hoplites from Athens, Phleious and Megara were initially harassed by Boiotian and Thessalian cavalry, but eventually closed with the main body of Theban infantry and overcame them, putting the Thebans to flight as well. The Tegeans and Spartans were temporarily unable to storm the Persian camp, which was protected by a strong stockade, but the arrival of the Athenians enabled them to storm the defences and capture substantial amounts of booty, as well as many prisoners.

Without waiting to recover any bodies, even that of Mardonios, Artabazos withdrew with what remained of the Persian army, still perhaps as many as 40,000. He marched straight out of Greece and back to Asia Minor. The Greek casualties were astonishingly light, amounting to only 91 Spartans, 16 Tegeans and 52 Athenians, although the Megarians and Phleiasians suffered badly at the hands of the Boiotian cavalry, leaving 600 dead on the plain. This resounding Hellenic League victory ended the Persian threat to the mainland of Greece. Eleven days after the battle the victorious Greeks marched on Thebes, the Greek city that had been a major base for the Persians after Thermopylai and which had contributed strongly to Mardonios' army. The Athenians were particularly keen to see their Boiotian neighbours made to pay for deserting the Hellenic cause. After a siege of 20 days the Thebans surrendered, offering up those of their leading citizens whom they judged were most to blame for their collaboration with the Persians. Pausanias disbanded his army, took the Theban prisoners to Corinth and executed them.

Pausanias was treated as the hero of the hour. He was awarded a tenth of all the booty from the Persian camp, which included many gold and silver items as well as expensive tents and other equipment for the Persian nobility. There were many non-combatants among the prisoners, including servants, concubines and other attendants. Pausanias had Mardonios' cooks prepare a typical Persian banquet in their master's richly decorated tent. Alongside this he had a standard Spartan meal displayed for comparison. With dry humour he remarked to the other commanders that it showed the folly of the Persians, who had so much luxury at their disposal but who still tried to plunder the poor Greeks. To commemorate their victory the states of the Hellenic League dedicated a golden tripod to Apollo at Delphi. It stood on a bronze column carved in the form of three

PHASE ONE Pausanias' army initially occupied the small ridge above the Asopos river, to the north east of Plataia and used the Gargaphia spring for water. Persian and allied Greek cavalry cut off their supply route from Plataia and rendered the spring unusable, so Pausanias ordered a retreat at night towards Plataia. At dawn his left wing (the Athenians and Megarians) was close to Plataia, with his centre (made up of Peloponnesians) alongside, but the right wing (Spartans, Perioikoi and Tegeans) were delayed. When the Persian cavalry made contact with the Spartans Mardonios ordered his whole army across the river Asopos to attack the Greeks.

PHASE TWO The Spartans and Tegeans defeated the Persians opposing them, killed Mardonios and drove his men back to the Persian camp. They were followed by the other Peloponnesians. The Athenians and Megarians were initially prevented from linking up with them by the Boiotians and other Greeks fighting on the Persian side. A total of 600 Megarians were killed as they crossed the plain towards the Spartans. Eventually the Athenians drove their opponents away and joined in the assault on the Persian camp.

intertwined snakes, emblems of Apollo. In the fourth century AD, Constantine took this monument to decorate the hippodrome of his new city of Constantinople. The lower parts of the snakes can still be seen there today. The Spartans had the names of the Greek states whose men fought against the Persians carved onto the coils of the snakes, but Pausanias put his own name on the base, claiming that it was his right to do so as principal commander of the Greeks.

The battle of Mykale

The defeat of Xerxes' fleet at Salamis encouraged some of the cities of the northern Aegean to rebel against the Persians. Among these the most important were Olynthos and Poteidaia. They were both besieged by the army of Artabazos, who had taken 60,000 men through Macedonia and Thrace to escort Xerxes back to Asia Minor. Olynthos fell to a determined assault and its population was massacred to discourage further revolts. Poteidaia was less easy to attack and Artabazos spent three months besieging it

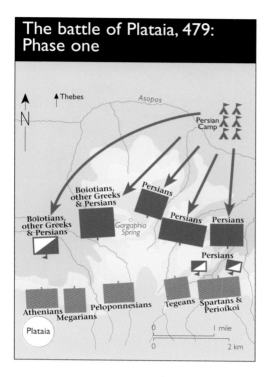

The battle of Plataia, 479: Phase one

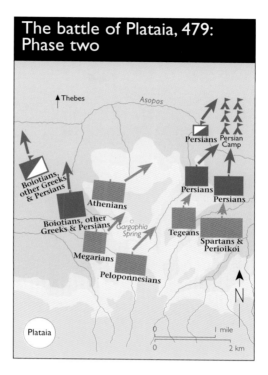

The battle of Plataia, 479: Phase two

before he had to give up and rejoin Mardonios. Nevertheless the Greeks felt that there was a strong likelihood of detaching more of their Ionian brethren from the Persians, so they sailed to Samos where Xerxes' fleet had been stationed for the winter, with a small army nearby, so that it could keep a watch on the Ionian Greeks.

The Greek fleet was much smaller than that which fought at Salamis, mainly because so many men were committed to the defence of the mainland. Herodotus says that only 110 ships gathered at Aigina in the spring under the command of the Spartan king, Leotychides. Themistokles was not as popular among the Athenians as he had hoped, probably because so many of them had lost their homes and property when the Persians sacked Athens, so he did not lead the small Athenian contingent, which was commanded by one of his rivals, Xanthippos. After the disaster of Salamis, however, the Persian commander, Tigranes, another cousin of Xerxes, was clearly unwilling to face the Greeks in a sea battle and he sent the best ships, from Phoenicia,

back to their home ports and disembarked the crews of the rest on the mainland promontory of Mykale, opposite Samos. They fortified their encampment and awaited the enemy. Leothychides also disembarked his crews and led the Greek soldiers against the Persian positions. As he approached the Persians he invited the Ionians among them to defect, which led the Persians to disarm the Samians, whose possession of a large island home might have made them more inclined to defy the Great King than those who dwelt on the mainland. Indeed, the paths leading over the mountain and away from the main Persian fortifications, which provided a possible escape route, were guarded by Greeks from Miletos, whose loyalty was not in question.

OVERLEAF This red-figure painted jug from Athens illustrates an artistic theme that was very popular in the fifth century. It shows a figure wearing Median dress of a patterned tunic and trousers and riding a horse. The rider is presented as one of the Amazons, a mythical tribe of women warriors, but the image symbolises the might of the Persians. (Ancient Art and Architecture)

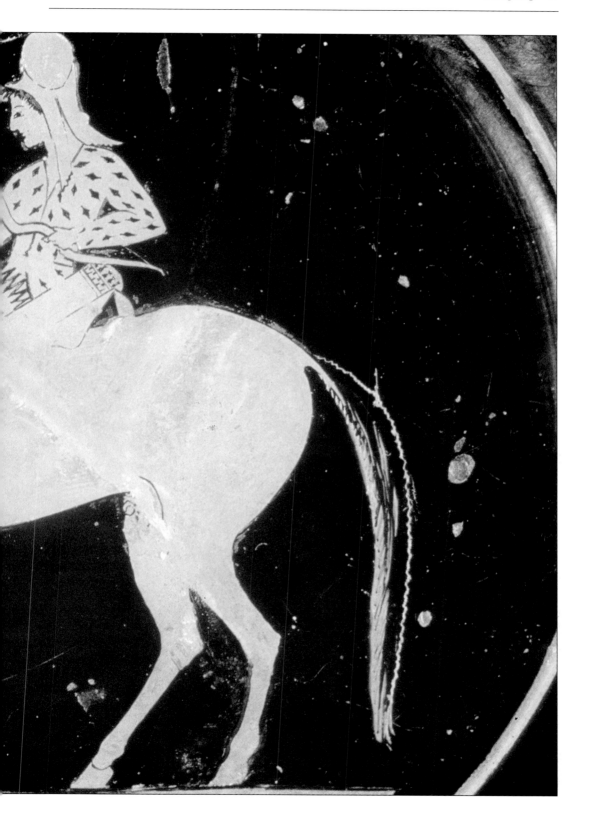

Leotychides and his men approached the Persian camp from the east and launched an attack. After prolonged fighting outside the camp the Persians retreated behind the stockade, which was soon breached, with some help from the Samians who were being held inside. Many of the Persians took their prepared escape route and eventually reached the satrapal capital of Sardis, but their commander Tigranes was killed. This victory on enemy territory encouraged wider rebellion among the Ionians and created something of a dilemma for the Hellenic League. How could they protect the rebel Ionians at such a distance and under the very noses of the Persian satraps? The Peloponnesians proposed transporting the Ionians back to Greece and giving them the cities of those Greeks who had medised. The Athenians objected strongly to this and eventually Leotychides was forced to admit those of them who were islanders, including the people of Samos, Lesbos and Chios into the League. They then sailed to the Hellespont, with the idea of destroying Xerxes' bridges, but they had already been broken up by a storm. Leotychides and the Peloponnesians sailed home, but Xanthippos and the Athenians remained in the Hellespont and took the city of Sestos after a siege. In the minds of the Athenians the emphasis was now shifting from defending Greece to making war on the territory of the Persian king.

Aristodemos the Spartan

One of the many individuals whom we encounter in the course of Herodotus' *Histories* is the Spartan citizen Aristodemos, who died at the battle of Plataia. From the details that Herodotus provides and from other sources of information we can trace his life and gain some revealing insights into the Spartan character. Aristodemos was born to a Spartan couple in one of the five villages that comprised the 'city' of Sparta, probably some time between 520 and 515. He was named after the mythical father of the first two Spartan kings. A Spartan father did not automatically have the right to raise his own sons. As soon as they were born he was obliged to show them to a group of older citizens who would inspect the infant and decide whether he was physically normal and likely to be a healthy child. Any children who failed this inspection were placed in an isolated gorge on Mount Taygetos and left to die. The boys who passed the inspection were deliberately toughened from an early age, by bathing them in wine, feeding them with plain food and getting them accustomed to enduring harsh conditions. On reaching the age of five, a boy was removed from his parental home and placed with other boys of the same age in a barracks. He stayed in this group until he reached manhood, around the age of 19 or 20, and was admitted to the ranks of Spartan citizens as one of the Equals.

Aristodemos' upbringing

The upbringing of Spartan boys was organised as a formal training called the *agoge*, aimed at preparing them for their future role as citizen soldiers. It therefore concentrated on skills and attributes thought appropriate to a hoplite. Discipline, conformity and group values were emphasised, as were physical and mental toughness. Singing and dancing were compulsory, with a focus on keeping in time and learning to recite by heart the choral poems of Tyrtaios. From the age of 10 athletic training, singing and dancing were also competitive, with regular prizes for the best boys and tests to determine if they were strong enough to proceed from one stage to the next.

The young boys went barefoot and wore very little clothing, being allowed only a single cloak for protection against the weather. They often exercised naked, as did the Spartan girls, who were not put through the *agoge*, but were raised to be fit and tough, so that they would produce strong healthy children. Food was simple and scarce, both to encourage a slim physique and to accustom the boys to function properly while hungry. This also encouraged them to steal additional food, which was not disapproved of, because it promoted stealth and resourcefulness, but they were severely punished if they were so careless as to be caught. A famous story was told of the Spartan boy who was caught by one of his elders and tried to hide a fox that he was carrying in his cloak. The fox gnawed through his stomach, but the boy did not cry out for fear of revealing it, so he died rather than be discovered. All stages of the *agoge* were supervised by older men, some of whom became close friends of individual boys. This practice often led to pederasty, but it was encouraged as a way of integrating the boys with the older men whom they would eventually join on a permanent basis as members of a *syssition*, or citizens' barracks.

The duties of a Spartan

Aristodemos passed all the tests and was elected to one of the *syssitia*. He was now a full Spartan citizen and had to be ready to be called up into action as part of a Spartan army, which usually comprised men aged between 20 and 40. When he reached his mid-20s he was required to take a wife. His choice of partner would to some extent have been his own, but it may have required the approval of the senior men of his village, and the girl's father would have had to approve of him as a husband. Men normally married women five or so years younger than them. The purpose of marriage was to produce more children for the Spartan state, so that the numbers of Spartans were maintained. A close emotional bond between husband and wife was not considered necessary. Until the age of 30 Aristodemos did not live with his wife, but stayed in the barracks with his *syssition* comrades. His visits to his wife were supposed to be carried out only in darkness and not too frequently. They were, however, expected to result in pregnancy. If they did not, he would not have been expected to keep his wife, but to repudiate her as barren and find another. Aristodemos did father at least one child, a son, and may have had more.

Once he turned 30 Aristodemos was considered a full Spartan citizen. He could now live in a house with his wife and family. He would join in the supervision of boys and young men and train with his messmates for war. The older Spartans were expected to be role models for the younger ones, examples of *andragathia*, meaning 'manly virtue'. A fine opportunity for Aristodemos to put his training into practice and demonstrate his manliness arrived in 480 when he marched off to face the Persians at Thermopylai. Aristodemos would normally have expected to go to war with the other mature men of his village, grouped in a regiment of up to 1,000 men, which was called a *lochos*. For Thermopylai special arrangements were made, because there was an important religious festival going on and it was considered insulting to the gods for the Spartan army to leave before it was completed. King Leonidas was chosen to command the Greek army and he obtained a special religious dispensation to take 300 men, as a bodyguard. He would normally have been assigned young men in their 20s, but in view of the likelihood that they might be defeated by the huge Persian army he decided to choose older men, who had already produced at least one son to maintain the ranks of the Spartans. Aristodemos was among those chosen and doubtless considered it a great honour to be singled out in this way.

Aristodemos at Thermopylai

At the pass of Thermopylai, while the Greeks were waiting for the Persians to make their move they had plenty of time to contemplate the enormous size of Xerxes' army. It was probably at this time that one of the local Trachinian men remarked that when the Persians finally got round to shooting off their arrows there would be so many of them that they would blot out the sun. One of the Spartans, called Dienekes, said to his comrades, 'What our friend from Trachis says is good news, for if the Medes hide the sun then we shall be fighting in the shade.' It is also likely that, as they waited, the Spartans recited some of the more inspiring of Tyrtaios' verses. King Leonidas is said to have particularly approved of Tyrtaios' poems as suitable for firing up the spirits of the younger men so that they would be brave and daring in battle. The following extract from fragment 12 shows clearly how Tyrtaios emphasised the hoplite virtues of bravery, standing firmly together and being ready to sacrifice one's life for the sake of others:

No man has high regard in war unless he is able to stomach the sight of blood and death, and fight the enemy at close quarters.
This is excellence, the best prize that men who are young and bold can win.
It does all the people of the state good whenever a man stands firm in the front ranks, holding his ground and steadfastly refusing to even think of shameful flight, risking his life with a stout heart and shouting encouragement to those around him.

Such a man has high regard in war.

He speedily forces back the ranks of enemy spears and his eagerness turns the battle's tide.

He who loses his life falling in the front ranks, brings glory to his father, his comrades and his city, his chest, his armour and his bossed shield pierced many times by blows from the front.

Young and old mourn him alike and the whole state is saddened by his loss.

His tomb and his children get pointed out as do his children's children and all his line.

Never do the name and glory of his bravery die out, but he is immortal even as he lies in his grave, whichever man the war god Ares slays as he fights for his homeland and his children, standing firmly and bravely.

This fragment describes more or less what happened to the Spartans with Leonidas at the pass of Thermopylai; all, that is, except for two. Aristodemos and another Spartan called Eurytos had picked up eye infections which became so acute that they were told by the king to remove themselves from the ranks of the 300 as they were incapable of fighting. They were taken to the nearby village of Alpenos by their helot attendants to recuperate. As the majority of the Greek army retreated past them, sent away by Leonidas before the Persians could surround them, the two Spartans argued over whether it was their duty to go back and die with their comrades, even though they could not see, or stay out of the battle as ordered. Eventually Eurytos forced his helot to lead him back to the battle and was promptly slain, though the helot managed to escape. Aristodemos obeyed orders and stayed put, thereby surviving the battle. One other Spartan, called Pantites, also survived because he had been sent off to Thessaly as a messenger before the battle started and by the time he got back it was over.

The 'trembler'

While Leonidas and his 298 dead Spartans were praised as great heroes, Aristodemos and Pantites found themselves despised when they got back to Sparta. It was generally felt that if they were true Spartans they would have died with their comrades. They were assumed to have been too afraid to fight, a slur on his manly virtue that Aristodemos felt very strongly. His sense of hurt would only have been compounded by the epitaph which was composed for the Spartans who died with Leonidas at Thermopylai. It was inscribed on a monument erected at the place where they made their final stand:

Stranger, tell the Spartans that we lie here in obedience to their words.

Yet Aristodemos had been ordered by Leonidas to retire from the battlefield and he obeyed the king's orders. It was only the difference of opinion with Eurytos, who had disobeyed his orders and returned to Thermopylai, that had caused the other Spartans to criticise Aristodemos for not doing likewise. Some people even suggested that he and Pantites had both been sent as messengers and had deliberately delayed their return to avoid the battle. In short they were both labelled cowards. The accusation of being a coward was the most damning that could be made against a true Spartan. Men who had run away from the enemy or refused to fight alongside their comrades were called *tresantes* meaning 'tremblers'. They were despised because they were the very opposite of the Spartan hoplite ideal. 'Tremblers' were required to wear coloured patches on their red cloaks to distinguish them and they were shunned by the rest of the Equals. Their own messmates from the *syssition* would have nothing to do with them, even to the point of refusing to speak to them. They could not hold any of the public offices and were unable to gain justice for insults or injuries, nor could they make legal agreements with other Spartans. No Spartan would allow his daughter to marry a 'trembler' and Aristodemos must have been concerned for the future of his own offspring, for no one would want to marry their children to the sons or daughters of a

This modern statue of the Spartan king, Leonidas, stands in the centre of the town of Sparta. Inscribed below is a famous two-word reply he is said to have given when the Spartans were invited by Xerxes at the battle of Thermopylai to surrender by laying down their arms. Leonidas answered him in Greek, 'Molon labe,' meaning, 'Come and take them.' (Ancient Art and Architecture)

'trembler'. Pantites found it all too much to bear and hanged himself, but Aristodemos endured the shame, hoping for an opportunity to restore his reputation.

Aristodemos at Plataia

That opportunity came the following year. In spite of the accusations of cowardice and his isolation from the rest of the Equals, Aristodemos was among those men who were called up by the ephors the following year to join the army that the regent Pausanias took to the battle of Plataia. The Spartans were anxious to have as large an army as possible so they probably sent almost all the citizens aged under 40, keeping only the oldest men back to guard Sparta against a possible Messenian helot uprising. Aristodemos marched with the men of his *lochos*, but he will still have been cold-shouldered by them. His only company would have been his personal helot attendant, carrying his equipment and cooking for him. As he approached the plain of Boiotia where the Persians were camped, his one aim will have been to show that he was not a coward, but a true Spartan. By an act of conspicuous bravery he could earn public honour and restore his reputation, even if it should cost him his life it would be worth it for the sake of his family.

Pausanias positioned his army on a ridge of hills near Plataia, but several days of cavalry attacks forced him to retreat by night. The Persians attacked the Spartans at dawn, first with cavalry and then infantry, who halted within bowshot of the Spartans and fired arrows at them from behind a wall of wicker shields. Pausanias needed to charge the Persians, but he delayed, waiting for reinforcements and good omens. It was usual for the commander, accompanied by the two ephors and his official diviners, to sacrifice a goat just before the ranks of the Spartan charged forward to engage with the enemy and to inspect its entrails to see if the gods were sending a good omen for the success of the battle. When the ephors and the diviners pronounced the omens favourable then the army could charge. The first time that Pausanias did this the omens were unfavourable, so he ordered the Spartans to wait. The men grew increasingly impatient as the Persians poured more arrows into their ranks, so Pausanias sacrificed again, and again, but still he did not give the order to charge. Eventually Aristodemos could take no more and, without waiting for the command, he broke out of the ranks of his *lochos* and charged at the Persians. To his left the Tegeans also rushed forward. Pausanias chose this moment to order the Spartans forward as well, as apparently the omens were now good. Aristodemos probably killed several Persians before he was cut down himself. The Spartans and Tegeans drove the Persians back, killed their commander Mardonios and won the battle.

Aristodemos certainly showed courage with his charge at the Persian ranks, and Herodotus felt that he was the bravest man on that day, but the Spartans did not agree. They refused to honour him as a hero of the state because they felt he had deliberately chosen to get himself killed. He had shown that he had the courage of a true Spartan, but he had failed to meet their high standards of discipline and obedience. Although he did not have his tomb and his children pointed out to later generations, nevertheless, thanks to the enquiries of Herodotus, he has achieved lasting fame.

Persian architecture

The Persians in Athenian tragedy

Twice each year the Athenians gathered in the theatre of Dionysos to watch and listen to choral competitions. By the early fifth century the format of these performances had evolved into dramatic plays, with carefully written scripts exploring tragic or comic themes. Some of the best examples have been preserved and they still have the power to enthral audiences nearly two and a half thousand years after their original performances. The tragic plays usually took their storylines from the rich traditions of Greek mythology, but occasionally a playwright would give his work a contemporary setting.

In 493 the Athenian tragedian Phrynikos presented a play entitled *The Capture of Miletos* in the theatre of Dionysos at Athens. The play, which took as its theme the recent fall of this great Ionian city to the Persians and the murder or enslavement of many of its people, was so moving that the audience was reduced to tears. This highly emotional reaction prompted the Athenians to fine Phrynikos and pass a decree that his play should never be performed again. The Athenians recognised that the fate of Miletos might be theirs if they resisted the Persians. Herodotus says that they fined Phrynikos because he reminded them of their own misfortunes and the looming threat of the Persian Empire. The text of the play has not been preserved.

In 472, however, eight years after the battle of Salamis, the great tragedian Aischylos, who had fought at Salamis and whose brother, Kynegeiros, had been killed in the battle of Marathon, produced a more popular play entitled *The Persians*. It was a great triumph for Aischylos and won first prize in the competition. The *choregos*, whose civic duty it was to pay for the production was Pericles, the son of the Athenian general, Xanthippos. The text of this play allows us to see part of the process by which the significance of the Persian Wars was defined for later generations. The dramatic action of the play takes place in the palace of the Persian king, Xerxes, where his courtiers and family are waiting for news of his expedition to conquer the Greeks. Through accounts of his actions Xerxes is characterised as an impetuous and dictatorial man whose pride and ambition will lead the Persians to disaster. This is a typical scenario for an Athenian tragedy, but the play is unique among the surviving examples of such works in its use of a contemporary subject and its presentation of the story from the perspective of the Persian court.

In the following extract (lines 230–45) Atossa, widow of King Dareios and mother of King Xerxes, is asking the Chorus, made up of elderly Persian men, to tell her more about the destination of her son's expedition, for she has had a dream that forebodes disaster. Shortly afterwards a messenger arrives with news of her son's defeat at Salamis.

Atossa: *This is something I want to learn my friends: where on the earth is Athens situated?*

Chorus: *Far away, as far as the point where the sun sets.*

Atossa: *Is this the city that my son is so keen to destroy?*

Chorus: *Yes, for so shall he make all of Greece subject to the king.*

Atossa: *Have they then so many men in their armies?*

Chorus: *Yes their army was strong enough to do the Medes great harm.*

Atossa: *What else is there about them? Are they a very wealthy city?*

Chorus: *They have a spring of silver, the earth's*
        treasury.
Atossa: *Do they arm themselves with bows and*
        arrows?
Chorus: *Not at all; they fight close with spears*
        and carry shields.
Atossa: *Who is their leader, the commander of*
        their army?
Chorus: *Of no man are they the slaves or the*
        subjects.
Atossa: *How then can they withstand an*
        enemy's onslaught?
Chorus: *Well enough to have destroyed the*
        magnificent army of Dareios.
Atossa: *What you say is terrible news for the*
        parents of our men.

This brief exchange shows that the
Athenians saw themselves as the liberators
of the Greeks through the bravery of their
hoplites, at Marathon, and the skills of the
navy, which they built from the profits of
their silver mines, at Salamis. They also
thought of themselves as superior to the
Persians because they were not 'slaves' to a
single ruler. This view that the Greek

The remains of the *Apadana* or audience hall of the royal
palace at Persepolis. There were originally 72 limestone
columns like these, rising to a height of over 20 metres.
They supported the massive roof beams of cedar, brought
from Lebanon. The *Apadana* was open on three sides to
allow light to get in and to provide the king with viewing
points to watch ceremonies and processions in the
courtyards of the palace. (Ancient Art and Architecture)

victories in the Persian Wars were a triumph
of Athenian democracy and liberty over
Persian monarchy and slavery disguises the
fact that the Athenians had many allies
whose regimes were far from democratic and
that they themselves were happy to make
other Greeks their subjects. Nevertheless it
was a powerful idea and has continued to
inform all subsequent discussions of the
wider significance of the Persian Wars.

Persepolis, pinnacle of Persian royal architecture

The Greeks were astounded that they had
managed to defeat the army and navies of
the Great King of Persia. They were used to

the idea that the Persians were fabulously wealthy and powerful and that the sheer size of their empire made them invincible. To a considerable extent this was an image that the Persian kings had deliberately fostered. In the Near-Eastern world of the fifth century there was nowhere that seemed as far away and yet so impressive as the Persian capital of Persepolis. For most people it took many months of travelling to reach it, at the heart of the Persian Empire, and few ever got to see it, but Persepolis represented the pinnacle of Achaemenid imperial architecture.

The king who started the building at Persepolis was Dareios. He wanted to have a new capital for the new dynasty that he had created. His work was continued by his son Xerxes and finished by Xerxes' son Artaxerxes. It was a monumental example of how effective the Persian kings were at utilising the resources of their vast empire. They took materials and craftsmen from all corners of the empire, even some Ionian Greeks are recorded among the craftsmen who built the palaces, and the numerous workers. The palaces were built to be impressive and to give visitors a sense of the overwhelming power and majesty of the Persian kings. Even as ruins they still convey that sense of power today.

Demokedes and Demaratos

Demokedes, a royal doctor

There are several stories in Herodotus' account of the Persian Wars of Greek exiles who had ended up living in Persia but who looked for an opportunity to return to their homeland. One of the most unusual ones concerns the doctor Demokedes, son of Kalliphon. He was a native of the Greek city of Kroton, in southern Italy, where a renowned school of medicine was developing. According to Herodotus, after learning the basics of the medical profession, as far as it was known at that time in Kroton, Demokedes quarrelled with his father and decided to leave Italy in 526 and try to make his fortune. He set himself up in Aigina, where he specialised in a form of medicine that, unlike the prevalent medical practices of the time, did not rely upon surgical instruments to cut and probe; he may have preferred the use of manipulation, massage and lotions. So successful were his techniques that after only a year Demokedes was being paid a retainer of 6,000 drachmas by the people of Aigina. The following year he was lured to Athens by Hippias, the son of Peisistratos, who paid him 10,000 drachmas, and the next year Polykrates, the tyrant of Samos, paid him 12,000 drachmas to come and practise there.

While he was in Samos Polykrates was captured and killed by the Persian satrap Oroites, who made slaves of the men of Polykrates' household, including Demokedes. Oroites was himself killed on the orders of King Dareios, who seems to have seen the ambitious satrap as a threat to his own position, and his slaves became the property of the king. Some time later Dareios dislocated his ankle when getting off his horse and the royal physicians, who were mostly Egyptians, were unable to heal the injury. In desperation, Dareios, in great pain and incapacitated by the injury, agreed to be treated by the Greek slave, whom one of his advisers remembered from his earlier days as the court physician to Polykrates. Demokedes reset the ankle and the king recovered completely, whereupon he installed Demokedes in his household and instructed all of his wives to reward him with gold for saving the king's life. He also cured the principal wife, Atossa, a daughter of Kyros the Great, of an abscess on her breast.

Demokedes could presumably have lived out his days as a respected member of the Persian king's retinue. He would have been housed and fed at royal expense, with allocations of grain, wine and other necessities provided for him from the royal storehouses. When Dareios was planning to extend his empire westwards, however, as a reward for curing queen Atossa, Demokedes contrived to be included in a reconnaissance expedition comprising 15 Persian nobles whom Dareios sent with two triremes and a supply ship to study the coasts and harbours of Greece and Italy. Having finished their survey of Greece the Persians proceeded to the city of Taranto in southern Italy, where Demokedes escaped from their supervision by telling the authorities that they were royal spies. From Taranto he made his way back to Kroton, where the Persians followed him and tried to apprehend him as a 'runaway slave of the king', but were resisted by the people of Kroton. The Persians eventually made their way back to Dareios, but only after being shipwrecked in the Straits of Otranto.

Demokedes' tale is typical of the oral sagas that Herodotus collected on his travels around the Mediterranean and the Near East. The basic outline may be reliable, although we cannot be certain about any of it, as no other records of Demokedes have survived. A renowned physician might indeed have moved from one Greek city to another and ended up working for the Persian king, who could afford to be far more generous than anyone else. Yet it is clear that many of the details that Herodotus was told are highly suspect. He claims that Demokedes at first pretended to Dareios that he was not a physician and had to be threatened with torture in order to admit to some medical knowledge, yet Dareios immediately surrendered himself to his care. Queen Atossa is supposed to have suggested the reconnaissance expedition to Dareios in their bedroom simply as a favour to Demokedes, who wanted to get back home. These embellishments make the story more entertaining, but they also provide ammunition for those who prefer to see Herodotus not as the Father of History, but as the Father of Lies.

Demaratos, a Spartan king in exile

Even a Spartan could find himself serving the Persian king. We first encounter the Spartan king Demaratos in Herodotus' account of what happened when a large Peloponnesian force invaded Attika in 506, led by both of the kings. The aim of the expedition was to overthrow the newly created democratic regime of Kleisthenes and to restore his defeated opponent Isagoras to power. Demaratos was persuaded by some of his allies, especially the Corinthians, that they were not justified in trying to force the Athenians to take back an exiled aristocrat and dismantle a regime that had come to power with popular support. Demaratos backed the Corinthian decision to pull out of the invasion, which had to be called off. As a

A golden *rhyton* or drinking vessel with its handle carved into the shape of a winged lion. The Achaemenid kings and the Persian aristocrats who accompanied them on their military expeditions took with them a large amount of gold and silver items such as these. When the Greeks captured Persian camps at the battles of Marathon and Plataia they were amazed at the wealth and luxury enjoyed by the barbarians. (Ancient Art and Architecture)

result of this disagreement between the two kings the Spartans decided that there should be no more jointly led expeditions, but that one king should always remain at Sparta.

The incident also sparked off a long-term feud between the two kings. Demaratos brought charges of corruption against the other king, Kleomenes, over the invasion of Attika and Kleomenes responded by plotting with Demaratos' cousin, Leotychides, to depose Demaratos. The grounds for this were, they claimed, that Demaratos was not the legitimate son of his predecessor, Ariston. There was some doubt over the matter because Demaratos' mother, who had been Ariston's third wife, gave birth prematurely and Ariston was thought to have had suspicions about the child's paternity. Eventually, in 491, rumours circulated by Kleomenes and Leotychides forced the ephors to act. As they usually did in moments of crisis the Spartan magistrates consulted the oracle of Apollo at Delphi. Kleomenes bribed the priests at Delphi to issue a false oracle saying that Demaratos was illegitimate. Consequently the ephors deposed Demaratos and made his cousin king in his place. Demaratos was briefly kept on at Sparta as a magistrate, but Leotychides forced him to leave Sparta. He sought refuge with the Persian king, Dareios, who gave him lands and made him a member of his court. He probably did this because he was about to invade Greece and wanted to use disaffected Greek aristocrats as governors of the newly conquered territories. Hippias, the former tyrant of Athens, was also among Dareios' courtiers. He went with the expedition of 490 but after the defeat at Marathon his chances of being reinstated as ruler of Athens disappeared and he died soon afterwards.

The grave monument of an Athenian citizen hoplite called Aristion. He wears a small bronze helmet and a cuirass made of toughened leather and linen, with a tunic beneath. He also has bronze greaves to protect his lower legs. His only weapon is a long spear. It was men like this who defied the army of the Spartan king, Kleomenes, that sought to prevent Kleisthenes' democratic reforms from being implemented in 507. (Ancient Art and Architecture)

According to Herodotus, Demaratos was ordered to accompany Dareios' son Xerxes on his invasion of Greece in 480. It is likely that Xerxes had promised to get him restored to his position in Sparta, as a subject ruler under the authority of the Persian king. Herodotus says that Xerxes consulted Demaratos several times about the strength and character of the Spartans. On the first occasion, after the crossing of the Hellespont, Demaratos, who had got used to the politics of the Persian royal court, is said to have asked whether Xerxes wanted a pleasant answer or a truthful one. On being asked to speak the truth he said that the Spartans would never submit to Xerxes, even if all the other Greeks were conquered, because their sense of freedom, duty and obedience allowed them to accept no master but their own laws, which had proven too strong even for Demaratos himself. On the second occasion, at Thermopylai, Demaratos' insistence that the Spartans were the bravest and most independent of the Greeks, and therefore the ones whom Xerxes must do his utmost to defeat, was greeted with scepticism. After the heroic defeat of Leonidas and his Spartan bodyguard, Xerxes changed his mind and asked Demaratos to advise how best to defeat the Spartans. The answer was to use his fleet to bypass the Isthmus of Corinth and to attack Sparta from the sea. His advice was supposedly rejected, although it may well be that it was with this strategy in mind that Xerxes sought to destroy the Greek fleet at Salamis, so that they could not contest any Persian landings on the Peloponnesian coast.

Demaratos never got the chance to return to Sparta as Xerxes' puppet ruler. He must have returned to Persia with Xerxes and lived out his life in exile at the Persian court. His descendants became minor aristocrats in the Persian-controlled territory around the Hellespont, where the Athenian historian Xenophon encountered them early in the fourth century.

Ironically Kleomenes was also deposed as king, because the Spartans discovered the deception that he had practised involving the Delphic oracle, and so he was forced to leave Sparta soon after Demaratos. He tried to get the Arkadians, Sparta's northern neighbours, to help him recover his position and the Spartans reluctantly allowed him to return. Almost immediately, however, he began to behave so violently that his family decided that he had gone mad and had to restrain him. He died almost immediately, but it is unclear whether he committed suicide or was killed by his family. His younger brother Leonidas succeeded him as king.

Demaratos' conversations with Xerxes must be treated with caution, as it is hard to see how Herodotus could have got such detailed information, but the basic story of his exile to Persia and the disappointment of his attempted return can be taken as historically reliable. He had the reputation of being a blunt, but likeable, man. He is once said to have replied in a council meeting to someone who asked him if he was keeping silent because he was stupid, or just at a loss for words, 'Certainly a stupid person would not know when to keep quiet.'

The Greeks attack the Persian Empire

The double victories of Plataia and Mykale were not the end of the Greek and Persian Wars. The Athenians had nurtured ambitions of controlling the Hellespont for several decades. They were increasingly involved in trade with the cities and tribes of the northern Aegean and Black Sea regions. This commercial interest partly explains why Xanthippos and his ships stayed behind in the Hellespont to capture Sestos. The following year, 478, Pausanias took command of the Hellenic League's naval forces and led them on two expeditions, firstly to Cyprus, where the Persians were driven out, and then to Byzantion, which also lost its Persian garrison. Pausanias had his own ambitions, however, and his autocratic style of command and extravagant behaviour now began to upset his allies. The Spartan ephors tried to rein him in but after a return to Sparta for a warning he attempted to set himself up as a tyrant in Byzantion. He was prevented from doing so by an Athenian force under the command of Kimon, the son of Miltiades. He returned to Sparta but quarrelled with the ephors again and had to take refuge in a temple. To avoid offending the gods the Spartans did not try to remove him, preferring to let him starve to death.

Disillusioned with Spartan leadership the Ionian Greeks now turned to Athens. A meeting was held on the island of Delos in 478/77 at which a new alliance was formed. Its members swore to continue the fight against the Persians and to ravage the king's territory in compensation for their own losses. They agreed to put themselves under Athenian leadership and to contribute warships or money to a league fund, administered by Athenian officials called *Hellenotamiai*, meaning 'treasurers of the Greeks'. The numbers of ships or amounts of tribute each island or city was to contribute

were worked out by Aristeides, who was the principal architect of the new alliance. It is known to historians as the Delian League because its treasury was established on Delos.

Themistokles had little to do with the new league, but he did persuade the Athenians to improve the fortifications of their own city and its main port, Peiraieus. The Spartans tried to prevent this development, but Themistokles forestalled their intervention and the Athenians began to turn their city into the strongest in Greece. Eventually they surrounded the whole city and its harbours and the narrow strip of land in between with a set of fortification walls. Themistokles fell out of favour again and in the mid-470s he suffered the indignity of being ostracised by the Athenian assembly. After living in Argos for a short while he went to the Persian court. The Persian king made him a local governor of Magnesia and he died there in 459.

The first major campaign of the Delian League, led by Miltiades' son, Kimon, was against Eion, the final Persian stronghold on the northern coastline of the Aegean. The town was captured in 476. The following year Kimon led the League's forces against a different objective, the island of Skyros, north-east of Euboia. The official reason for conquering this island was that its inhabitants had been practising piracy against merchants sailing through the area, but this seems to have been just the excuse to disguise an act of Athenian imperialism. Kimon 'discovered' a huge human skeleton on the island, claimed it was the bones of the Athenian hero Theseus and returned them to Athens in triumph. Soon afterwards Skyros was settled by Athenians. Another place that felt the growing power of Athens was Karystos on Euboia, which had refused to join the Delian League but was compelled

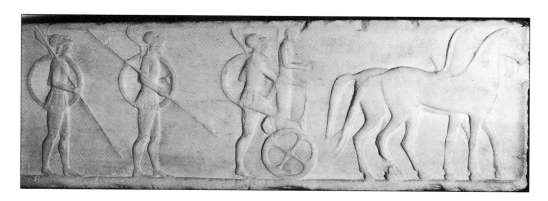

to do so by another Athenian-led military expedition. When Naxos tried to leave the League in 470 she was attacked, forced to surrender her ships and dismantle her walls and made to pay a monetary tribute. The Delian League was becoming more and more like an Athenian Empire, modelled on the Persian one. That is not to say, however, that the Athenians neglected the aim of making war on the Persian king's territory. In 466 Kimon commanded a large fleet of Delian League ships in a campaign along the south-western coast of Asia Minor to drive the Persians out of the region. It culminated in a battle at the river Eurymedon in Pamphylia at which the Great King's Phoenician fleet of 200 ships was destroyed. Xerxes died in 465 and his son Artaxerxes I failed recover the territory lost to the Delian League. Another major revolt in Egypt between 459 and 454 was aided by an Athenian fleet, but the Persians eventually overcame them and regained control. Soon

This relief sculpture depicting hoplites and a chariot in a formal procession was originally part of the base of a statue. It was probably set up around 490. In 478 the statue base was dismantled and, along with many other pieces of sculpture, it was incorporated into the walls of Athens. The Athenians were in a hurry to complete the walls before the Spartans could interfere and prevent them doing so, and they did not have time to cut and prepare new stones for all of them. (Ancient Art and Architecture)

afterwards Kimon was killed fighting against the Persians in Cyprus and in 449 a peace treaty known as the Peace of Kallias was negotiated between Athens and the Persian king, bringing a halt to their conflicts. By the terms of this treaty the autonomy of the Ionian Greeks was guaranteed, the Persian king agreed that his ships would not sail westwards beyond the Gelidonya islands and that his satraps in Asia Minor would not allow their soldiers to come within a day's ride of the Greeks cities on the coast. In return the Athenians agreed not to make war against the king's territory.

Messenger:

At once ship into ship battered its brazen beak.
A Hellene ship charged first, and chopped off the whole stern
Of a Phoenician galley. Then charge followed charge
On every side. At first by its huge impetus
Our fleet withstood them. But soon, in that narrow space,
Our ships were jammed in hundreds; none could help another.
They rammed each other with their prows of bronze; and some
Were stripped of every oar. Meanwhile the enemy
Came round us in a ring and charged. Our vessels heeled
Over; the sea was hidden, carpeted with wrecks
And dead men; all the shores and reefs were full of dead.

Then every ship we had broke rank and rowed for life.
The Hellenes seized fragments of wrecks and broken oars
And hacked and stabbed at our men swimming in the sea
As fishermen kill tunnies or some netted haul.
The whole sea was one din of shrieks and dying groans,
Till night and darkness hid the scene. If I should speak
For ten days and ten nights, I could not tell you all
That day's agony. But know this: never before
In one day died so vast a company of men.

(Aeschylus, *The Persians*, p. 134 [trans P Vellacott, Penguin, London, 1961])

The Persians was produced in 472 BC, only eight years after the battle of Salamis. It is the only Greek tragedy to take its story from history rather than myth and it is likely that Aeschylus himself either took part in the battle or witnessed it. The play celebrates the Greek victory and was performed before an audience of Athenian citizens who may also have taken part in the battle.

Part II
The Peloponnesian War
431–404 BC

Thucydides the Athenian wrote the history of the war fought between Athens and Sparta, beginning the account at the very outbreak of the war, in the belief that it was going to be a.great war and more worth writing about than any of those which had taken place in the past. My belief was based on the fact that the two sides were at the very height of their power and preparedness, and I saw, too, that the rest of the Hellenic world was committed to one side or the other; even those who were not immediately engaged were deliberating on the courses which they were to take later. This was the greatest disturbance in the history of the Hellenes, affecting also a large part of the non-Hellenic world, and indeed, I might almost say, the whole of mankind. For though I have found it impossible, because of its remoteness in time, to acquire a really precise knowledge of the distant past or even of the history preceding our own period, yet, after looking back into it as far as I can, all the evidence leads me to conclude that these periods were not great either in warfare or in anything else.

(Thucydides, *History of the Peloponnesian War*, 1.1, p. 35 [trans Rex Warner, Penguin, London, 1954])

Introduction

This book gives a concise account of one of the key periods of Classical Greek history. The Peloponnesian War, which lasted from 431 to 404 BC, was a conflict between the Greek city-states of Athens and Sparta. It was a confrontation between the leading land power of the time, Sparta, and the leading sea power, Athens. In a wider sense it was also a clash between a cautious, traditional oligarchy and an ambitious, innovative democracy. It is called the Peloponnesian War because Sparta was the head of an alliance of Greek states from the Peloponnese, the southernmost peninsula of mainland Greece. The stories of the Peloponnesian War feature some of the great personalities of the Classical World, including the revered Athenian statesman Perikles, the bold and resourceful Spartans Brasidas and Gylippos, the flamboyant Athenian general Alkibiades and the Spartan leader Lysandros, who eventually achieved the decisive naval victory that the Spartans needed to win the war.

The enduring fame of the Peloponnesian War is due in no small way to its principal historian, Thucydides, an Athenian citizen who took part in some of the early stages of the war as a naval commander. He was exiled from Athens in 424 and he decided to write a detailed account of the war because, in his view, it was such an important war that it was more worthy of a written history than any previous conflict. He carefully gathered as much information as possible, from eye-witnesses and documents, so that he could offer as accurate and well considered an analysis of events as possible. He was aware that this sort of history might not appeal to those who preferred a more romanticised and sensational account of the past, but he observed in his introduction: 'This is a possession for all time, rather than a prize piece that is read and then forgotten.'

Thucydides' work is incomplete, tailing off literally in mid sentence, just as he is explaining what happened after an Athenian naval victory in 411. It is likely that he had either died, or at least stopped working on it by 396 because he does not seem to know about an eruption of Mount Etna on Sicily that occurred in this year. We do not know whether he simply had not written any of the remaining books which would have covered the period 410 to 404 (there were probably to be two more), or whether he had drafts or notes but no final versions.

Another Athenian historian, Xenophon, continued the story of the war from a point just a few months after the latest events recorded by Thucydides. This could imply that Xenophon had a version of Thucydides' work which was slightly longer than the one which now survives, for it seems clear that he intended his to be a continuation of Thucydides', although he is less detailed and analytical than Thucydides. Xenophon called his work the *Hellenika*, meaning an account of the doings of the Hellenes, which was the Greeks' name for themselves. We can supplement these two main accounts from the works of many later classical writers, who provide biographical and historical details not mentioned by Thucydides or Xenophon, along with a small number of original documents from the time of the war, mostly decrees of the Athenians inscribed on stone.

Thucydides was the first writer who, in explaining the origins of a war, made a clear distinction between the immediate, publicly proclaimed reasons for the conflict and the longer-term, underlying causes of tension between the two sides. This explanatory scheme is still regularly employed by modern historians when they seek to account for the outbreak of more recent wars. It is a testament to the fascination of Thucydides' subject and the quality of his work that, even in the twenty-first century, students of history, politics and warfare in universities and military academies across the world regularly study the events of the Peloponnesian War for the lessons it can teach them about politics, diplomacy, strategy, tactics and the writing of history.

This helmet was worn by a Greek heavy infantry soldier, or hoplite in the sixth century. By the start of the fifth century the city-states of Classical Greece had already fought many small scale wars, mostly as the result of border disputes with their neighbours. The Peloponnesian War was on a much grander scale than anything the Greeks had previously seen. (Ancient Art and Architecture)

The rise of Athens

The origins of the Peloponnesian War lie in the rise to power of its two protagonists, the city states of Athens and Sparta and their political estrangement during the middle part of the fifth century BC. Athens and Sparta had been the two leading states in the alliance of Greek city-states formed to combat the Persian king's invasion in 480. Both could claim to have been instrumental in saving the Greeks from conquest by the Persians, since the Athenians had taken the leading role in the naval victory over the Persians at Salamis in 480, but the following year the Spartans led the Greek army that defeated King Xerxes' land forces and ended the threat of Persian conquest.

After the Persians had been driven out of mainland Greece the alliance began to break up. The Spartan regent Pausanias led a victorious expedition to liberate Greek cities in the Eastern Aegean from the Persians, but he behaved with great arrogance and his treatment of the Eastern Greeks angered many of them. The Spartans recalled Pausanias and withdrew from the war against the Persians, leaving the alliance bereft of leadership. The Athenians were invited by several of the leading Greek states, particularly the cities and islands of Ionia, to lead them in a continuation of the war against the Persians. In 477 they created a new alliance to ravage the territory of the Persian king in compensation for the subjugation of the Ionians and the invasion of Greece. Each of the allies agreed to contribute men, ships or money to a common pool of resources which was administered and commanded by the Athenians. This alliance is called the Delian League by modern historians because its official treasury was established at the sanctuary of Apollo on the tiny island of Delos, in the centre of the Cyclades.

This painted water jug was produced in Athens after the Peloponnesian War. It shows a Greek hoplite (heavy infantryman) and an archer fighting a cavalryman who is dressed as a Persian. The hoplite carries a large, round shield on his left arm and uses a spear of between eight and 10 feet in length. Aside from his essential helmet he wears no other armour. (Ancient Art and Architecture)

The Spartans already had their own alliance known as the Peloponnesian League. It was made up mainly of the small city-states in the Peloponnese, but some larger ones, such as Corinth, belonged, as did most of the cities of Boiotia, the region to the north of Athens. They had far greater autonomy than the members of the Delian League and they could vote on equal terms with the Spartans in the League conferences. It was essentially a defensive alliance that was only activated when there was a clear threat to the security of one or more of its members.

A bronze statue of Athena, patron goddess of the Athenians c. 450. The statue shows Athena wearing a hoplite's helmet. Her right arm originally held a spear and on her left can be seen the remnant of a strap for a large, round hoplite shield. The base bears an inscription saying, 'Melisso dedicated this as a tithe to Athena.' (Ancient Art and Architecture)

whole League force was lost. Kimon had been exiled in 461 but he returned in 451 to lead further campaigns, including an invasion of the Persian held island of Cyprus, where he died in 449. Later that year the Athenians negotiated a formal peace treaty with Persia, known as the Peace of Kallias.

The Delian League had proven a remarkably successful alliance in terms of its victories over the Persians and the security and prosperity it earned for its members, but what had started out as a League of Greek states under Athenian leadership gradually took on the character of an Athenian Empire. As early as 470 the Aegean island state of Naxos tried to opt out of its obligations, but was forced back into line. Its contribution to the League was changed from a certain number of ships for each campaign to a fixed annual 'tribute' of money, a process that was applied to more and more states. In 465 the island of Thasos tried to revolt; its citizens endured a two-year siege but eventually capitulated. They were reduced to tribute status and made to pay an indemnity, collected by the Athenians. In 454 the League's treasury was transferred to Athens. This move has made it possible for historians to study the finances of the League in some detail, because the Athenians gave one sixtieth of the annual tribute to their patron goddess Athena each year, recording the payments on stone slabs. Many of these so-called 'tribute lists' have survived and they show both the widening extent and the increasing wealth of the Athenian Empire. Allied revolts were put down with considerable ferocity and in some cases the Athenians appropriated land from the recalcitrant allies and established colonies of Athenian citizens there, to act in part as garrisons.

The Athenian Empire

The Delian League successfully waged war against the Persians, culminating in a magnificent victory under the command of the Athenian general Kimon at the Eurymedon river in 466. A Persian fleet of 200 ships was destroyed and with it the main threat to the security of the Greeks in the Aegean. In 459 the Delian League sent 200 ships to the Nile Delta to assist in an Egyptian revolt against the Persians, but four years later this revolt was crushed and the

Inscribed records of decisions of the Athenian Assembly routinely refer to the allies as 'the cities which the Athenians rule'. Athens dominated the economic life of her subject allies, particularly their maritime trade. Some of the profits of the Empire were spent on the Athenian navy, on pay for Athenian citizens who carried out public offices and, it was rumoured among the other Greeks, the magnificent public buildings which adorned the city of Athens from the 440s onwards.

The 'First' Peloponnesian War

The major turning point in relations between the Athenians and the Spartans came in 462 BC. Two years earlier an earthquake had devastated Sparta, killing thousands. It sparked off a major revolt among the Helots of Lakonia and Messenia, who were servile populations under direct Spartan rule. Some of the Messenians successfully resisted Spartan attempts to bring them to heel and established themselves on Mount Ithome in Messenia. In 462, in response to a Spartan appeal to all her allies for help, Kimon persuaded the Athenians that he should lead a small army to assist them. Kimon and his force had not been in Messenia for very long when they, alone of all the allies whom the Spartans had invited to help them, were dismissed. The reason for this seems to have been a growing sympathy for the Messenians' cause among the Athenians.

Kimon was exiled on his return by the Athenians, who felt humiliated and insulted by the Spartans' actions. From 460 to 446 there was constant political tension between the two sides, with both Athens and Sparta forming alliances with each other's enemies. In some cases the tension resulted in a series of military conflicts which exacerbated the rivalry. These conflicts are sometimes called the First Peloponnesian War, although to some extent they lack the continuity and coherence which is characteristic of a single war.

In the fifth century BC, the Greeks felt that going to war in order to resolve a dispute or assert a claim to something was a right and proper thing to do. This certainly did not mean that they always resorted to violence in order to settle arguments, but the attempt to decide matters by armed force was accepted as a normal way of behaving for communities and states. If a state was felt to deserve punishment, it was not unusual for the inhabitants to be sold into slavery; in extreme cases the men might all be executed. Given the small size of most individual states, it was natural that treaties for mutual defence against third parties were regularly made, with each side promising to come to the aid of the other in the event of an attack. A common formula for such alliances was that both parties agreed to have the same friends and enemies.

One of the first things the Athenians did to vent their anger against the Spartans, therefore, was to make an alliance in 460 with Argos, Sparta's most powerful neighbour in the Peloponnese and her long-standing enemy. They also took advantage of a border dispute between their western neighbour, Megara, and her neighbour Corinth to detach Megara from the Peloponnesian League. To make Megara more secure from attack the Athenians built fortifications which linked the port of Nisaia to the city of Megara proper. The Athenians were acting out of self-interest in strengthening Megara. A Peloponnesian attack on their own territory would probably have to come through the Megarians' territory, known as the Megarid; an Athenian garrison was established in Megara. In 459 the Athenians began building their own fortifications, known as the Long Walls, to link the city of Athens to its main port at Peiraieus.

Another Athenian alliance, with the Thessalians, improved both their military and strategic position. The extensive open plains of Thessaly were ideal country for breeding and training horses, so the Thessalians were among the best cavalrymen in the Greek world, whereas mountainous Attika did not suit the breeding of horses and produced few cavalrymen. The Thessalians were also the northern neighbours of the Boiotians, whose southern borders with the Athenians were the subject of several disputes. In Thessaly and Megara the Athenians saw opportunities to weaken the Spartans by putting pressure on their allies.

In 457 the first major clash between the two sides occurred. The Peloponnesians bypassed Megara by taking their army by sea across the Gulf of Corinth. They encountered an Athenian army at Tanagra in Boiotia. The ranks of the Athenians were swelled to over 14,000 men by their allies, including 1,000 Argives, a large contingent from the Ionian states of the Delian League and a force of Thessalian cavalry. The Spartans and their allies numbered less than 12,000, but after two days of heavy fighting, during which the Thessalians changed sides, the Spartans won a prestigious victory. Once they had returned to the Peloponnese, however, the Athenians defeated the Boiotians in a separate battle at nearby Oinophyta, gaining control over much of central Greece as a result.

In 456 the Athenian general Tolmides took a force of 50 ships and, stopping at Gytheion on the coast of Lakonia, burnt the Spartan's dockyard facilities. The Athenians also ravaged some of the surrounding territory, then headed north into the Corinthian Gulf, capturing the Corinthian-held city of Chalkis on the northern shore of the narrow entrance to the Gulf. This expedition demonstrated the strategic advantage of Athens' massive fleet. A more significant outcome, however, was the capture of the small city of Naupaktos, also on the northern shore of the Gulf of Corinth. Here the Athenians established a large group of Messenians who had been allowed to leave by the Spartans as the only way of ending the Messenian revolt. They were to play a major role in the future confrontations between Athens and Sparta. The Athenians made more sorties north to punish the Thessalians for their treachery at Tanagra and in 454 they sailed into the Corinthian Gulf once more to discourage naval activity by the Corinthians and harry their allies and friends in Western Greece. But the destruction of the Athenian expedition to Egypt, increasing difficulties in

This model shows an Athenian trireme at rest in one of the specially constructed ship-sheds around the Peiraieus. As well as the ships and their crews a Greek city needed to invest in substantial facilities in order to maintain an effective navy. For many of the cities in the Delian League the cost was too great, so they contributed money rather than ships to the League's war efforts. (J F Coates)

A sixth-century black-figure Athenian painted vase showing two warriors fighting. Although Greek armies regularly consisted of several thousand men, artists preferred to paint scenes of individual duels in the tradition of the Greek heroes of the Homeric epic the *Iliad*. (Ashmolean Museum)

Scenes of parting like this one are quite common on Athenian painted pottery from the fifth century. Athens and her allies were at war with Persia or their fellow Greeks almost continually from the Persian invasion of 480 to the conclusion of the Thirty Years' peace in 446. (Ancient Art and Architecture)

controlling the Athenian Empire, and the reluctance of the Spartans to venture out of the Peloponnese reduced the belligerence of both sides. A five-year truce was agreed in 451, as well as a Thirty Years' Peace between Sparta and Argos.

In 446 the Boiotians began to agitate against Athenian domination and a punitive expedition led by Tolmides was defeated at Koroneia, with many Athenians taken captive. In order to secure their safe return Athens abandoned all of Boiotia except the southern city of Plataia. A federal political structure was created by the Boiotians, with their largest city, Thebes, taking a leading role. This move inspired the island of Euboia to revolt from Athens. While the Athenians were trying to suppress the Euboians, the Megarians, encouraged by Corinth and Sikyon, also revolted, killing their Athenian garrisons, and the young Spartan king Pleistoanax led the army of the Peloponnesian League into the Megarid to consolidate the revolt of Megara. The Athenian general Perikles rushed his forces back from Euboia to confront Pleistoanax, who had reached Eleusis. The Spartan king withdrew without any attempt at battle, leaving Perikles free to return to Euboia and suppress the revolt. There were accusations that he had bribed the Spartan king and Pleistoanax's senior adviser, Kleandridas, was

This photograph shows an impression taken from one of the huge stones on which the Athenians recorded the dedication of ¹/₆₀ of their annual tribute to the goddess Athena. By studying the details of these 'tribute lists' historians have discovered how some of the cities that revolted from the Delian League were punished through loss of territory and the imposition of colonies of Athenian settlers, which resulted in their payments being reduced. (Archive of Squeezes, Oxford)

Athens and Peiraeus during the war

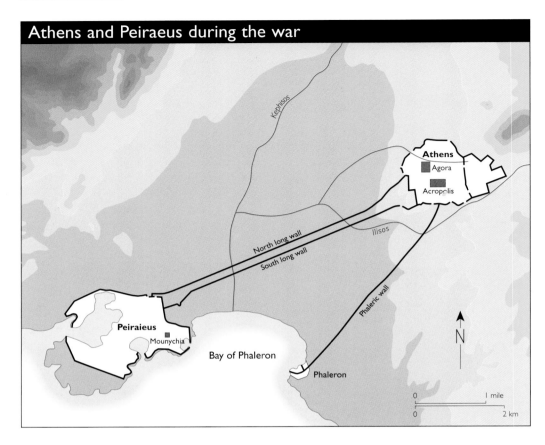

condemned to death for treason and forced into exile to avoid execution. He eventually settled in Thurii, an Athenian colony in Southern Italy, where he became a leading military commander and was influential in bringing the city into an alliance with the Peloponnesians in 435. Pleistoanax himself was tried and acquitted, but he nevertheless went into exile as well.

In 446 the Athenians agreed a peace treaty with the Spartans, to last for 30 years. Its terms were that each side should retain its territory and alliances. Athens gave up any claim over Boiotia and agreed to stop trying to expand her empire at the expense of the Peloponnesian states, but she kept control of Naupaktos. An important clause in the treaty provided for independent arbitration of any disputes that might arise over the observance of its terms. The mutual dislike and suspicion which had caused the 'First' Peloponnesian War was not dispelled by the Thirty Years' Peace, however, and both sides continued to look for ways to disadvantage each other. When the island of Samos in the Eastern Aegean revolted against Athens with Persian help in 441, the Spartans tried to take advantage of this and go to war with Athens, but at a meeting in 440 they could not persuade a majority of members of Peloponnesian League to vote with them. Nevertheless there was a growing sense among the Greeks that a decisive confrontation between Athens and Sparta was looming. In the historian Thucydides' view, although there were several short-term justifications for the main Peloponnesian War, it was 'the increasing magnitude of Athenian power and the fear this caused to the Spartans that forced them into war.'

Athens and Sparta

In the fifth century BC Greece was divided into hundreds of independent city-states; the Greek word for this type of state was *polis* (plural *poleis*). The size of these states varied considerably, but most comprised an urban centre, where much of the population lived, and where the principal public buildings were located, plus a surrounding rural territory. Although there were many differences in the ways that each state was organised and governed, broadly speaking they came in two types: either a democracy, where decision making was in the hands of the majority of the citizens, or an oligarchy, in which effective control of decision making was limited to a minority of the citizens.

Greece in the Peloponnesian War 431–404

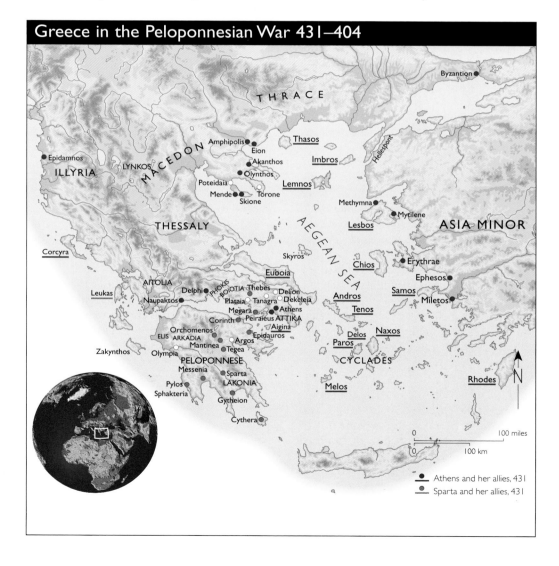

● Athens and her allies, 431
● Sparta and her allies, 431

Athens

Athens was a relatively large state comprising the peninsula of Attika, with the city of Athens as its political and religious centre. The Athenians had a very broadly based, democratic constitution. The major decisions were taken by the Assembly, attendance at which was open to all adult male citizens. The Assembly met regularly to debate proposals on important issues put before it by a committee, but anyone who wanted to could speak out in a debate, or make their own proposal, as long as it was not contrary to one that had already been voted into law. The Assembly could not meet every day, so mundane financial and administrative matters and the day-to-day running of the state's affairs were in the hands of several smaller committees. The most important of these was the Council, consisting of 500 men who were selected by lot from citizens over the age of 30. It was the Council that prepared the agenda for meetings of the Assembly. A sub-committee of 50 members of the Council was permanently on duty each month, living in a special building next to the Council chamber. Membership of the Council and the other committees changed every year, which meant that there were plenty of opportunities for ordinary citizens to participate in government.

Although in theory any Athenian citizen was entitled to speak out in the Assembly, in practice meetings tended to be dominated by a handful of individuals. These politicians were often men of aristocratic birth, whose wealth, education, family connections and military experience commanded respect among the ordinary citizens. Kimon, the leader of several successful Delian League expeditions against the Persian Empire was one such figure, but the most influential politician in the mid-fifth century was Perikles, the son of Xanthippos. As well as being rich, well bred and a good military commander, Perikles was an excellent orator. He was able to persuade the citizens in the Assembly to elect him as a general year after year and to vote in favour of his proposals for using the political power and financial resources of the Athenian Empire for the benefit of the poorer citizens. After Perikles' death in 429 many other politicians competed for popularity and influence over the Athenians, but none ever managed to attain such a dominant position again.

A photograph of the remains of the Athenian Acropolis. The rocky outcrop in the middle of Athens had been a citadel and a sanctuary for many centuries and had several temples. Around 447 Pericles persuaded the Athenians to transform it by building a monumental set of marble buildings which were to be the most magnificent in the Greek world. They served as potent symbols of the wealth, power and pride of the Athenians. (Ancient Art and Architecture)

Sparta

Sparta was the name of the city in the centre of the fertile territory of Lakonia (also called Lakedaimon). Unlike Athens Sparta had few monumental buildings and it was essentially a loose amalgamation of five villages. The Spartans had gradually evolved a system that combined monarchical and democratic elements within an oligarchy. Over the preceding centuries most of the Greek states had expelled their kings, or reduced them to purely ceremonial functions, but the Spartans retained two kings who acted as leaders in warfare and religious matters. In most respects, however, Sparta was a typical oligarchy, with its public business in the hands of a few men. Major decisions were referred to an assembly of adult male citizens, but there was little or no chance for the ordinary citizens to discuss or debate them. They were simply expected to indicate their agreement or disagreement with what their leaders suggested. Debates on important issues were restricted to smaller groups of elected officials. Every year the Spartans elected a board of five overseers or *ephors*, who had wide ranging executive, disciplinary and judicial powers over all the people of Lakonia, including the two kings. Although they were not subject to any written laws and they had the authority to prosecute any Spartan citizen, regardless of their official status, the ephors were only in power for a year and they could not be re-elected at any time.

The Spartans did not have a deliberative council that routinely discussed all public business, as the Athenian Council of 500 did. Instead they had a council of senior citizens, called the *gerousia*, whose 28 members were elected by their fellow citizens for life, but they normally did not achieve this status until they were over 60 years of age. This high age limit is not particularly surprising given the ancient Greeks' traditional respect for age and experience. Men who had reached 60 were considered to be in physical decline, and so no longer suited for the

rigours of warfare, but still in full possession of their mental faculties. The main function of the members of the *gerousia* was to oversee observance of Sparta's laws and customs, particularly in relation to the upbringing and discipline of citizens. They could act as a consultative body for the kings and the ephors on major public decisions, although there is no clear evidence as to their role in determining foreign policy. They discussed and prepared proposals which were put before the assembly of Spartan citizens, and they acted as a court for political trials, or inquests into the conduct of kings and other leading Spartans. The two kings were also members of the *gerousia*. They could exercise a leading role in its deliberations through informal ties of patronage and friendship with its members.

An interesting difference in the way the citizen assemblies of Athens and Sparta operated was that, whereas the Athenians assessed the size of a majority by counting raised hands, the Spartans judged decisions on the basis of how loudly the assembled citizens shouted in favour of a proposal, or a candidate for election. Such a method was less precise and the outcome could be more easily manipulated by the presiding magistrates. It is indicative of a strong reluctance among the members of the ruling oligarchy to allow the citizen body to have true sovereignty over public affairs. This antipathy towards full democracy, as practised by the Athenians and many of their allies, was one of the fundamental causes of tension between the two sides.

Military hierarchies

The command structures of the two sides also reveal a lot about their different political and social systems. Athenian armies were usually commanded by one or more members of a board of 10 generals, who were elected annually by the citizens. Successful generals, like Kimon or Perikles, were often re-elected and they exploited their popularity and prestige to play a leading role in Athenian politics, whereas unsuccessful, or unpopular generals would not be re-elected. The generals could be held to account for their actions by the Assembly, which sometimes acted as a court sitting in judgment over

them. Even the great Perikles suffered the humiliation of being deposed and fined early on in the war because the Athenians did not regard his strategy as being successful. The ultimate sovereignty of the Athenian citizens over their generals tended to have an inhibiting effect on their actions.

The full Spartan army could only be commanded by one of the kings, or a regent if the kings were unable to take command in person. The kings were accompanied on campaign by two ephors,

The two men on this Spartan relief are probably citizens. The Spartans prided themselves on their constant readiness to fight for their city. They were expected to value their city and their comrades above themselves and their families. Until the age of 30 they did not even live in their own homes, but stayed in their mess halls and visited their wives occasionally. (Ancient Art and Architecture)

A Roman bust of Perikles based on an Athenian original. Perikles was so good at persuading the Athenians to vote for his proposals that the historian Thucydides felt that although the Athens of his time was called a democracy, in fact it was ruled by its leading citizen. (Ancient Art and Architecture)

but the kings seem to have exercised complete authority while the army was on active service. The ephors could, however, prosecute the kings before a court consisting of themselves and the *gerousia*, if they considered that they had acted inappropriately while in command of the army. During the Peloponnesian War the full Spartan army rarely took the field. Instead one of the kings led armies consisting of a small proportion of Spartan

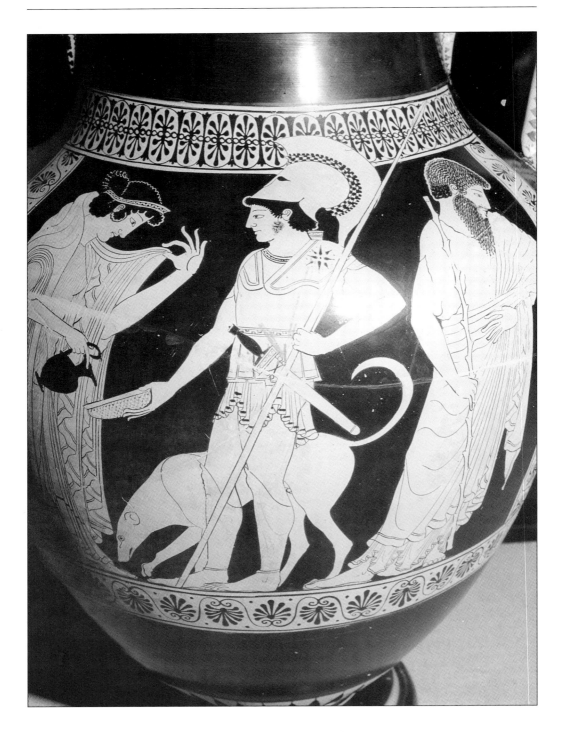

This Athenian vase depicts a soldier taking leave of his family as he goes off to war. It was part of the public duty of an Athenian citizen to fight when called upon. Normally it was only the fairly prosperous citizens who could afford the equipment of a hoplite. The poorer citizens were more likely to serve as oarsmen or sailors in the fleet. (Ancient Art and Architecture)

citizens, along with the combined forces of their Peloponnesian League allies on campaigns in Southern and Central Greece. For expeditions further afield they sent much smaller Spartan detachments, led by specially appointed Spartan officers. These men were allowed a great deal of latitude in deciding how to conduct their operations, but internal rivalries and jealousies were commonplace among the Spartans. At several points during the war successful commanders were refused reinforcements or prevented from carrying on their achievements because other Spartans did not want them to gain too much prestige.

Athenian manpower

It has been estimated that the total number of adult male Athenian citizens in 431 was around 40,000. Of these about 1,000 were wealthy enough to serve as cavalrymen, which involved maintaining their own horses. Of the rest as many as 20,000 may have been eligible to serve as hoplites, the heavily armed infantrymen who usually formed the core of a Greek citizen army, but less than half of them would be called upon to fight at any one time. In practice the forces that Athens mobilised during the war were composed of her own citizens and those of her allies, supplemented by mercenaries. Athens commanded fleets and armies drawn from her Delian League allies many times during the fifth century but only on a few occasions are we able to get a clear idea of the proportions of Athenian to allied forces involved in the campaigns of the Peloponnesian War. The most detailed breakdown is provided by Thucydides when he describes the forces sent on an expedition to Sicily in 415. There were 5,100 hoplites, or heavy infantrymen, of whom 2,200 were Athenian citizens, 750 were mercenaries from the Peloponnese, and the remaining 2,150 were supplied by Athens' subject allies of the Delian League. The fleet of 134 trireme warships was made up of 100 Athenian vessels and 34 from the

allies, principally the large and populous island of Chios. It is unlikely that the allies regularly contributed as many as half of the soldiers involved in all the military undertakings of the Peloponnesian War. Athens despatched troops to many parts of the Greek world during the war and often there will have been only a few allied soldiers involved, mostly serving as mercenaries.

Naval manpower requirements were on a far larger scale. Few cities, even one a populous as Athens, had the necessary resources to man a large fleet, since a trireme normally required 150-170 oarsmen, plus skilled sailors and steersmen, who were especially hard to find. In 433, for example, when the Corinthians were preparing a major expedition against Corcyra, they offered very generous rates of pay to potential rowers from all over the Greek world in a desperate attempt to recruit enough oarsmen to man their ships. Similarly, it was vital for the Athenians to be able to recruit from as wide a pool of naval manpower as possible and they had to pay recruits well enough to prevent them from deserting to the other side, or returning home.

Spartan manpower

Male Spartan citizens (*Spartiates* in Greek) were almost constantly in training as hoplites. They did not have any other occupation and their farmland was worked for them by slaves. Their training began at a very early age, usually five or six years and continued through various stages until, at 18 years' old, they were allowed to attend meetings of the citizen assembly and go abroad on military expeditions. At this age they were admitted to a mess group (the Greek word for which is *syssition*). Each mess group was made up of about 15 Spartans who trained, exercised, dined and fought together. In theory they were all of equal status and contributed food and other resources to a common stock of supplies. If they could not afford to make their regular contributions they could be deprived of their full citizen status.

The total number of full Spartan citizens was never very large. Even when it was at its greatest extent, towards the end of the sixth century BC, it was probably less than 10,000, and by the start of the Peloponnesian War there may have been only half that number of adult male citizens available for military service. So from where did the Spartans obtain the manpower for their armies? To some extent they relied upon the non-Spartan population of Lakonia, especially those men who lived in the towns and villages around Sparta and were called the *Perioikoi*, which means 'dwellers around'. The Perioikoi lived in autonomous communities, some of which were large towns or even small cities. Unlike the Spartans they worked for a living, as farmers, traders and craftsmen. It was the Perioikoi who made the armour and weapons used by Spartans as well as day-to-day items like pottery, furniture and cloth. Usually they fought as hoplites alongside the Spartans themselves.

When they needed to assemble a large army to take on another Greek state, like Athens or Argos, the Spartans called upon the allied states of the Peloponnesian League. The nearest of these were the cities of Arkadia, the mountainous region to the north and west of Lakonia. The main Arkadian cities of Orchomenos, Tegea and Mantinea were not very large, but each of them could easily muster several hundred soldiers. Larger contingents were contributed by more distant states like Corinth and Thebes. These allies probably provided the majority of hoplites in any Spartan army, especially when serving outside of the Peloponnese.

The Helot curse

The Spartans also made considerable use of the large, publicly owned, slave population of Lakonia and its neighbouring region,

Messenia. These slaves were called *Helots* and they were the descendants of people who were conquered and enslaved by the Spartans in a series of wars from about 950 to 700 BC. The Messenians proved very difficult to control and organised major revolts against the Spartans on several occasions. The Helots of Lakonia were less rebellious and substantial numbers of them normally accompanied the Spartans to war, acting as baggage carriers and fighting as light armed soldiers. During the Peloponnesian War they were used as oarsmen and sailors on Spartan naval vessels. In exceptional circumstances Helots were equipped and trained to fight as hoplites, on the understanding that they would be given their freedom at the end of the campaign for which they were recruited.

An important feature of the Spartan system for maintaining discipline and obedience was the regular use of physical violence. From the start of their boyhood training Spartans were beaten by their elders and superiors. Spartan citizens were especially encouraged to use violence against the Helots. Each year the Spartan ephors declared a ritual war on the Helots, thus justifying the killing of any troublesome Helots and keeping the rest in a constant state of fear. Yet for all their heavy-handed domination and control of the Helots, the Spartans could not do without them. It was the labour of the Helots that furnished the individual Spartan citizens with natural products for their contributions to the communal messes.

Throughout the Classical period the Spartans' main priority was always to keep their dominant position over the Helots, who were so essential to their own way of life. But this was no easy task, even for men who were constantly prepared for war. The Messenian revolt of 462–456 showed how fragile the Spartans' control was, and the abrupt dismissal of Kimon and his Athenian contingent indicates how sensitive Spartans were to any interference in their relationship with the Messenians. The

This bronze statuette of a hoplite was probably made in Lakonia and dedicated by a Spartan citizen at the sanctuary of Zeus in Olympia. The Spartans were famous for their zealous observance of religious rituals. Many similar offerings have been found in sanctuaries around the Peloponnese and elsewhere in Greece. (Ancient Art and Architecture)

continual need to subjugate this conquered population was the main reason why the Spartans were reluctant to commit large numbers of citizens to campaigns outside the Peloponnese. In the words of the modern scholar Geoffrey de Sainte Croix, who studied the history of the Peloponnesian War in great detail: 'The Helot danger was the curse Sparta had brought upon herself, an admirable illustration of the maxim that a people which oppresses another cannot itself be free.'

Fear and suspicion lead to war

The most immediate, short-term cause of the Peloponnesian War, according to Thucydides, was the judgment of the Spartans, endorsed by their allies, that the Athenians had broken the terms of the Thirty Years' Peace. A key clause was a guarantee that no state would be deprived of its autonomy. This did not mean that the Athenians could not demand tribute from their subject allies, nor that the Spartans had to relinquish control over the Peloponnesian League. Rather it meant that no state should be deprived of the freedom to run its own affairs, insofar as it had done before the peace treaty was agreed. The Athenians were accused of failing to respect this clause by several of the Greek states.

The case against Athens

The Spartans were under considerable pressure from their allies in the Peloponnesian League to restrain the Athenians. In 432 they invited all interested parties to put their case before a meeting of the Spartan Assembly. Prominent among the states arguing for war was Corinth. There were two main Corinthian complaints. One was the action of Athens on behalf of Corcyra (modern Corfu) against the Corinthians. In 435 the Corinthian colony of Corcyra was involved in a dispute with her colony at Epidamnos, in modern Albania. This dispute escalated to involve the Corinthians, on the side of Epidamnos, in a naval battle in 432 with the Athenians, who had made a defensive alliance with Corcyra in 433. Corcyra had a large navy of her own and the Corinthians and other Peloponnesians feared that their alliance might make the Athenians invincible at sea. They also saw the Athenians' involvement as unjustifiable interference in their affairs, contrary to the terms of the Thirty Years' Peace.

The other Corinthian complaint was over Athens' treatment of the city of Poteidaia. This city, located on the westernmost spur of the Chalkidike peninsula, had originally been founded by Corinthians and still received its annual magistrates from Corinth. It was a tribute-paying member of the Delian League and of great strategic importance because of its proximity to the territory of the Macedonian king, Perdikkas, who was a former ally of Athens. Perdikkas was now encouraging the cities of Chalkidike to revolt from Athens. They had formed a league with its political and economic centre at Olynthos. The Poteidaians had been ordered by Athens to send their Corinthian magistrates back home and dismantle their fortifications. While they negotiated with the Athenians they sent an embassy to the Peloponnese and obtained an assurance from Sparta that if the Athenians attacked Poteidaia, Sparta would invade Attika. The Athenians were fearful that they might lose control of this prosperous area, which provided some seven per cent of their tribute revenue, so they sent forces to lay siege to the city, which had been reinforced by troops from Corinth and mercenaries from the Peloponnese. The Corinthians complained that Athens was breaking the terms of the Peace and demanded that the Spartans invade Attika.

A further complaint against Athens was made by the people of Megara, who complained that they had been excluded from access to the harbours and market-place of Athens by a decree of the Athenian Assembly. The purpose of what is known as the Megarian decree seems to have been to put pressure on the Megarians to abandon their alliance with Sparta and the Peloponnesians and resume their alliance with Athens, which they had abandoned in 446. The Megarians' territory

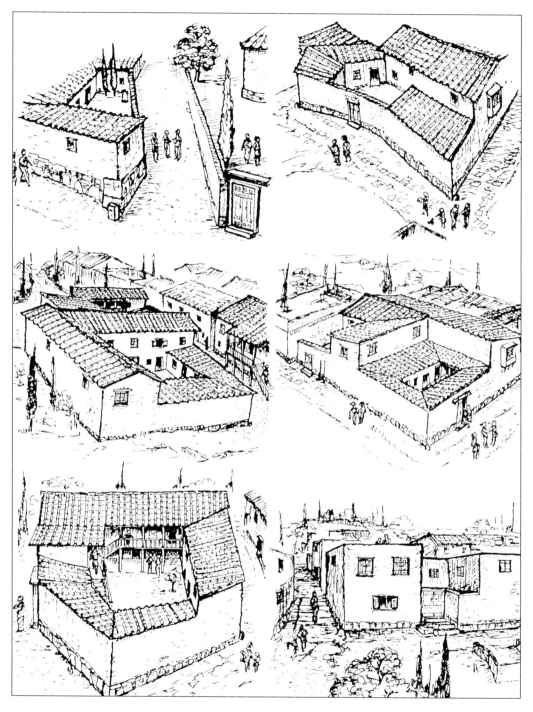

These sketches show reconstructions of typical Athenian houses based on archeological remains. The walls were built of sun-dried clay bricks and the roofs were covered with large pottery tiles. The windows had no glass, only wooden shutters. Most houses were built around a small courtyard and those of wealthier families would usually have an upper storey. (John Ellis Jones)

bordered on Attika in the east and provided potential access for a Peloponnesian army to attack Athens. The exclusions from Athenian harbours and markets seem to have had a very severe effect on Megarian trade. This is not surprising as Athens was the largest city in Greece and her commercial harbour at Peiraieus was a major centre of maritime trade.

Representatives from the island state of Aigina also complained that their autonomy was being infringed by Athens. Aigina had been part of the Athenian Empire since 458, but is not unlikely that the Athenians had recently begun to behave more aggressively towards Aiginetans for similar reasons to those which were causing them to put pressure on Megara. The Athenians must have been conscious of the fact that Aigina provided a potential base for naval attacks on Athens and her maritime trade. Autonomy was fine for some of the more distant islands or cities in the Aegean, but for places on their doorstep the Athenians preferred the same kind of close control as the Spartans exercised over their Messenian neighbours. An Athenian garrison was installed on the island by 432 and, although the Aiginetan tribute payments were reduced by over half, this meant an effective end to the Aiginetans' right to govern themselves freely, again contrary to the key clause of the Thirty Years' Peace.

The Athenians claimed that they had the right to do as they pleased regarding their empire, which they had won for themselves at considerable cost. They probably had not expected their treatment of Aigina to become an issue, given the fact that in the case of Samos in 440 the Corinthians themselves had upheld the right of Athens to police its own empire. In the case of Corcyra they felt that they were doing no more than responding to a defensive request from an ally, although it is unlikely that they entered into the alliance without some expectation of clashing with the Corinthians. They pointed out that Poteidaia was one of their tribute-paying allies and had been encouraged to revolt by the Corinthians, who were openly fighting against them on the side of the Poteidaians. The Megarian decree, they claimed, was simply a set of religious sanctions imposed because the Megarians had cultivated some land which was supposed to be left untouched as it was sacred to the gods, as well as some disputed territory on the border between Attika and the Megarid. They also accused the Megarians of sheltering runaway Athenian slaves.

The Spartans and their allies vote for war

Having heard the complaints and the counter-arguments of the Athenians, the Spartans removed everyone except the full Spartan citizens from the assembly place so that they could discuss the matter among themselves. The vast majority of the Spartans were angered by what they had heard. Their allies had convinced them that the Athenians had broken the terms of the Thirty Years' Peace and were acting with unreasonable aggression. In consequence there was great enthusiasm for immediately declaring war on Athens. At this point one of the two kings, Archidamos, introduced a note of caution. He seems to have argued that it was premature of the Spartans to rush into war a with Athens, whose extensive empire provided her with the resources to fight a protracted war more easily than the Spartans. He pointed out that Athens' chief strength lay in her naval power, while Sparta was essentially a land power. He advised sending diplomatic missions to try to seek negotiated settlements of the various disputes, while at the same time recruiting new allies, accumulating resources and preparing for a war in which expensive naval campaigns would be necessary to obtain victory. He had to put his arguments carefully, in order to avoid offending the Spartans' sense of duty towards their allies and their great pride in their martial prowess, whilst at the same time pointing out to them the true size of the task that lay before them. Thucydides' version of a key part of his speech is as follows:

No-one can call us cowards if, in spite of our numbers, we seem in no hurry to attack a single city. Their allies are no less numerous than ours and theirs contribute money. And in war it is the expenditure which enables the weapons to bring results, especially in a conflict between a land power and a sea power. Let us gather our resources first and not get rushed into premature action by the words of our allies. We shall have to bear the brunt of it all, however things turn out. So let us consider the options in a calm fashion.

In response to Archidamos' sensible and cautious arguments the ephor Sthenelaidas appealed to the sense of outrage at the Athenians' high-handed behaviour and exhorted the Spartans to take decisive action against them. Thucydides' version of his speech dismisses Archidamos' concerns over resources and emphasises the need to respond decisively to the demands of Sparta's allies:

For while the other side may have plenty of money, ships and horses, we have good allies whom we cannot betray to the Athenians. Nor is this something to be decided by diplomacy and negotiations; it's not through words that our interests are being harmed. Our vengeance must be strong and swift ... So vote as befits you Spartans, for war! Do not allow the Athenians to become stronger and do not utterly betray your allies! With the gods beside us let us challenge the unrighteous!

In spite of the fervour of his rhetoric, when Sthenelaidas, as the ephor presiding over the Spartan assembly, put the matter to a vote, he claimed that he could not tell whether the shouts were louder for or against going to war. So he told the Spartans to separate into two groups and then it was clear that the majority favoured war. All that remained was for the Spartans to call a congress of the Peloponnesian League to get their allies' approval for a war against the Athenians. The vote was not unanimous, but the Corinthians persuaded a majority of the Peloponnesians to declare that Athens

had broken the terms of the Thirty Years' Peace.

Even now the Spartans were reluctant to act. They sent an embassy to Athens to try to negotiate a settlement. The autonomy of Poteidaia and Aigina was raised in these discussions, but the main sticking point seems to have been the Megarian decree, which the Athenians refused to rescind. Eventually a Spartan envoy delivered the message, 'We want peace and we want the Athenians to let their allies be free.' Perikles told the Athenian Assembly that the Spartans could not be trusted to stop at these demands, but would try to force them to give up more and more in the name of freedom for the Greeks. He encouraged the Athenians to tell the Spartan envoys that they too should stop interfering in the affairs of their own allies, and submit the problem of supposed infringements of the Thirty Years' Peace to arbitration. At this point the Spartans abandoned the negotiations. As Thucydides stressed, the underlying cause of the war was Athens' growing power and the fear that caused among the Spartans and their allies. No amount of diplomacy would change the reality of that power or the fear that it was generating.

The Thebans strike first

The Boiotians also had grievances against the Athenians going back nearly 30 years. Plataia was the only Boiotian city which had not joined the Boiotian League, in which the Thebans were the dominant force. It is not entirely surprising, therefore, that the opening encounter of the Peloponnesian War was not a Spartan led invasion of Attika, but a pre-emptive strike on Plataia by the Thebans, who were anxious to secure as much of their border with Attika as possible. They were acting in concert with a group of Plataians who were unhappy with their city's long-standing alliance with Athens and wanted to bring it over to the Spartan side in line with most of the rest of Boiotia.

The majority of the Plataians were unaware of this plot and they were taken completely by surprise. When an advance force of around 300 Theban hoplites entered the city and told the Plataians that they should join the League of Boiotian cities, they were initially cowed, but once they realised that the rest of the Theban army had been delayed by heavy rain their anti-Theban and pro-Athenian feelings reasserted themselves. After a vicious struggle at night, in the pouring rain, which involved not just the Plataian citizens but many of their women and slaves, 120 Thebans were dead and the rest surrendered. The main strength of the Thebans did not arrive until later the next morning and they withdrew after being promised that the prisoners would not be harmed. The Athenians were told about the attack and sent a herald to urge the Plataians not to act rashly. By the time this message arrived, however, the Plataians had gathered all their property into the city and executed their Theban prisoners. There was now no doubt that the Thirty Years' Peace was over and Plataia was reinforced by the Athenians, who evacuated the women, children and men who were too old to fight. The attack on Plataia provided an early indication of the level of bloodshed which was to become commonplace in the Greek world over the next three decades.

The first twenty years

The Archidamian War

The first 10 years of conflict between Athens and Sparta were considered by many of the Greeks to have constituted a separate war. At the start of the war the Peloponnesian strategy was to invade the territory of Attika by land, damaging crops and buildings and forcing the Athenians to come out of their city and settle the war in a decisive pitched battle. The Peloponnesians were confident that they would win such a battle. If no such confrontation was achieved, the Peloponnesians hoped that the Athenian citizens would soon grow weary of the attacks and look for a settlement on terms favourable to their opponents. For the first few years the Peloponnesian army was led by the only available Spartan king, Archidamos, whose name is given by modern historians to this part of the war.

The Athenians also doubted their ability to defeat Sparta and her allies in a major hoplite confrontation, so, at the urging of Perikles, they retreated behind their fortifications and waited for the Peloponnesians to give up and go home. They struck back by using their superior naval forces to attack the territory of

The young man featured on this Athenian wine jug of about 430 BC is equipped with the typical large round shield, long spear and short sword of the hoplite. He wears no body armour, only a heavy tunic and a headband to ease the fit of his bronze helmet. The lion device on his shield is a personal one. At the start of the Peloponnesian War most Greek cities did not have standardised symbols for their soldiers, which sometimes caused confusion in battle. (Boston Museum of Fine Arts)

Sparta and her allies, hoping to make them lose their enthusiasm for the conflict. This strategy could not win them the war, but it could prolong the stalemate and might discourage enough of the enemy to force them to make peace. The strategists on both sides probably thought that there would be only a few years of fighting before a settlement was reached.

In fact the annual invasions of the Archidamian War, of which there were five between 431 and 425, did not always last very long, nor, indeed, did they succeed in doing much damage. Athenian cavalry harried the light troops on the Peloponnesian side and even the longest invasion, lasting 40 days in 430, failed to cause much harm. Athens could import much of its food, particularly grain, via the shipping routes secured by Athens' maritime empire and powerful navy. In any case it proved difficult to assemble the Peloponnesian forces at the right time to strike against Attika's agricultural resources, in part probably because many of the soldiers wanted to be at home on their own farmland. In 429 the Peloponnesians were persuaded by the Thebans to make a determined attempt to overcome the resistance of Plataia. The Spartan king Archidamos, conscious of the historical significance of Plataia as the site of Sparta's great victory over the Persians in 479, tried to negotiate a surrender, but assurances from the Athenians that they would not abandon the Plataians convinced those still inside the city walls to hold out. The Spartans built a circuit of wooden siege fortifications to prevent any forces from getting in to relieve the 600 or so remaining people. A breakout was achieved during a winter storm by about 200 men, who climbed over the walls using ladders, but they could not persuade the Athenians to send a force to relieve the siege.

In the summer of 426 the new Spartan king, Agis, son of Archidamos, was leading another expedition of Peloponnesian forces into the Isthmus of Corinth on their way to Attika when there was an earthquake, which forced them to turn back before they had even reached Athenian territory. In the following year a similar expedition, also led by Agis,

arrived in Attika early in the summer, when the crops were still a long way from ripening and the weather was very stormy. This made it difficult for the Spartans to feed themselves while they were camped on Athenian territory and the troops began to complain. Then news arrived of a serious Athenian incursion at Pylos on the western coast of the Peloponnese and the whole army was withdrawn, having stayed in Attika for only 15 days.

A devastating plague struck Athens in 430, with further outbreaks in 429 and 426. The second year it killed Perikles himself, but even this misery did not convince the Athenians to seek peace. If anything it probably made them keener to cause harm to their enemies in return and the scale and range of naval counter-strikes was stepped up after Perikles' death. The Peloponnesians themselves made limited use of their naval forces, which were principally furnished by the Corinthians. A grandiose scheme was hatched to involve the Western Greeks of Sicily and Southern Italy in the war and create a huge fleet of 500 triremes, but this came to nothing and the Athenians took the initiative in the west by sending expeditions to Sicily. They went at the invitation of an old ally, the city of Leontini, which asked for their help against the larger city of Syracuse. Two small Athenian fleets were sent to Sicily in 427 and 425, partly with the aim of disrupting grain supplies from the island to the Peloponnese, but also with an eye towards adding as much of the island as they could to the Athenian Empire. In 424, however, the Sicilian cities came to an understanding among themselves and the Athenians returned home without anything to show for their efforts.

The revolt of Mytilene and the end of Plataia

The next major setback of the war for the Athenians was a revolt in 428 on the island of Lesbos, led by the largest city, Mytilene. The cities of Lesbos had been founders of the Delian League and their contributions to its resources were crucial to the Athenian war effort. With the exception of Methymna they had oligarchic governments and they decided that in her severely weakened state Athens would not be able to respond effectively to an attempt to break away from her control. The Athenians despatched a small army and a fleet to blockade Mytilene, which was dependent on reinforcements and food supplies from overseas. The Mytileneans asked Sparta and the Peloponnesian League for help and a relief force was slowly assembled under the command of the Spartan Alkidas. The Athenians moved faster, however, sending a second fleet of 100 ships early in 427, in spite of the losses caused by the plague. The oligarchic regime at Mytilene distributed weapons to the mass of the population to stiffen their defences, but this plan backfired and the newly empowered citizens demanded a general distribution of grain to feed the starving population. When this did not materialise they surrendered the city to the Athenian commander Paches, who sent the leaders of the revolt back to Athens.

A debate ensued in the Athenian Assembly about the appropriate punishment for the Mytilenean rebels. The politician Kleon persuaded the citizens that an example had to be made of the people of Mytilene in order to discourage further revolts. He proposed that all the adult male citizens should be executed and the women and children sold into slavery. The Assembly voted in favour of this and despatched a ship to tell Paches to carry out this brutal decree. The next day, however, many people realised the injustice of the decision. A second meeting of the Assembly was called and the citizens voted to rescind their decree and only to punish those who were guilty of leading the revolt. A second trireme was sent out with the revised orders. Its crew rowed in shifts, not putting in to land at night, as was normal on such a voyage. Ambassadors from Mytilene supplied them with food and drink while they rowed and promised great rewards if they could make up the 24 hours start that the previous ship had on them. Eventually they reached Mytilene just as Paches was reading the orders delivered by the first ship. The mass of the citizens were saved, but Mytilene was deprived of her fleet and much of her territory.

At about the same time the small garrison of Plataia finally succumbed to starvation and surrendered to the Spartans. They were treated very harshly on the insistence of their neighbours the Thebans. All of the 225 surviving men were subjected to a 'trial' by the Spartans, at which they were each asked: 'Have you done anything of benefit to the Lakedaimonians (i.e. the Spartans) and their allies in the current war?' As none of the defenders could answer yes to this question, the Spartans decided that they were justified in executing all of them. The 110 women who had stayed behind were sold as slaves.

Naval warfare

At sea the war was fought almost entirely between fleets of triremes. These were warships rowed by up to 170 oarsmen and manned by 30 or more sailors and soldiers. The number of rowers could be varied so that a trireme could carry enough troops to act as an assault ship for small forces, or it could be used to tow and escort troop carriers if a larger army needed to be transported. When fully crewed the ships were dangerous offensive weapons in themselves, each sporting a heavy bronze ram on its prow, which could damage an enemy vessel's hull if it impacted with enough force. Consequently the best naval tactics involved manoeuvring behind or to the side of an enemy ship and rowing hard enough to smash the ram against its hull and rupture it. Another, more dangerous, tactic was for the helmsman to steer close into the enemy on one side and break off their oars, having signalled his own rowers to ship their oars just before the vessels made contact. The triremes were lightweight vessels that did not easily sink when they were holed, but instead they would often remain afloat, or perhaps partially submerged, and they could be towed away by whichever side was the victor. The crews of damaged ships were very vulnerable, however, and unless their own ships came quickly to their rescue they might be captured, or if the ship was completely awash with water they could easily drown. Surprisingly few Greeks were strong swimmers, since they did not swim for pleasure. Even if there was an accessible coastline close by it might be held by enemy troops who could kill or capture those men who did make it ashore.

Athenian naval superiority

In 429 the Peloponnesians sent out a fleet under the command of the Spartan Knemon to challenge the Athenian squadron under the command of Phormio based at Naupaktos. This naval base was strategically located to intercept Peloponnesian fleets sailing to and from Corinth, the Northern Peloponnese and Eastern Boiotia. Phormio had only 20 ships, whereas Knemon had a total of 47, drawn from Corinth and Sikyon. Nevertheless Phormio attacked and succeeded in putting the Peloponnesians on the defensive. They formed most of their ships into a circle with the prows facing outwards, their aim being to prevent the Athenians from getting behind any of them. Five of the best ships were stationed in the centre of the circle to attack any Athenian vessel that managed to get inside the formation. Phormio's response to this tactic was to tell the commanders of his own ships to sail around the fringes of this circle, getting gradually closer to the Peloponnesians and forcing them to back in towards each other. Eventually, with the help of a strong early morning wind, the circle of ships became too tightly packed and were unable to maintain their formation without colliding with each other. When it was clear that the Peloponnesians had lost all semblance of order Phormio attacked, sinking several of the enemy and capturing 12 ships.

The superior seamanship and tactics of the Athenians were rewarded with another success soon afterwards when a larger force of 77 Peloponnesian ships drove Phormio into the narrow stretch of water at Rhion, hoping to trap them against the northern shoreline, thus negating the greater speed and

manoeuvrability of the Athenians. After initially losing nine ships to this overwhelming force, Phormio and his remaining commanders broke away and retreated towards Naupaktos. The Peloponnesians pursued, but their lead ships became too spread out to support each other. As the final Athenian ship reached Naupaktos it went behind a merchant ship at anchor in the bay and turned on the foremost of the pursuing vessels, ramming it amidships and causing the rest to stop rowing and wait for their comrades. This decision left them sitting in the water and vulnerable to the swift counter-attacks of the Athenians, who now rowed out and rejoined the battle. Because they were now very close to the shore some of the Peloponnesians ran aground, or came close enough for the Messenians who were based at Naupaktos to swim out, some in their armour and swarm aboard some of the ships. The Athenians recaptured most of their own ships, which the Peloponnesians had been towing behind them. They also took six Peloponnesian vessels, on one of which was a Spartan commander called Timokrates, who killed himself rather be captured by the Athenians. From this point onwards the Peloponnesians generally avoided naval confrontations with the Athenians until the Athenian navy had been seriously weakened by the Sicilian Expedition. In 425, when the Peloponnesian fleet sent to Corcyra was recalled to assist in removing Demosthenes' forces from Pylos, they chose to drag their ships over the narrow isthmus of Leukas rather than risk a meeting with the Athenian fleet, which was heading for Corcyra.

Nevertheless the Athenians did not have things entirely their own way at sea. In 429 the Spartans with Knemon were invited by the Megarians to transfer their surviving crews to 40 ships docked at Niasia, the Megarian port nearest to Athens. These ships could then be used to make a surprise attack on the Athenian port of Peiraieus, which was not well guarded. Strong winds and, in Thucydides' view, a lack of courage, caused them to abandon the idea of attacking Peiraieus and to strike at the island of

A sketch showing how the Athenian harbour at Mounychia in Peiraieus may have looked in the fourth century. Early on in the Peloponnesian War a daring attempt by the Spartans to attack the harbour showed the Athenians that they needed to fortify it. The entrance is narrow and there is a chain stretched across it to prevent unauthorised ships from getting in. (J F Coates)

Salamis instead. They captured three Athenian ships on the north of the island and did a considerable amount of damage before the arrival of an Athenian fleet and concerns over the state of their ships forced them to withdraw. The episode had demonstrated that Athenian territory was also vulnerable to seaborne attack and steps were taken to close off the harbour entrances at Peiraieus and station more ships on guard duty in the future.

Spartan defeat at Pylos

In the spring of 425 the Peloponnesian army, led by the young Spartan king Agis, again invaded Attika. They settled down to spend the summer devastating as much Athenian territory as possible and to try, once more, to force the Athenians into a major

confrontation on land. Meanwhile, the Athenian generals Eurymedon and Sophokles were taking 40 ships to Sicily, via Corcyra. They made a detour into the area of Pylos on the western coast of the Peloponnese to attempt a scheme devised by the general-elect Demosthenes who was travelling with them.

Demosthenes' plan was to turn Pylos into a fortified post for a detachment of the Messenian exiles from Naupaktos to use as a base for conducting raids against Peloponnesian territory. From Pylos they could easily penetrate Messenia and, with their ability to speak the local dialect, their knowledge of the land and their kinship with the Messenians, they could stir up trouble for the Spartans in their own back yard. Demosthenes seems to have had some difficulty convincing the two current generals to carry out his plan, but eventually an improvised set of fortifications was built and Demosthenes was left there with five ships while the rest of the fleet sailed on towards Corcyra.

Initially the Spartans, did not see any serious threat from this Athenian foothold on their territory, but when King Agis and his advisers heard the news they abandoned

This bronze hoplite's helmet is in the style known as Corinthian. Such helmets afforded good protection to the wearer, but they severely restricted vision and hearing, making the hoplites heavily dependent on the coherence of their formation. This example is inscribed with the name Dendas, perhaps the person who dedicated it in a sanctuary. Many men preferred simpler helmets such as those seen in the illustration on page 86. (Ancient Art and Architecture)

their invasion of Attika and hurried to Pylos, gathering forces for a strike against Demosthenes. A Peloponnesian fleet that had been on its way to Corcyra was recalled to assist them. Demosthenes also sent for help and the Athenian fleet turned round at Zakynthos and headed back to Pylos.

This fifth-century sculpture from the temple of Aphaia on Aigina shows the hero Herakles, recognisable by his lionskin headress. He is in the act of shooting an arrow from a kneeling position. Archers were often carried on warships and would target the officers, steersmen, sailors and soldiers on enemy ships. (Ancient Art and Architecture)

The Spartans were determined to remove the enemy before their reinforcements could arrive. They attacked the Athenian position from the land and the sea for two days. They landed a small force of hoplites on the island of Sphakteria as part of the attempt to blockade the fort by land and sea. The Spartans were wary of the advantage that the Athenians had over them in naval confrontations, and seem to have decided that occupying the island would restrict Athenian access to the bay behind and prevent them from putting forces in the rear of the Spartans' own positions on land. Demosthenes beached his few remaining ships and deployed their crews as makeshift infantry. He and his men held out resolutely against almost continuous Spartan attacks. The Spartans' efforts took on a frantic edge, with one of their trireme commanders, Brasidas, putting his ship and his own life at risk by running his ship aground inside the area fortified by the Athenians and trying to force his way onto the land. He was badly wounded and lost his shield, but his bravery earned him much praise. The next day the Athenian fleet arrived, now numbering 50 vessels with the addition of ships from Naupaktos and four allied triremes from Chios.

The character of the confrontation changed dramatically once the Athenians had a strong naval force at their disposal. They easily drove the 43 Spartan ships away from the promontory of Pylos and onto the beaches in the bay, disabling some and capturing others. The blockade of the fort was lifted and the Spartans were left camped on the mainland watching helplessly as the Athenians sailed around Sphakteria unopposed. The most unfortunate result of this reversal of fortune was that 420 Peloponnesian hoplites and their Helot attendants were left stranded on the island.

The Spartans immediately sent a delegation from the *gerousia* and the ephorate to assess the situation. Their appraisal was an honest but bleak one. The situation was untenable for the men on Sphakteria because they could not be rescued and the Athenians could put their own soldiers on the island and eventually overwhelm them with sheer numbers. Even that might not be necessary, however, as there was virtually no food on the island, so they might easily be starved into surrender. The official delegation went straight to the Athenians and negotiated a truce, which allowed them to get provisions to their men and halted Athenian attacks. In return the Spartans surrendered what remained of their fleet and all the other triremes that they had back in Lakonia (a total of 60 ships), and sent an embassy to Athens to discuss a full peace treaty.

These negotiations could have ended the war, but instead they came to nothing. The Spartan envoys were prepared to make huge concessions to recover their men, but they refused to do so in front of a full session of the Athenian Assembly, which was what the Athenians insisted upon. Such a public display of weakness and humility was simply too much for the proud Spartans, accustomed as they were to having their most important decisions settled by a small group of senior citizens in a private meeting. There was a substantial body of opinion in Athens that favoured coming to terms now, but the more belligerent and arrogant feelings of Kleon and his supporters carried the day. When Kleon accused them of lacking sincerity the Spartans gave up and returned home. The truce was over and the Spartans requested the return of their ships, but the Athenians held on to them claiming that some of the details of the agreement had not been adhered to by the Spartans. Thus they were able to bring an end to Spartan naval activity for the time being and increase the pressure on the men trapped on Sphakteria.

More Athenian forces came to Pylos and a stalemate ensued. The conditions for the Athenians were not easy, as despite being masters of the sea, they did not control much of the coastline. Their fort was still under attack from the Spartan army on the mainland and Demosthenes had less than 1,000 soldiers to defend it. The Spartans offered cash rewards to anyone who was prepared to dodge the Athenian triremes patrolling around the island and bring food to the men there, either by swimming or in small boats. Enough Helots and Messenian fishermen volunteered to maintain the food supply. Eventually the Athenians began to feel the difficulty of supplying their own forces at such a great distance and in a confined space with nowhere to beach their ships in safety.

Back in Athens, Kleon's arrogant handling of the Spartan peace envoys put the onus on him to find a solution. He tried to deflect it by blaming the lack of progress on the board of generals. They should make a determined assault on the island and kill or capture the men there, he said. He would have done so already, if he were a general. One of the current generals, Nikias, took him at his word and invited him to select whatever forces he required and show them how to do it. The mass of citizens cheered this suggestion and shouted for Kleon to take up the challenge. Kleon was trapped by the kind of crowd-pleasing rhetoric that he normally used against others. He obtained a mixed force of tough, experienced hoplites from the Athenian citizen colonies of Lemnos and Imbros, and plenty of light infantry, both peltasts (light infantryman armed with javelins) and archers. He promised to destroy or capture the Spartans in 20 days.

The most amazing thing

Kleon's boast that he could resolve the situation in 20 days, coming from a man who had never previously held any military command, was probably a piece of sheer arrogance. However, he did have enough

This photo shows the bronze covering of a hoplite shield; the wooden core has long perished. It is pierced with letters that tell us it was booty taken from the Spartans at Pylos in 425 by the Athenians. The taking and dedicating of trophies was a key part of Greek warfare. They served as physical reminders of a god-given victory over the enemy. (American School of Classical Studies at Athens: Agora Excavations)

understanding of warfare to choose Demosthenes, the energetic commander whose plan had started the whole affair, as his chief adviser. Between them they came up with a tactically sound approach. They landed 800 hoplites on the island from both sides at dawn and caught the weary Spartan sentries completely by surprise. Once bridgeheads were established they flooded the island with the Messenians from the fort at Pylos, plus archers, peltasts and several thousand ordinary rowers from the fleet, whose only offensive weapons were sling stones and rocks. By holding the hoplites back from a direct engagement with the superior Spartan troops, and using the rest of his force to harry the enemy with missiles Demosthenes forced the Spartans to retreat rather than be gradually picked off where they stood. If they could have achieved close-quarter combat with the enemy the

Spartans might have been able to defeat them, but their heavy armour slowed them down. It also proved insufficient protection against the showers of arrows, javelins and stones from unarmoured men who easily ran off before they could be engaged by the lumbering hoplites. The Spartan commander, Epitadas, was driven back to an old fort on some high ground at the north end of the island where his surviving men, many of them severely wounded, prepared to make a stand. The Messenians, however, clambered over the cliffs and came up behind the Spartans, who were now surrounded and hopelessly outnumbered.

Before all the Spartans were killed Kleon and Demosthenes decided to offer them a chance to surrender. Epitadas was dead by this time, and his second in command was too badly wounded to move, so the third in command, Styphon, asked permission to consult his superiors among the Spartans on the mainland. A tense exchange of messages followed between Styphon and the dismayed Spartan officers across the bay. Finally the following instruction was issued: 'The Lakedaimonians (i.e. the Spartans) order you to do whatever you think is in your own best interests, provided you do not act dishonourably.' This remarkably unhelpful message was the final straw for the 292 men who were still alive. After a brief discussion they laid down their arms and surrendered to the Athenians. One hundred and twenty of them were full Spartan citizens.

'To the rest of the Greeks the most amazing thing that occurred in the whole of the war,' was how Thucydides chose to describe the Spartan surrender at Sphakteria. It was unthinkable that a Spartan force, however hard pressed, would give in to their opponents. They were expected to fight to the death, as King Leonidas and his 300 Spartans had chosen to do against the might of the Persian army at the battle of Thermopylai in 480. The blow to Spartan prestige was tremendous, and the boost to Athenian morale was equally great. The captured men were taken back to Athens by the fleet. A series of Spartan embassies tried to negotiate

their release, but the Athenians demanded more than they could give in return.

The strategic value of Demosthenes' plan was demonstrated because the Pylos fort now became a thorn in the side of the Spartans, as the Messenians, emboldened by their success on Sphakteria, launched raids into the surrounding countryside and caused many Helots to desert. Nikias and the other Athenian generals took a force of 80 ships and raided the territory of the Corinthians, doing considerable damage and establishing another fortified post at Methana, from where it was possible to ravage much of the Eastern Peloponnese.

Athens in the ascendancy

The following year, 424, the Athenians began to reap the benefits of having over 100 Spartan citizens as hostages. There was no Peloponnesian invasion of Attika this year because the Athenians had told the Spartans that they would execute the prisoners if this happened. On the contrary, it was the Athenians who took the initiative by attacking Kythera, a large island off the Peloponnesian coast to the south of Lakonia. The inhabitants were free men of Perioikoi status and their loyalty to the Spartans was guaranteed by their proximity to Lakonia and the Spartan practice of posting a garrison there with a Spartan commander. Nikias, Nikeratos and Autokles sailed there with 60 ships and an invasion force of 2,000 hoplites. They defeated the Kytherans and their garrison in a brief battle and persuaded them to swap sides, having already made them aware through messages from Nikias that their lives would be spared and they would be allowed to remain on the island if they gave in quickly. Kythera became another tribute-paying island in the Athenian Empire. From here it was easy for the Athenians to raid the coast of Lakonia, rendered especially vulnerable by the Spartans' rash decision to surrender their ships as part of the truce negotiated at Pylos. It was now the Spartans' turn to post cavalry

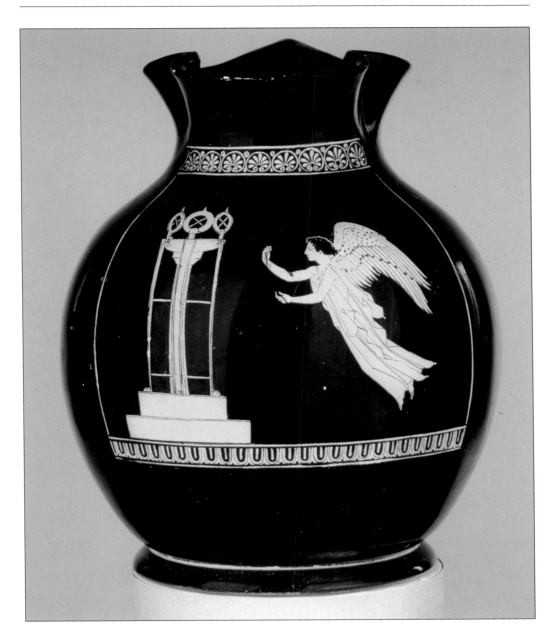

The scene on this Athenian red-figure wine jug shows Nike, the goddess who personified Victory, decorating a bronze tripod with a ribbon. Nike was usually portrayed with wings because the Greeks believed that it was the gods who told her whose side to fly to and no men could force her to stay with them.(Ashmolean Museum)

detachments and scatter small units of troops to defend their farmland from enemy attacks.

Nikias and his fellow generals took their fleet on to the eastern coast of the Peloponnese and attacked Thyrea, on the border between Argos and Lakonia. This was where the Spartans had settled refugees from Aigina. The local Spartan garrison, fearing a repeat of the Sphakteria episode, fled and left the hopelessly outnumbered Aiginetan exiles to the mercy of the Athenians. The Athenians killed many of them on the spot and transported the rest back to Athens for public execution. In this respect they

The small temple on the Acropolis dedicated to Athena Nike (Victory) was built in the 420s. It may reflect the Athenians' sense of triumph over their Peloponnesian enemies, but it was mostly decorated with scupltures showing mythological scenes or depicting the famous Athenian victory over the Persians in 490. (Ancient Art and Architecture)

behaved no better than the Thebans and Spartans had done towards the unfortunate citizens of Plataia.

The next Athenian target was Megara, where a pro-Athenian democratic faction in the city was plotting with Demosthenes to let an Athenian army into the city at dawn to force the Peloponnesian garrison to surrender. The plot was only partially successful but it did enable the large Athenian army to take control of the nearby port of Nisaia. The garrison of Peloponnesian troops stationed there offered to pay a ransom for themselves and hand over the Spartans among them in return for safe passage. This was doubtless another symptom of the low esteem in which the Spartans were held after the Sphakteria débâcle. The city of Megara itself was not captured, however, partly thanks to the resolute action taken by the Spartan Brasidas, who was at Sikyon recruiting troops for an expedition into the Thracian region. He quickly assembled a force of 4,000 hoplites who linked up with some Boiotian cavalry to check the Athenian advance on the city. The hoplite force that Brasidas used was largely composed of Corinthians, whose territory bordered Megara and who were likely to suffer the most from further Athenian gains in the area. At this point in his narration of the events of the war Thucydides makes the following comment on the Athenian citizens' ambition and overconfidence:

So completely were they taken in by their current good fortune that they assumed that no-one could possibly stand against them; and they believed that both the possible and the impossible alike could be accomplished, regardless of whether their resources were great or meagre. The reason for this was the completely unlooked for success in whatever they did, which greatly raised their expectations.

Athenian defeat at Delion

The Athenians were content to retain the port of Nisaia and turned their attention to the Boiotians, their neighbours to the north of Attika, who were dominated by the city of Thebes, Sparta's principal ally outside of the Peloponnese. Demosthenes and his fellow general Hippokrates had devised a complex plan to capture and fortify Delion, a position on the coast of Boiotia, near Tanagra. From there they hoped to force most of the Boiotians to revolt against Theban control. The plan called for two armies to converge on Delion from the north and south. Demosthenes' army was to include allies from Akarnania in Western Greece, some Phokians and Boiotians from Orchomenos, while Hippokrates led an army composed largely of Athenian citizens. The plan went wrong from the outset. Demosthenes' intentions were betrayed to the Thebans and he was prevented from making the rendezvous. Hippokrates and the Athenian hoplites reached Delion and fortified it, but as they were heading back to Attika they were confronted by the Thebans and most of the other Boiotians. As often happened in a hoplite battle the right wing of each army drove back its opponents, but the superior Boiotian cavalry forces scattered the Athenian right wing and the heavy concentration of Theban hoplites forced the Athenian left into headlong flight. Over 1,000 Athenians were killed, including their general Hippokrates.

Brasidas fights back

In 424 the Spartans decided to strike at a vulnerable area of the Athenian Empire, the Greek cities of the north-eastern Aegean, especially the peninsula of Chalkidike. Unable to mount any naval expeditions, they sent a small army overland from the Peloponnese to Northern Greece. It was under the command of Brasidas, the Spartan who had fought so bravely at Pylos and was beginning to gain a reputation as a skilful tactician. The Spartans were not prepared to risk more of their own citizens so far from home, so his force consisted of 1,000 hoplite mercenaries, from various parts of the

This photo is of the Hellenic naval vessel *Olympias*, a working reconstruction of an Athenian trireme. Such warships routinely used their sails for long voyages, but they were propelled by their oars alone during battles; the masts were removed and stored on land. Some triremes were used to transport soldiers and a few were even converted to carry up to 30 horses. (Ancient Art and Architecture)

Peloponnese and 700 Helots who had volunteered to fight as hoplites in exchange for their freedom. Funding came from the king of Macedon and the recently formed League of the Greek cities of Chalkidike, all of whom wanted to reduce Athenian influence in the area.

One of Brasidas' first successes was against the city of Amphipolis. He had already persuaded the Chalkidian cities of Akanthos and Stageira to revolt from Athens, but Amphipolis was a more difficult, though tempting target. It had been founded under Athenian direction in 437/436 to control a strategically vital crossing point of the river Strymon, a major trade and communication route, and to provide a base for exploitation of the natural resources of the Pangeion mountain region, principally timber for ship-building,

silver and gold. It had a population drawn from all parts of Greece, with only a small Athenian element. The strength of these citizens' loyalties to the Athenians was dubious, but there was an Athenian hoplite garrison there, commanded by the general Eukles.

The sudden appearance of Brasidas, accompanied by Chalkidian forces from the cities that had joined him, caught the inhabitants of Amphipolis completely unprepared. Many of them were outside the city walls, working on their farmland. Nevertheless Eukles managed to despatch a ship to alert the historian Thucydides, who was an Athenian general for this year and had a force of seven triremes on the island of Thasos, less than a day's sail away to the south east.

The news of Brasidas' arrival was communicated to Thucydides as quickly as possible. The distance between Amphipolis and Thasos is about 50 miles (80km) and the journey would normally have been a relatively straightforward one for experienced mariners. It was winter however, and navigating across to the mainland, along the coast and up the river Strymon in poor weather and failing light could have been quite hazardous. Thucydides does not say how difficult his voyage was, but his failure to cover the distance in less than six hours is certainly not indicative of incompetence or hesitancy. He says that he set out 'immediately' and 'at full speed' with his seven ships from Thasos, but he still failed to reach the city in time to prevent its surrender, and nearly failed to save the city of Eion, further down the river Strymon.

Thucydides says that even the Athenians in Amphipolis did not expect relieving forces to arrive quickly, which suggests that they were uncertain when, or possibly whether, their call for help would reach him, in spite of the fact that he was close by. Perhaps there was an additional worry about what his reaction to the news would be? They would only know if he had heeded their call when they saw his ships coming up the river from Eion. Yet Brasidas decided to offer them generous, remarkably un-Spartan surrender terms, allowing the inhabitants to retain their possessions and political rights in exchange for acknowledging Spartan authority. Those who did not wish to stay under these terms were allowed to take their possessions and leave unmolested. In contrast, when the Plataians finally surrendered in 427 all of the men, except those who could claim that they had been helping the Spartans, were killed and the women who had stayed with them were enslaved. Unlike many other Spartan commanders during the war, Brasidas was operating a long way from home and had no-one overseeing his actions, but his leniency to the inhabitants was based on his own expectation that a relief force would arrive quickly and that Thucydides would easily be able to exploit his local connections to summon up further forces to challenge Brasidas.

So why did Eukles and his compatriots not come to the same conclusion and determine to hold out even for a single day? Thucydides says that the population of Amphipolis felt they were better off surrendering on Brasidas' 'generous terms' and they would not listen to

the Athenian commander. It would seem that a lack of firm information on the prospects of relief, combined with the certainty of lenient treatment by Brasidas, caused a catastrophic loss of confidence in the Athenians. It was easier to believe in the visible Spartan forces than in the unseen fleet of Thucydides whose approach could only be presumed to be happening. Without any means of communicating quickly with each other over long distances, Greek commanders were constantly plagued by doubts and fears of betrayal and abandonment. Brasidas was able to exploit this weakness to seize control of a vital Athenian outpost. The consequence for Thucydides was that the Athenian Assembly chose to blame him for the loss of Amphipolis and he was exiled from his home city. His loss was posterity's gain, however, as he was able to travel around the Greek world gathering vital information for his history of the Peloponnesian War.

The fragile truce of 423

Brasidas continued to campaign in the area, but he met some determined resistance from the local Athenian garrison in the city of Torone, until some of its population opened the gates and the Athenians were forced to flee by ship. Emboldened by his successes he put the resources of Amphipolis to good use by building triremes on the banks of the river Strymon.

The Athenians clearly had to find a way to put a stop to what Brasidas was doing and their possession of the Spartans taken at Pylos in 425 gave them a strong bargaining position in peace negotiations. Sparta persuaded her allies to agree to offer a truce for one year as a preliminary step towards a long-term settlement. The Athenian assembly accepted and oaths were taken by representatives of both sides in the summer of 423. The terms of the truce included a clause allowing each side to keep its own territory, specific restrictions on movement of troops and communications with strategically sensitive areas, particularly around Megara, restrictions on Peloponnesian movement at sea and a ban on accepting any deserters from the other side, whether they were free men or slaves. This would have included any more Messenians fleeing to Pylos and should also have put a stop to the defections from Athens' tribute-paying cities in Northern Greece.

In the midst of the negotiations for this truce Skione, one of the Chalkidian cities, revolted. Brasidas, who had persuaded the Skionians to come over to his side, claimed that it was not contrary to the terms of the truce because it happened before the oaths were taken. The Athenians were furious with the Skionians, however, and Kleon persuaded the assembly to vote for a decree that the city should be sacked and its citizens executed as a punishment. This harsh decision did not deter Skione's neighbour Mende from changing sides as well, although in this case there was no doubt that it happened after the truce was ratified. Brasidas might have made even greater gains had he not had to divert most of his forces to a joint campaign with his royal ally and paymaster King Perdikkas of Macedon. The Athenians took advantage of his absence to send an expedition to the region under the generals Nikias and Nikostratos. They managed to recover Mende, whose citizens changed sides again in time to avoid the full wrath of Athenian retribution, but Skione held out longer. Brasidas might have been able to raise the siege there too, if Spartan reinforcements had managed to get through Thessaly, but they were blocked with the connivance of King Perdikkas, who had fallen out with Brasidas and was now co-operating with the Athenians.

Deaths of Kleon and Brasidas

The war continued in a sporadic fashion despite the truce. The Athenians tried to revive their interests in Sicily by encouraging opposition to Syracuse, but no significant progress was made. A Boiotian force captured, through treachery, the fort of Panakton on the border between Athens and Boiotia. This was not a serious defeat for the Athenians,

but it increased the vulnerability of Northern Attika to raids and made it more difficult for the Athenians to bring supplies into their city from the island of Euboia. In the meetings of the Assembly there was a growing sense of impatience, which led to demands for some decisive activity on the part of their generals. This sense of frustration made it easier for Kleon to persuade the Athenian assembly to vote for a strong expedition to be sent to the north to deal with Brasidas. The Assembly authorised Kleon to take command of 30 triremes, with 1,200 Athenian hoplites, 300 cavalry and a strong force drawn from the subject allies. He gathered further troops from those besieging Skione and attacked Torone. The city was quickly taken by a combined land and sea assault. The Toronian women and children were sold into slavery, while the surviving 700 men, consisting of some Toronians, some Chalkidians from other cities and a few Peloponnesians, were taken back to Athens to join the other enemy prisoners.

The main target for Kleon's expedition was the recovery of Amphipolis. Brasidas also realised the importance of the city and he hired additional Thracian mercenaries to bolster his defences. Kleon based himself at nearby Eion, but he took his army close enough to Amphipolis to observe the dispositions of Brasidas' forces inside the city. When they appeared to be preparing to come out for battle he ordered his men to withdraw. But Brasidas had selected 150 of his best hoplites as a strike force and he rushed out of the gates while Kleon was still trying to turn his army round and organise it for the march back to Eion. As more of Brasidas' men poured out of the city to engage them the Athenians panicked and fled. Kleon was killed by a Thracian mercenary along with about 600 hoplites. On the other side there were only seven casualties, but they included Brasidas, who had once again chosen to lead by example and was fatally wounded. He survived long enough to hear the extent of his victory and the jubilant citizens of Amphipolis gave him a magnificent funeral and installed a shrine

The Propylaia of the Athenian Acropolis was a monumental gateway to the sanctuary which contained temples altars and other sacred buildings. Ritual processions of men, women and children passed through it during the many religious festivals that were celebrated by the citizens in honour of their gods. (Ancient Art and Architecture)

to him as their honorary founder, in place of the original Athenian founder. When news of Brasidas' death was brought back home he was hailed as the best of the Spartans, but his mother is reputed to have said: 'My son Brasidas was indeed a fine man, nevertheless he was not as good as many other Spartans.' For this display of traditional Spartan reticence and patriotism the ephors decided to award her public honours.

The Peace of Nikias

The deaths of both Brasidas and Kleon took a lot of the momentum out of the war between Athens and Sparta. Both had been energetic and ambitious in proposing and carrying out schemes to wear down the other side. Their simultaneous deaths were taken by everyone involved as symbolic of the stalemate that had been reached after nearly 10 years of war. Those who advocated peace were now able to push along negotiations for a long-term treaty. By the end of 422 the Spartans were faced with the prospect of further Helot revolts if the raids from Pylos and Kythera continued. More urgent, however was the need to recover over 100 full Spartan citizens from the Athenians. Why were these few Spartans who became trapped on Sphakteria so precious that their imminent capture brought the Spartan war effort to a standstill and securing their return dominated Spartan thinking for nearly four years? There were other, allied prisoners to be exchanged, of course, including those captured by Kleon at Torone. The Spartan manpower shortage referred to earlier must also be part of the explanation. In addition, Thucydides tells us that some of them were important people back in Sparta, with relations among the Spartan citizens who held high office, yet after their return they were condemned as cowards and deprived of their citizen rights for surrendering instead of fighting on. Ultimately it may have been the symbolic and emotional significance of these prisoners that made the Spartans desperate to wrest them from the grasp of the gloating Athenians. As long as they remained in Athens they were living, walking proof that, for all their training, discipline and haughty disregard for others, the Spartans were not the bravest and the best of the Greeks. Once they were back home they could be stripped of their Spartan status and replaced by some of the other, braver Spartans that Brasidas' mother had ranked above even her remarkable son.

For the Athenians there was also a growing manpower shortage, as the deployment of allied troops in Kleon's forces illustrates. They also would have welcomed the prospect of recovering prisoners held by Peloponnesians and their allies, and they were probably just as concerned about the heavy toll that the war effort was taking on their financial reserves and the revenues from their slightly diminished empire. The confidence that the Sphakteria victory had produced must have been severely dented by the defeats at Delion and Amphipolis. The Athenian general Nikias played a leading role in the negotiations that produced a peace treaty, so modern scholars have named the treaty after him.

It is clear that the aim was to conclude a treaty similar to the Thirty Years' Peace which had been negotiated in 446, but with an initial duration of 50 years. Each side was supposed to give up any territories that it had gained by force during the war, such as the border fortress of Panakton. The Thebans refused to restore Plataia and the Athenians insisted on holding onto the Megarian port of Niasia, both claiming that these places had surrendered voluntarily. The Athenians recovered the strategically vital city of Amphipolis, but the other Chalkidian cities were allowed to declare themselves autonomous, as long as they resumed their payments of tribute to Athens. The rebellious citizens of Skione were less fortunate. Their change of sides had so angered the

Athenians that, when they first heard of it, they were persuaded by Kleon to vote for a harsh punishment. The men were to be executed and the women and children sold into slavery. This time, unlike the situation over the revolt of Mytilene, there was no change of heart. Skione's stubborn resistance seems to have hardened the attitude of the Athenians, who were not prepared to be merciful towards subject allies who had tried to break away from their empire.

The Spartans' main requirements were met with the return of Pylos and Kythera to them and a general exchange of prisoners. They also concluded a new treaty with Athens that included a clause promising Athenian help in the case of another Helot revolt. Nevertheless, they could hardly claim that their grandiose mission to liberate the Greeks from the tyranny of Athens had been achieved. The Athenians and their empire were still there.

The peace of Nikias certainly did not last for 50 years. Within months of the Athenians and Spartans agreeing to cease hostilities and exchange conquests their relationship had deteriorated into mutual suspicion. Gradually the tension escalated as it had done in the 430s, until both sides were openly at war with each other again. Indeed, Thucydides, looking back on these events with the benefit of hindsight did not think it was a proper peace at all, but merely a break in open hostilities directed against the territory of the two protagonists. Outside of Attika and Lakonia, he argued, each side did much to harm the interests of the other until the renewal of the conflict was inevitable. In part the failure to maintain peace can be blamed on the reluctance of the allies on both sides to accept the terms of the treaty. The Corinthians and the Boiotians both refused to be bound by it, particularly as it was made without their consent and included a provision for alterations to be made by mutual agreement between Athens and Sparta, without reference to any allies. The Boiotians demonstrated their disapproval by holding on to Panakton until they had destroyed its fortifications.

Athenian irritation with what they saw as failure by the Spartans to keep their side of the agreement was exploited by an ambitious young politician called Alkibiades, a relative of Perikles. He persuaded the Assembly that the way to get back at the Spartans was to encourage trouble for them in the Peloponnese. An excellent opportunity to do just this came about because the peace treaty which had been concluded between Sparta and Argos in 451 was about to expire. Throughout the Archidamian War the Argives had maintained a neutral position to their own benefit. Unlike many of their neighbours they were not economically and socially worn out from 10 years of inconclusive warfare. The people of Argos were also very well aware of their former glories, celebrated in myths and stories of Argive kings leading the Greeks. A democratic faction in Argos started working with Alkibiades and his supporters in Athens to create a new, anti-Spartan coalition by recruiting cities like Elis and Mantinea who resented the extent of Spartan influence in the Peloponnese.

In 419 the Argives attacked Epidauros, in order to secure their eastern flank against the Corinthians and to provide a convenient landing point for Athenian forces, which could not enter the Peloponnese by land because the Corinthians blocked their route. The Spartans had to respond to this show of Argive force, so they reinforced Epidauros by sea. The Argives were dismayed that the Athenians, whose naval strength was far superior to the Spartans, did nothing to hinder this move. What the Athenians did decide to do was to add an additional section to the public inscription recording the terms of the Peace of Nikias, claiming that the Spartans did not keep their oaths. In 419 the Spartans gathered a substantial army in the Peloponnese to attack Argos, and summoned further troops from their more distant allies, including Corinth and Boiotia. The Argives marched into the heart of the Peloponnese to try to prevent these forces joining up, but they were unsuccessful. Dividing his forces, the Spartan king, Agis, manoeuvred the

Argives into a vulnerable position between a small Spartan-led force and a larger one comprising the Boiotians, Corinthians and other allies of Sparta. But instead of pressing on to what seemed like certain victory, Agis met with a few representatives of the Argives and, without consulting any of his allies, agreed to withdraw under a truce that was to last for four months.

Agis was severely criticised back in Sparta, but the pious and tradition-bound Spartans felt obliged to observe the truce. He was, however, obliged by the ephors to accept a 10-man board of special advisors to prevent him making any similar political errors. In 418 the Argives gathered their allies once more and set out to force other Peloponnesian states to join their coalition. They easily persuaded the city of Orchomenos to come over to them and moved south to Mantinea, intending to use the city as a base from which to put pressure on Tegea. The Spartans were forced to respond to a direct threat to one of their principal allies.

The battle of Mantinea

Led by Agis, the Spartan army marched into the territory of Mantinea and implemented their standard policy of ravaging the enemy's land in order to force them to come out and offer battle in defence of their crops. Unfortunately, in that part of the Peloponnese the harvest was mostly completed by this time, and the damage did not amount to much. The allies were not eager to risk a battle as they were hoping for reinforcements in the shape of a large force of about 3,000 hoplites from Elis and a further 1,000 from Athens. When they eventually did emerge from Mantinea, instead of marching directly against the Spartans they took up a defensive position on the slopes of the nearby hills and waited for Agis and the Spartans to make the next move.

Agis was determined to force a battle, so he ordered his army to advance towards the enemy, up an increasingly steep slope.

Thucydides says that when the two armies were close enough to throw javelins or cast stones at each other, one of the older men in the Spartan ranks called out to Agis, saying that he was trying to make up for one mistake with another. He meant that Agis was trying to atone for his earlier, ignominious withdrawal from Argos by leading a reckless attack on a strong enemy position. It may well be that the old man whose words brought Agis to his senses was one of the members of the *gerousia*, the Spartan council of elders; he may even have been one of the 10 advisers. Whatever its origin, the rebuke seems to have worked, as Agis ordered a last-minute about turn, taking the army back to the city of Tegea. He was fortunate that his foolhardy advance and sudden retreat confused the commanders of the Argive coalition. They did not immediately try to pursue the retreating Spartans, probably because they were concerned that their opponents might turn about once more and attack them when they were no longer in such a strong position.

King Agis and his allies were still faced with the problem of how to draw the coalition allies down from their commanding position and into a more favourable location to engage them in battle. They decided that as an alternative to threatening the Mantineans' crops, they would threaten their water supplies by diverting the course of the main river in the area so that, when the rains came in the autumn, it would flood the territory of the Mantineans and ruin their land. In order to prevent this the enemy would be forced to come down from the hills and onto the flood plains of the river, where the flat land would not give an advantage to either side. This idea must have been suggested by the Tegeans who had a long history of disputes with the Mantineans over how to manage the flood plains.

In the meantime the Argives and their allies were on the move. The senior commanders of this coalition force were members of the aristocracy of Argos, the Thousand, whose relations with the Spartans had usually been good, but who were under pressure from their own citizens to demonstrate that they would not come to terms with the enemy in order to avoid a battle. They were also expected to fulfil on the promises offered by the new alliance to places like Mantinea, which were looking for a genuine alternative to the traditional dominance of Sparta in the Peloponnese. The Argives and their allies, therefore, moved down from the hilltop and onto the plain to the south of Mantinea. They lined up in the order of battle they had decided upon for the confrontations with the Spartans.

Their right wing, traditionally the strongest in a hoplite battle, was occupied by the Mantineans, whose home territory was now under threat, and by hoplites from some of the smaller cities of Arkadia. Next to them were the elite 1,000 hoplites from Argos, while the bulk of the Argive hoplites occupied the centre and the left wing, along with 1,000 hoplites and some cavalry from Athens.

Meanwhile the Spartans had advanced towards Mantinea, unaware that the opposing army had left its previous position and was now much closer to them. Emerging from a wood, they were surprised and disconcerted to find the enemy drawn up for battle in front of them. Agis hastily arranged his forces for the battle, adopting the usual Spartan procedure of putting the Skiritai, hoplites from the Skiris region of Arkadia, on his left wing, alongside hoplite companies formed from freed Helots, including those men who had returned from Brasidas' expedition to Thrace. At the centre were the Lakonian hoplites, both Spartans and Perioikoi. The Spartans' other Arkadian allies, including the Tegeans, were stationed on the right wing, with some Spartan officers to stiffen their resolve. At the extreme ends of each wing Agis stationed a couple of hundred Spartan cavalry. Both sides had some cavalry and a small number of light-armed troops, armed with bows, javelins and slings, but the bulk of each army consisted of hoplites, 8,000 on the Argive side and about 9,000 on the Spartan side. These were very large numbers for a hoplite confrontation and the ensuing battle demonstrated several of the key strengths and weaknesses of this form of massed infantry warfare.

Thucydides observes that there is a marked tendency for a hoplite phalanx to move to its right as it approaches the enemy. This is the result of the fact that each man's right side feels vulnerable because his shield cannot fully cover that side of his body. To compensate he moves closer to the protruding shield of the man on his right, and so on down the line, resulting in a general drift to the right of the whole army. So, as both armies advanced, each one began to extend its right wing beyond the opponents' corresponding left wing. At the battle of Mantinea this tendency was exaggerated by the fact that the Spartan army was larger and its front was wider, so that the line of the Tegeans and Spartans on Agis' left extended well beyond that of the Athenians and Argives opposite them. Conversely, on Agis' left wing the line of the Skiritai and freed Helots did not extend as far as the line of the Mantineans.

Worried that his left would be outflanked and easily defeated, Agis ordered the men there to move towards their left. However, this threatened to open up a significant gap in the line, so, as the two armies closed with each other Agis told two Spartan company commanders to take their men from the right of the Spartan hoplite line and fill the developing gap between his left wing and centre. They refused, being experienced Spartan officers who understood that to do so would leave an even more dangerous gap between the right wing and the centre. Agis tried to get his left wing to move to the right again, to close up the front line of his army, but it was too late and as the armies clashed there was a considerable gap between the freed Helots and the Spartans.

This relief sculpture comes from a large tomb built for a local aristocrat in South Western Asia Minor around 400. It shows hoplites fighting in a phalanx formation. If the discipline and cohesion of the formation was maintained it was very difficult to overcome. An unexpected attack, or one coming from the flank or rear, could easily panic the hoplites and break up their formation. (Ancient Art and Architecture)

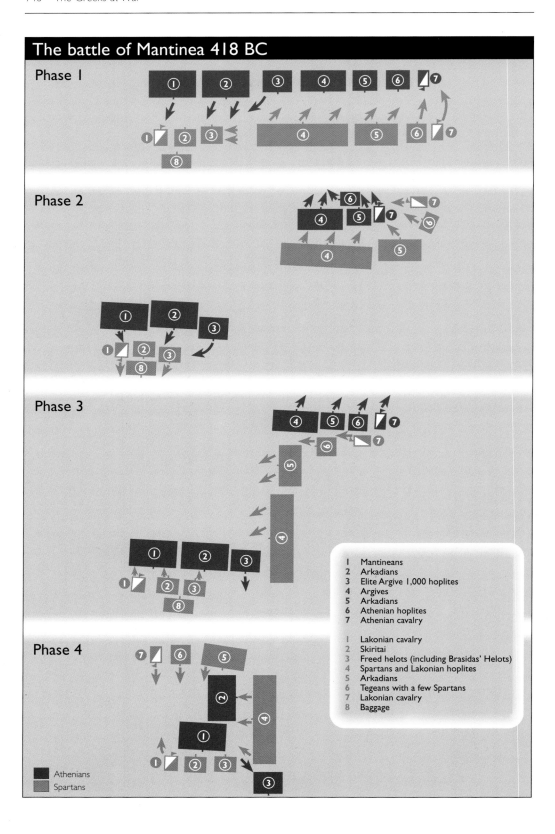

The battle of Mantinea 418 BC

Phase 1

Phase 2

Phase 3

Phase 4

1   Mantineans
2   Arkadians
3   Elite Argive 1,000 hoplites
4   Argives
5   Arkadians
6   Athenian hoplites
7   Athenian cavalry

1   Lakonian cavalry
2   Skiritai
3   Freed helots (including Brasidas' Helots)
4   Spartans and Lakonian hoplites
5   Arkadians
6   Tegeans with a few Spartans
7   Lakonian cavalry
8   Baggage

Athenians
Spartans

The Mantineans, their Arkadian allies and the 1,000 Argives exploited this gap, driving Agis' left wing back and nearly encircling it. If they had slowed down, consolidated the split between the two parts of Agis' army and then moved to their left, attacking the main formation of Spartan hoplites from the flank and rear, they might have won a remarkable victory. Instead they rushed forward, breaking up Agis' left wing and driving the men before them until they reached the baggage train, which was guarded by a few older men, many of whom they killed. Meanwhile, their own centre and left wing were faring badly. The Spartans easily overcame the Argives in front of them, who panicked and fled after only a brief show of resistance. They were older men, less well trained than the 1,000 elite hoplites who were pursuing Agis' defeated right wing, and more accustomed to fear the Spartans. The Athenians on the extreme left of the Argive army were being encircled. It was only the brave action of their cavalry that prevented a complete rout. So the battle had become divided into two separate groups of victorious hoplites pursuing their defeated and demoralised enemies. Such circumstances were typical of hoplite confrontations and, as was often the case, it was the army which retained the most discipline and cohesion after the initial stage of the engagement that was able to win the day. Agis, seeing his left wing in disarray, ended the pursuit of the

enemy centre and left so that he could turn the bulk of his army against the Mantineans, Arkadians and elite Argives, encircling them and inflicting heavy casualties.

Once again, however, an experienced senior Spartan officer intervened. This was Pharax, one of the men appointed to advise Agis after his last campaign against Argos. Pharax drew King Agis away from the front line where he was fighting and told him to give orders to leave an escape route for the 1,000 elite Argive hoplites. The historian Diodoros says that this was because they were so determined and desperate that they might have inflicted serious damage on the Spartan forces, but it may well be that there was a political angle to Pharax's advice. The elite Argive hoplites were men from the richest families in Argos and they were those most likely to support an oligarchic regime, which was what the Spartans wanted. If they were slain, however, their influence would have been lost and the pro-Athenian, democratic element in Argos would have found it easier to continue governing and pursuing its anti-Spartan alliances. It was, therefore, the Mantineans, the ordinary Argives, the Athenians and the Arkadians who suffered the most casualties at the hands of the Spartans, losing over 1,000 men between them, while the elite Argives got away almost unscathed.

The immediate consequence of this victory was the restoration of the Spartans' military reputation, but it did not produce a long-term resolution of the conflicts between the Greek states. Reluctant allies of Sparta also knew what to expect if they looked elsewhere for support. They had defeated the rival city of Argos, bringing a halt to her scheme to dominate the Peloponnese in place of Sparta. The following year the oligarchic faction in Argos was able to overthrow the democratic government with Spartan assistance. A democratic revival followed soon after, however, while the Spartans were busy with one of their many religious festivals, and the oligarchic regime was removed. New overtures were made to the Athenians and there were further plans for joint operations in the

1. As the two armies approached Agis ordered the men on his left wing to move to their left. The Spartans who were told to fill the gap between his left and centre did not do so. Both armies drifted to their right as they came closer.

2. The Mantineans, Arkadians and elite Argive 1,000 drove the left wing of Agis' army back towards their baggage. The Spartan centre and right defeated and panicked the Argives, Arkadians and Athenians in front of them.

3. Agis turned the soldiers on his right and centre to help his stricken left wing. Before the elite Argive 1,000 were surrounded Pharax advised Agis to leave them an escape route.

4. As the elite Argive 1,000 escaped the Spartans surrounded the remaining Mantinean and Arkadian hoplites, inflicting heavy casualties.

Peloponnese. The Athenians, meanwhile, were re-establishing a healthy financial position. Peace with Sparta made it easier to draw in revenues from trade and the tribute of their allies, while at the same time it reduced expenditure on military pay and equipment. In 416 they launched an expedition to take control of the small island of Melos, whose population might have hoped for assistance from the Spartans, but who were abandoned to the less than tender mercy of the Athenians.

Athens and Sicily

In the spring of 415 an embassy arrived at Athens from her ally Egesta, one of the smaller cities of Sicily, located in the North Western part of the island. Athens' alliance with Egesta dated back to the 450s when the Athenians were looking for opportunities to make alliances with enemies of the Spartans and their allies. They had also made alliances with the Sicilian Greeks of Rhegion and Leontini around this time and they had intervened in Leontini's struggle with Syracuse in 427, to counter the potential for Syracuse and her Sicilian allies to send assistance to the Peloponnesians. Syracuse had been founded by settlers from Corinth, and it would have been natural for the Syracusans to join the line up alongside their mother city against the Athenians.

The Egestans were seeking help against their southern neighbour Selinous, an ally of Syracuse. Realising that the Athenians would not send significant help if there were no funds available to pay for it, the Egestans insisted that they would be able to cover most of the expenses of a large fleet and army. Initial Athenian interest was tempered by the need to have proof of the availability of the funds, so an investigative embassy was despatched to Egesta. They returned bearing 60 talents of silver with them and the promise that there was plenty more where that came from because the Sicilians were very wealthy. In fact they had been fooled by the Egestans who invited the envoys to dine in a different

house each night and plied them with rich food and plenty of wine, served in expensive gold and silver dishes and cups. What the overindulging Athenian envoys had failed to notice, however, was that the same silver and gold utensils were being used on each occasion, so the impression of a highly prosperous city with riches was all a clever ruse.

Having heard this news of an apparent abundance of money to finance an expedition to Sicily the citizens of Athens debated what proportion of their own men and materials to commit to it. The Athenian forces that had operated in Sicily in the years 427–424, ostensibly on behalf of Leontini, had made some headway in securing allies, obtaining funds and using their limited military resources to thwart the imperial ambitions of Syracuse and prevent any assistance coming from Sicily to the Peloponnesians. It is likely that Alkibiades and his ambitious supporters played on renewed fears of Syracusan intervention in the war, but at the same time they invited the Athenians to revive their dream of conquering Sicily and helping themselves to the wealth and resources of the Western Mediterranean. They painted a picture of weak opponents, so divided by internal strife that they could not possibly resist the military might of Athens. Most of the Athenians had no idea how large the cities of Sicily were, or how strong and determined their citizens might be. Alkibiades played on this ignorance to make the success of the expedition seem almost inevitable. The older, more cautious leaders like Nikias advocated rejecting the request altogether and concentrating on problems closer to home, especially the recovery of the coastal regions of Thrace. This objective, they argued, was more realistic and more important than a wild adventure into the West.

The ambitious, imperialist argument prevailed, however, and the assembly voted to send 60 ships under the joint command of three generals, Alkibiades, Nikias and a veteran commander called Lamachos. The official tasks of the generals were to help Egesta against Selinous and to re-establish the city of Leontini, which had been broken up by

Syracuse in 424. There was also a third, very vague directive given to the generals: 'If the war were to be going well for them, they were also to manage matters in Sicily in whatever manner they might feel was in the best interests of the Athenians'. Thucydides was in no doubt that this meant that the real intention of the expedition was to conquer Sicily. He was sure that the lure of fabulous wealth and limitless conquests had won out over Nikias' warnings against overambition. When Nikias tried to dissuade the assembly by insisting that the forces allocated were too small and that a huge, expensive commitment was needed to bring about success, he expected the citizens to have second thoughts. Instead they voted to allow the generals to take as large a force as they thought fit.

Shortly before the expedition set sail an ominous act of religious vandalism occurred. All over Athens, at cross-roads, public sanctuaries and outside the entrances to many private houses there were statues called herms. They usually consisted of marble blocks surmounted by busts of the god of travellers, Hermes, often with ithyphallic appendages. One night a group of men went round the city systematically mutilating these statues. The timing and scale of the damage clearly implied an orchestrated attempt to create an omen that would cause a delay or even cancel the expedition. A general call for information about the apparent conspiracy produced no immediate suspects, but accusations were brought against several wealthy citizens, including Alkibiades, of religious sacrilege. They were accused of conducting obscene parodies of the Sacred Mysteries, archaic fertility rituals celebrated twice each year by initiates in the cult of the goddess Demeter and her daughter Persephone at Eleusis, near the border with Megara. Alkibiades demanded an immediate trial, but it was decided to allow the expedition to sail while further enquiries were carried out. A series of dubious denunciations and confessions followed, some concerned with parodies of the Mysteries and others the equally mysterious mutilation of the herms. The ordinary Athenian citizens suspected,

without much clear evidence, that a group of the wealthiest citizens were hatching a plot to overthrow the democracy and install an oligarchic government. Several individuals fled the city and it was eventually decided to recall Alkibiades to stand trial.

When the expedition reached Athens' ally of Rhegion, on the toe of Italy, they were denied entry to the city, but a market was set up and they drew their fleet out of the water and onto the beach. Three ships were sent off to Egesta and they returned with the bad news that there was no more money available from that particular source. The people of Rhegion, despite their Ionian kinship with Leontini, refused to join in the war and declared their neutrality. The three Athenian generals considered their options, but they disagreed on how to proceed. Nikias suggested sailing round to Egesta on the western side of Sicily to try to obtain further funds. With or without this money they could settle the dispute between Egesta and Selinous, by force if necessary, and then come back around the southern coastline, allowing the cities a good view of the powerful Athenian fleet. If an opportunity should present itself they might also sort out the quarrel between Leontini and Syracuse. Alkibiades was in favour of delaying any offensive action until they had gathered more allies among the Sicilians, both the native population and the Greek cities. Lamachos' proposal was the simplest, an immediate direct assault on Syracuse, before the enemy had made adequate preparations. He argued that the Syracusans' lack of readiness, combined with the fear induced by the appearance of such a large Athenian force would give them their best chance for a quick victory.

Eventually Lamachos was persuaded to agree to Alkibiades' plan and so Nikias was outvoted two to one. The Athenians set off to persuade more of the Greek cities of eastern Sicily to side with them. At Messene they were not allowed into the city, but Naxos agreed to join their alliance and Katana was won over. Soon after the success at Katana, however, a trireme arrived from Athens with a summons for Alkibiades and several others to return to stand trial for their parts in the

Sicily during the Peloponnesian War

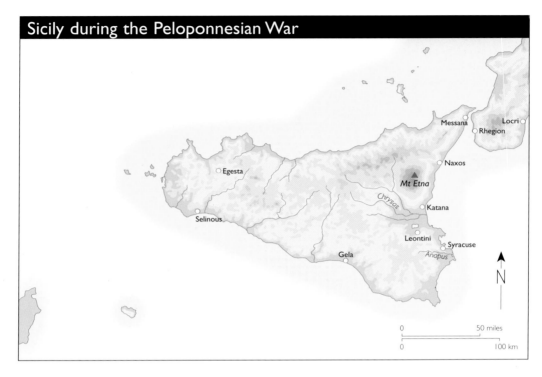

scandalous parodying of the Eleusinian Mysteries. Alkibiades was reluctant to go back, fearing, with some justification, that his political opponents in Athens had been conspiring against him in his absence and that he could not expect a fair trial because of the atmosphere of panic and suspicion that had been created back in Athens. When they reached Thurii in Southern Italy he escaped and eventually made his way to Sparta, where he was given a cautious welcome. He was condemned in his absence and sentenced to death, as were several others.

Nikias and Lamachos attempted to press on with the campaign in Sicily, raising some funds and making a sudden attack on Syracuse, which resulted in a defeat for the Syracusans outside their city. The battle indicated that the Athenian forces needed cavalry support and more money to wage a successful war against Syracuse and because it was getting late in the year the two Athenian generals decided to abandon military action and retire to Katana for the winter.

The siege of Syracuse

In the spring of 414 the Athenians moved on to the offensive and attacked Syracuse in earnest. They brought 250 cavalrymen from Athens and 300 talents of silver to finance their activities. The Athenian fleet landed the army to the north of Syracuse and took control of the heights of Epipolai, a plateau above the city. From there they set about building siege walls. The Syracusans tried building counter-walls to prevent their city being entirely cut off from the land. In a battle to wrest control of the Syracusan fortifications Lamachos was separated from the main Athenian forces with only a few other hoplites around him. A Syracusan officer called Kallikrates then challenged him to single combat; they both killed each other, but the Syracusans easily overcame Lamachos' companions and took his body, stripping the armour from it and taking it back to the city. Nikias, who was too ill to participate in the main battle, managed to beat off an attack on the main Athenian fortifications and the Syracusans were then

Siege of Syracuse

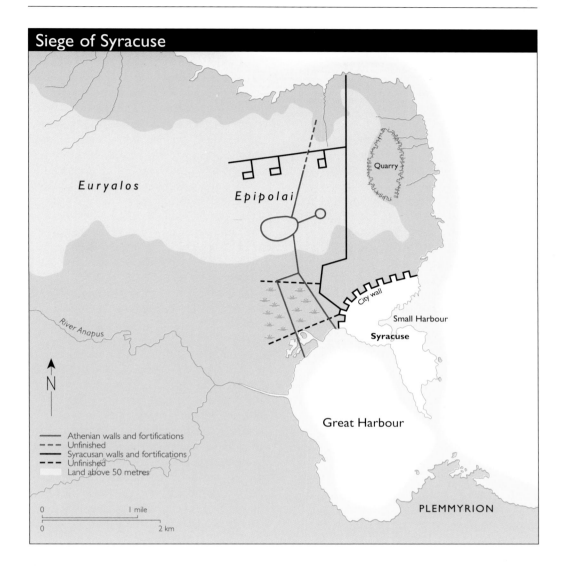

dismayed to see the Athenian fleet sailing into their Great Harbour.

The Syracusans had sent urgent messages to the Peloponnese asking for assistance and Corinth, as the mother-city of Syracuse, had pressed the Spartans to act. Corinth and Sparta sent only a few ships and troops, but the Spartans supplied a determined and resourceful commander in the mould of Brasidas. His name was Gylippos. It was the news of his arrival, slipping past the ships that Nikias belatedly sent to try to intercept him, that halted discussions among the disheartened Syracusans about negotiating a truce with Nikias. Gylippos managed to

gather some soldiers from other parts of Sicily and he encouraged the Syracusans to take the offensive, inflicting the first significant defeat on the Athenians through his skilful use of cavalry. The Syracusans continued with their counter-walls and succeeded in building them out to a point where the Athenians were unable to complete their circumvallation of the city. While the Syracusans began training their naval forces to take on the Athenians, Gylippos went in search of more reinforcements. Nikias also decided that help was needed and he sent a letter back to the Athenians asking either for permission to return home or for massive reinforcements.

He also requested a replacement general because a serious kidney disease was making it difficult for him to carry out his duties.

Athenian defeat in Sicily

In view of their ambition and determination in the earlier stages of the war, it is no great surprise that the Athenians rejected the idea of recalling the whole expedition. Nor did they allow Nikias to step down, but they did appoint two of his officers to assist him and, more importantly, they sent Demosthenes, the hero of Sphakteria, to Syracuse with a large fleet of reinforcements. Before these forces arrived, however, Gylippos and the Syracusans managed to seize the main forts and stores at Plemmyrion on the southern side of the Great Harbour after a combined land and sea operation. This defeat forced the Athenians to crowd into an inadequate camp in unhealthy, marshy ground on the west side of the Great Harbour.

The Syracusans also modified their triremes to utilise a new tactic against the highly

A silver coin from Syracuse dating to about 400 and showing, beneath the main image of a chariot racing victory, a trophy of captured armour. Such trophies were usually erected at the site of a battle by the winning side, using armour from the defeated enemy. This coin may be meant to commemorate the defeat of the Athenians in 413. (Ancient Art and Architecture)

skilled Athenians. The Syracusans adopted a Corinthian idea that involved shortening the bow sections of their triremes and fitting extra beams across the hulls at the point where the anchors were usually housed. The effect of this was to transform the sleek, sharp-prowed vessels designed for penetrating the vulnerable hulls of enemy triremes, into stockier, blunt-nosed ships which were capable of ramming the lighter-built Athenian ships head on and disabling them, without being badly damaged themselves. In the relatively confined waters of the Great Harbour at Syracuse such tactics were far more effective than those employed by the Athenians, who preferred to row round an enemy ship and strike them from the side or rear.

When the Syracusans were ready to try out their new tactics they also used another Corinthian stratagem. They challenged the Athenians at sea in the morning and then broke off, apparently giving up for the day; but they had arranged for food to be brought directly to shore so that their crews could take a quick meal and then set out again while the Athenians were unprepared and hungry. In the fighting which followed many of the Athenian triremes were badly damaged by the heavy prows of the Syracusan ships and seven were lost completely.

Just when things were looking bleak for Nikias and his men, however, Demosthenes sailed into the Great Harbour with 73 ships, 5,000 hoplites and thousands of light infantry. With his characteristic decisiveness Demosthenes recommended a strong attack on the Syracusan counter-walls, but this was beaten off. A risky night attack from the heights of Euryalos attempted to take the fortifications in the rear, but the Syracusans, reinforced with non-Spartan troops from Lakonia and 300 elite Boiotian hoplites, routed the Athenians and drove them back once more. Demosthenes concluded that there was now no alternative but to abandon the siege and sail back to Athens. Nikias took some persuading, however, since he was still hopeful of getting a negotiated surrender through the activities of pro-Athenian faction within Syracuse, and he expected that the

Assembly would blame him for the expedition's failure. However, the situation was made worse for the Athenians by the arrival of more allies to help the Syracusans and Nikias agreed to depart. Just as the Athenians were about to leave, however, an eclipse of the moon occurred. Nikias and many of the Athenians took this as an omen that the gods disapproved of their plans and some diviners among them prescribed a wait of 27 days before deciding what to do next.

The Syracusans took the initiative once more. First they challenged the Athenians to another battle and destroyed 18 of their ships, wiping out the numerical advantage that Demosthenes' arrival had created. Then they blockaded the entrance to the Great Harbour, which was less than a mile wide. The Athenians tried to force their way through, but they were so comprehensively defeated that the following day the Syracusans were able to tow away the surviving Athenian ships without any resistance. The Athenians were demoralised, exhausted and dangerously short of supplies. There was no alternative now but to attempt a retreat overland to a friendly Sicilian community in the interior of the island. They abandoned their sick and wounded and set off in two columns, one led by Demosthenes and the other by Nikias. The Syracusans caught them up, however, and Demosthenes quickly surrendered, after being given assurances that the men would not be starved or executed. Nikias' men tried to push on, but when they finally reached a watercourse their discipline broke and they became easy prey for the Syracusans and their allies, who set about slaughtering them in the river bed. Nikias, who had worked so hard to make peace between Athens and Sparta, surrendered to Gylippos, in the hope that the Spartan's influence would prevent him from being executed. It did not, as the Corinthians were eager to prevent him being ransomed and some of the Syracusans wanted to ensure that he did not reveal, under torture, details of their earlier negotiations to hand over the city to the Athenians. He and Demosthenes were

executed and the rest of the survivors were shut up in the nearby quarries for 70 days, where many of them died of exposure and starvation. Eventually most of them were sold as slaves. Page 78 recounts how some of them managed to get back home.

News of the defeat was slow in reaching Athens and when it did the Athenians could scarcely believe that their magnificent invasion force had been totally destroyed. The first person to bring news of the disaster seems to have been a travelling merchant who disembarked in the Peiraieus and went to a barber's shop. There he began chatting to the barber about it, assuming that it was common knowledge. The barber, on realising what he was referring to, ran up to the city and rushed into the market place to tell the magistrates what he had heard. They convened a meeting of the people's assembly and presented the barber before them with his story. Because the man could not give a satisfactory explanation of the source of his information – he did not know the stranger's name or where he had heard the news – he was assumed to be an agitator deliberately spreading malicious rumours. Indeed, he was being tortured to reveal more of his supposed plot when further messengers arrived with full details of the events.

Dekeleia

After his arrival in Sparta Alkibiades had recommended that the Peloponnesians take a leaf from the Athenians' book of strategies by seizing and occupying a fortress in Athenian territory. He suggested Dekeleia on the southern slopes of Mt Parnes, but the Spartans were reluctant to commit themselves to offensive action while the Peace of Nikias was potentially still valid. In the summer of 414, however, an Athenian fleet of 30 ships was assisting the Argives in their ongoing border war with Sparta and it made several incursions into Lakonian territory. The Spartans were satisfied that the enemy had violated the treaty and prepared to march out and occupy Dekeleia the following spring.

When Agis and the Peloponnesians invaded Attika in 413 they opened a new phase in the war. Instead of ravaging as much as they could of the Athenians' territory for a short while and then going home, they now set up a permanent garrison in the fort of Dekeleia. From there they made raids across large parts of Attika. The Athenians had to disperse their military strength in garrisons of their own, but much of their agricultural land was rendered too vulnerable to farm, and they were prevented from using the overland route from Oropos to bring in supplies from the island of Euboia. This had been a key source of food for the city of Athens during the Archidamian War, and was one reason for the Athenians' ability to continue the struggle far longer than their enemies had expected. They could still bring resources into Athens, but now they had to come by sea, round Cape Sounion and into the harbour at Peiraieus. A further effect of the occupation of Dekeleia was to encourage slaves to escape from their masters and take refuge in Dekeleia. Thucydides estimated that 20,000 such runaways fled from the towns, farms and, above all, the silver mines of Southern Attika.

Even this increase in pressure on the Athenian homeland was not enough to force them to come to terms with the Spartans. As long as they could draw on the extensive resources of their maritime empire they could continue the war. In order to deprive them of access to these resources the Spartans and their allies had to mount a major naval offensive in the Eastern Aegean. They began this task in 412/411, when several of Athens' key allies defected, after the news of the Sicilian disaster reached them and they realised that Athens had been severely weakened. In 412 the Spartans received a welcome boost to their own naval strength with the arrival of 25 Syracusan ships, but the bulk of their fleets had to be provided by Sparta and her Peloponnesian allies, especially Corinth. The cost of this sustained naval effort was beyond them, so Sparta had to persuade the king of Persia to fund and support her overseas operations. Even with Persian aid it still took another seven years before Athenian resistance was worn down and their last fleet was captured in the Hellespont.

These ancient stone quarries near Syracuse were used to imprison and punish the Athenians captured after the defeat of the Sicilian expedition in 413, many of whom died there from exposure and starvation. Most of those who survived were sold as slaves. (AKG Berlin)

A ship's captain at war

The trials of a young trierarch

Some of the best sources of information on individual Athenians are the written versions of speeches delivered in the law courts. Several of these give details of the military activities of specific people during the Peloponnesian War. One of the most detailed of these accounts derives from a speech made by a defendant who was put on trial in the year 403/402 for embezzlement of public funds. If found guilty he would be stripped of his citizen rights and his property. As part of his defence he recited his war record to the court.

Athenian trials normally took place at one of several designated sites in or near the Agora, the main market place in Athens, which was surrounded by public buildings. They were presided over by an official called an *archon* whose main function was to ensure that proper procedures were followed. Verdicts were decided by the votes of a jury consisting of Athenian citizens, aged over 30, who had registered themselves for a year and volunteered to act as jurors on the day. Two hundred or more jurors would be assigned to each court in the morning and they might hear several cases in a day. From the middle of the fifth century they were paid two obols for the day, a measure proposed by Perikles. This was later raised to three obols, on the proposal of Kleon, but it was still far less than a strong, healthy man might be able to earn for a day's work. Consequently many of the volunteers were men who were short of money or unfit for hard work, particularly the poor and elderly. *The Wasps*, a famous comic play written by Aristophanes characterises the jurors as bad-tempered old men who attended the courts for the money and the chance to inflict punishments on the rich and powerful. For cases involving major political issues a meeting of the citizen assembly sometimes acted as a law court.

An Athenian trial was essentially a contest between the prosecutor and the defendant, each of whom attempted to persuade the jury to vote in their favour. They were given a certain period of time to put their case and they had to speak for themselves. The speakers would, as in a modern trial, try to prove guilt or innocence of the specific charge by referring to known facts, citing evidence and offering the statements of witnesses. They might also argue that the interpretation of a particular law did or did not allow it to be applied in this case, but they were also able to make more generalised arguments about themselves or their opponents which most modern courts would not allow. The large number of jurors and the random allotment to courts made it impossible to bribe the jury, but the prosecutors and defendants might try to gain their sympathy, flatter them, or appeal to their sense of self-interest in order to secure a favourable verdict. At the time of the Peloponnesian War it was becoming common for litigants to hire someone to write a persuasive speech for them. For this case the defendant hired Lysias, the son of Kephalos, a non-Athenian businessman who had considerable skills as a speech writer. The speech he composed for this defendant was preserved and later published along with many others written by Lysias. Most of what follows is directly attested in the speech; other details are deduced from the speech and a combination of other historical sources, mainly Xenophon's *Hellenika*.

The name of the defendant in this particular trial is not known, but we do learn that he was a sponsor of dramatic choruses (*choregos*) and a trierarch. This means that he was one of the wealthiest Athenian citizens.

This fragment of a Classical Athenian marble relief clearly shows the three levels of oars which propelled a trireme. Only the topmost level of oarsmen are visible, because they rowed through an outrigger, whereas the lower two put their oars through ports in the side of the ship's hull. Constant practice was needed to co-ordinate the efforts of up to 170 oarsmen on each ship and the Athenians prided themselves on having the best trained crews in Greece. (Debra de Souza)

The duty of a *choregos* was to supervise and pay for the training and performance of a festival chorus, a group of singers and dancers who would take part in one of the many public religious festivals of the Athenians. By spending lavishly on these choruses, and hopefully winning prizes, a wealthy man could gain much prestige and goodwill from his fellow citizens.

The main duties of a trierarch were to ensure that the trireme assigned to him was fully equipped, properly crewed and operationally effective throughout the campaign period. These were primarily financial obligations. The basic wages for the crew, plus a daily maintenance allowance so that each man could buy provisions, were supposed to be paid from the state funds allocated for each particular expedition or campaign. But the money available to the generals in command of the fleet was often inadequate, forcing the trierarchs to meet the immediate costs out of their own resources.

In order to prevent the crews from spending too much money on things which might make them unfit for service, such as wine and unhealthy foods, the Athenians usually allowed only half of the wages to be paid whilst the ships were active, with the rest being handed over when they returned to Peiraieus at the end of the campaign. When manpower was in short supply, however, the trierarchs could be tempted to offer full pay, or additional bonuses in order to attract skilled sailors or experienced oarsmen. The young trierarch emphasised at his trial the extra amounts of money he spent on his ship and his crew to ensure that they were the best in the fleet.

A trierarch was normally expected to command the ship in person, although there was no guarantee that he would have appropriate military experience or navigational competence. Lysias' client claims to have inflicted great damage on enemy ships during the various sea battles in which he was involved, but that claim is not supported with any details and is exactly the sort of thing he might expected to say in order to make the jurors think well of him. In practice an inexperienced trierarch will have relied upon the knowledge and judgment of his helmsman or *kubernetes*, who was usually a professional sailor. A very experienced, skilful helmsman could demand that a trierarch pay very high wages for his services. Ideally the trierarch and his helmsman would form a close partnership, which is exactly what Lysias' client had to do when hiring a renowned helmsman called Phantias, who stayed with his ship for seven years.

The defendant was very young, having only recently come of age and passed the formal scrutiny, or *dokimasia* which all young men had to undergo before they could be officially entered on the rolls of Athenian citizens. It normally took place in their eighteenth or nineteenth year and involved checking the candidate's entitlement to participate in the public life of the city. The defendant's first term as a trierarch seems to have been in the Athenian year 411/410. He continued in this capacity for the next seven years, participating in a series of naval battles in which the Athenians experienced both resounding success and abject failure. By reciting his record of service as a trierarch in the recent war the defendant hoped to win the sympathy of the jury. He could argue that for the jury to convict him, depriving him of his property and his citizen rights would only harm their own interests. He could do far more for them if he remained a wealthy citizen, than if he lost his citizenship and all his property.

The generals' favourite

The young trierarch's war service started when the charismatic Athenian general Alkibiades was resuming his military career. He was elected as one of the 10 generals for the Athenian year 411/410 and took a position of joint command over the fleet which was operating in the Aegean. Alkibiades was notorious for his luxurious lifestyle, even when on campaign. He was wealthy enough to maintain his own trireme, with his close friend Antiochos as its helmsman. Rather than place his bedroll on the ship's deck, as the other officers and trierarchs did, he had a section of the deck cut away to make a large cabin area wherein he hung a hammock to provide him with a more comfortable night's sleep. Once he had joined the main Athenian fleet, however, Alkibiades decided to make use of the young trierarch's well maintained vessel. He liked to lead detachments of the fastest ships from the fleet to lure the enemy into an ambush, or to make swift surprise attacks against enemy bases and coastal cities. He could have done this in his own trireme, but he seems to have preferred to use the trierarch's vessel on these occasions, presumably because it was faster and had a better crew. The next few years of the war saw an upturn in the fortunes of the Athenians under Alkibiades, with several minor victories and a major triumph over the Peloponnesian fleet at Kyzikos in 410.

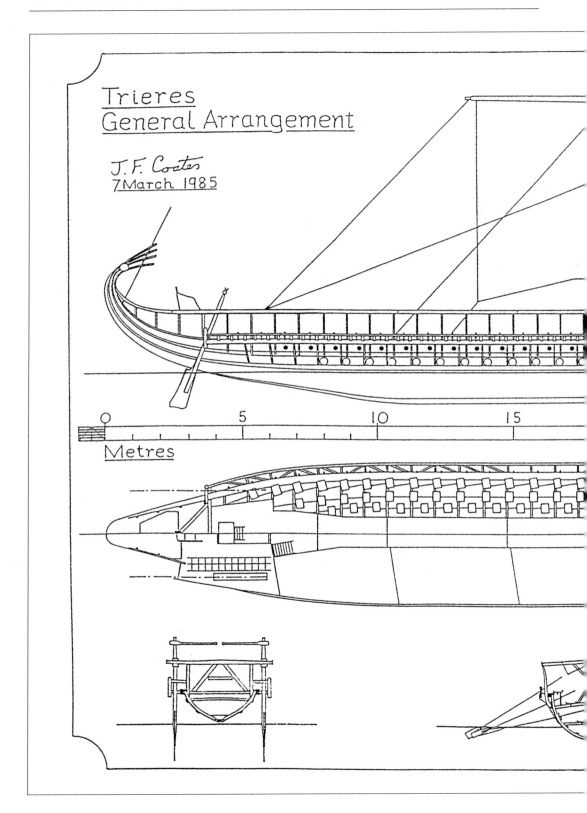

Trieres
General Arrangement

J.F. Coates
7 March 1985

0   5   10   15

Metres

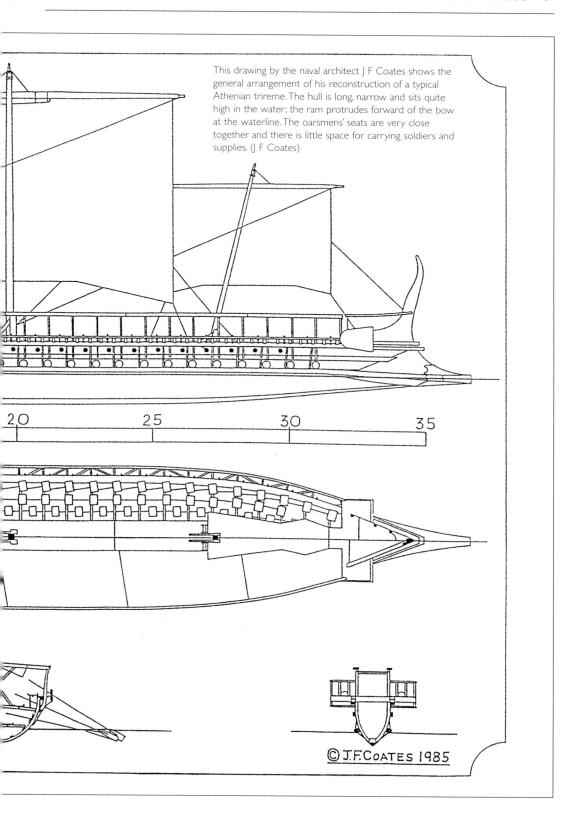

This drawing by the naval architect J F Coates shows the general arrangement of his reconstruction of a typical Athenian trireme. The hull is long, narrow and sits quite high in the water; the ram protrudes forward of the bow at the waterline. The oarsmens' seats are very close together and there is little space for carrying soldiers and supplies. (J F Coates)

20　　　25　　　30　　　35

© J.F. COATES 1985

This Athenian gravestone bears the name Demokleides, son of Demetrios and depicts a lone man seated above the prow of a trireme. Many Athenian and allied citizens were lost at sea in the Peloponnesian War. Their relatives were often upset at not being able to conduct proper funerals rituals for them. (Ancient Art and Architecture)

The young trierarch told the jury at his trial, 'I would have done anything not to have him sailing with me.' He pointed out that he was not related to Alkibiades, nor were they friends, or even members of the same tribe, but he was forced to accept him on board the ship because he was the overall commander of the fleet. It may well be, however, that the trierarch was exaggerating his dislike for Alkibiades in order to avoid seeming to have been too closely associated with someone who had fallen out of favour on two occasions. The jury at the trierarch's trial would have contained some passionate supporters of the restored democracy, who might consider Alkibiades a traitor and take a similar attitude to anyone who was closely associated with him.

Early in 406 the trierarch's ship was once more detached from the main fleet, now based at Notion, while Alkibiades sailed to join in an attack on the city of Phokaia. Against Alkibiades' instructions, his personal helmsman, Antiochos, who had been left in charge of the main fleet, got into a battle with the Spartan fleet under Lysandros and was defeated with the loss of 22 ships. This defeat was only a setback for the Athenians, but it provided an opportunity for Alkibiades' rivals and enemies to bring his dominance to an end. Back in Athens he was blamed for the defeat and heavily criticised for entrusting command of the main fleet to Antiochos, a mere helmsman. A new board of 10 generals was elected and Alkibiades was not one of them. Several citizens threatened to take out lawsuits against him, which they could easily do once he ceased to be a general. Understanding that his popularity and influence had been so badly undermined that any jury in Athens was likely to be very hostile, he took his own trireme and sailed off to his private fortresses in the Hellespont.

The young trierarch now had a new general on board, Archestratos, one of those who had been elected following the downfall of Alkibiades. In the summer of 406 Archestratos ordered the trierarch to sail with Konon's (the new commander) fleet from Samos to try to prevent the new Spartan commander, Kallikratidas, from capturing the city of Methymna on the island of Lesbos. Archestratos, the general who was sailing on the trierarch's ship, was killed at this point and yet another of the Athenian generals, Erasinides, commandeered the trierarch's vessel for his own use. Soon afterwards the Spartan fleet was defeated by the Athenians in a major sea battle off the Arginousai islands, but Erasinides and five of his fellow generals were tried and executed back in Athens for failing to rescue the crews of the stricken Athenian ships.

The young trierarch's next major battle was the disastrous defeat at Aigospotamoi, in the summer of 405. On this occasion the Athenian fleet was attacked by the Spartans while the crews were dispersed looking for supplies. The young trierarch was in full command of his ship on this occasion, having no general on board, and his crew were not caught napping, probably because he spent extra money to ensure that there were plenty of supplies available to them without the need for extended foraging. His experienced helmsman, Phantias, may also have advised him to keep his crew in a state of readiness. As a result of his preparedness, when the Spartans attacked he was able to get his trireme away and to rescue another Athenian ship as well. All but a handful of ships from the Athenian fleet were captured by the Spartans and the Athenian citizens among their crews were executed. Soon afterwards the Athenians, with their city now blockaded by land and sea surrendered to the Spartans.

Buying the goodwill of the people

The defendant proudly claimed to have spent the huge sum of six talents during his time as a trierarch, which was far more than was legally required. Patriotic fervour may partly account for this, but there are hints in his speech that he had other motives for being so generous on behalf of his fellow-

Battle of Arginousai, phase one

Arginousai
Islands

N

—— Athenian or allied ship
—— Spartan or allied ship

| 0 | 1,000 yds |
| 0 | 1,000 m |

LEFT AND RIGHT

1. The Athenians drew up their 155 ships with two groups of 60, one on each wing and 35 in the centre. The ships on the wings were arranged in two staggered lines, one behind the other, to discourage the Spartans from breaking through the line to attack ships from the side or rear. Those in the centre used the westernmost of the Arginousai islands to protect them. The Athenian wings moved forward while their centre held station. The 120 ships in the Spartan fleet feared that they might be outflanked and attacked from the side or rear, because the Athenian lines extended beyond theirs. So they moved away from the centre and engaged the wings, gradually separating into two sections.

2. After a fierce battle the Spartan left wing was defeated, Kallikratidas was killed and the surviving ships fled south. The Spartan right wing fought harder, but it was also defeated. As the Spartans fled the 35 ships in the Athenian centre joined in the pursuit. The Spartans lost 77 ships while the Athenians lost only 25.

brief struggle between oligarchic and democratic factions among the Athenian fleet at Samos. This would explain why Lysias' speech fails to mention any patriotic deeds performed by the father on behalf of the Athenians. It was better to avoid all mention of a man whose record was suspect and concentrate instead on the zealous contributions of his son to the Athenian cause.

The young trierarch's own political sympathies are only hinted at, but they seem also to have been oligarchic, rather than particularly democratic. At his trial he tried to distance himself from Alkibiades, who was one of the instigators of the oligarchic revolution in 411, but he could not hide the fact that the infamous general spent a lot of time on his ship. They were both very wealthy men, with a marked preference for the best that money could buy and may have become good friends. The trierarch was very vague about his own activities in the crucial year 404/403, when Athens was under the control of the so-called Thirty Tyrants, a ruthless and unpopular oligarchic government imposed by the Spartans after the Athenians surrendered. He continued to perform his public liturgies and at the very least it seems that the oligarchs made no attempt to condemn him and confiscate his property, which they did to many of their political opponents.

citizens. It is very likely that the young trierarch's father was actively involved in the oligarchic revolution of 411. Like his son he would have been a very wealthy man and probably also served as trierarch. Thucydides says that the trierarchs with the fleet at Samos played a major part in plotting the overthrow of the democracy back at Athens and the young trierarch's father may even have been a member of the infamous council of 400, a group of wealthy citizens who took control of affairs in Athens for several months in 411. The circumstances of his death are not mentioned, but it may have occurred in the

Battle of Arginousai, phase two

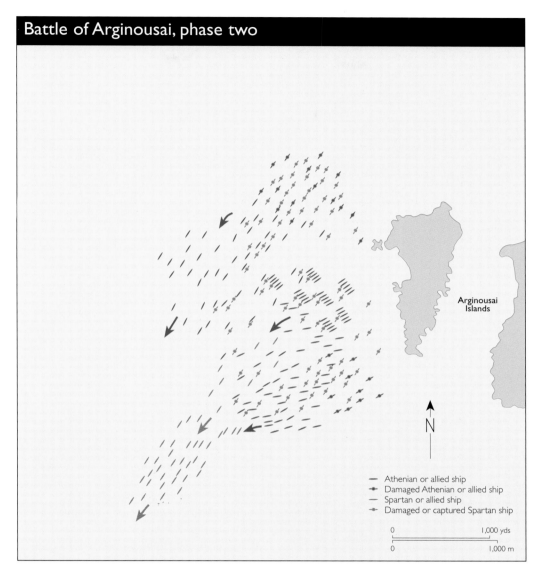

Arginousai
Islands

N

— Athenian or allied ship
→ Damaged Athenian or allied ship
— Spartan or allied ship
→ Damaged or captured Spartan ship

0   1,000 yds

0   1,000 m

How typical were the wartime experiences of this particular trierarch? In terms of his participation in raids and battles there was nothing unusual, although other trierarchs would not have had to play host to a succession of generals on their ships. To have served as a trierarch for seven consecutive years was highly unusual, however, and it cannot be a coincidence that in this particular case the seven years were, in effect, the last years of the war. The financial position of the Athenians had deteriorated as the war dragged on. From 413 they were

losing the revenues of their maritime empire as more and more states defected to the Spartans, whether willingly or under duress. The cost of combating this was enormous, as it involved maintaining fleets and armies overseas all year round. The trierarch also paid large contributions to the war tax during this period and he was one of many wealthy citizens who must have felt that they were being made to bear the financial costs of the belligerent policies of the less wealthy majority of citizens. This was one reason why so many of the trierarchs supported the oligarchic revolution in 411 which promised to make peace with the Spartans.

We do not know the outcome of the trial. The defendant had been accused of embezzlement, but there is no reason to think he was guilty. He hints in his speech that his opponent has been put on trial recently on charges of impiety. Accusations made for personal or political rivalry were common in Athens and prominent men could expect to face several during their lives.

Politics and culture

Democracy and oligarchy

The Peloponnesian War affected the lives of most of the people in the Greek world at the end of the fifth century BC. One of the most important political effects of the long war between Athens and Sparta was the polarisation of much of the Greek world into blocks of allies and supporters of either the Athenians or the Spartans. Many of the states involved in the war adopted or retained political constitutions that were similar to that of the state to which they were allied. Those on the Spartan side tended to have oligarchic constitutions, whereas the allies of Athens tended to favour democracy. The Spartans found it much easier to deal with oligarchies than democracies. They were suspicious of large citizen bodies with broad decision making powers, whereas the Athenians saw such groups of people as their natural allies, and vice versa. The Spartans claimed to be fighting the Athenians in order to 'liberate' the Greeks from their tyrannical rule, but the form that they preferred this liberation to take was often the repression of a broadly based, democratic regime and its replacement by a much narrower oligarchic one. As the war dragged on many cities were subject to revolutionary changes, according to whether a pro-Spartan or a pro-Athenian faction had the upper hand. The result was a series of parallel conflicts that raged in many of the city-states of Greece. Thucydides wrote a scathing condemnation of these civil wars in his account of the Peloponnesian War. He blamed them on people whose ambitions and lust for power, coupled with fanatical devotion to their political friends, made them blind to the need for moderation and compromise in their dealings with their fellow-citizens. The widespread tendency to exact revenge for each atrocity simply prolonged the hatred.

We noted on pp. 28-30 how the dispute over Epidamnos escalated to such an extent that Corcyra became involved in a war with Corinth. Corcyra in turn drew the Athenians into this war, and eventually through Corinth the Spartans became embroiled as well. Athenian expeditions intervened in the internal affairs of Corcyra in 427 and 425 on behalf of the democratic faction, who drove their oligarchic opponents out of the city. The exiled oligarchic faction established themselves on the mainland opposite Corcyra and launched piratical raids on the territory held by their opponents. They tried to persuade the Corinthians and the Spartans to take up their cause once again and restore them to power by force, but without success. Eventually they decided to abandon their mainland bases and cross back over to the island. They established a fortified base in the mountains to the north of the city and continued their guerrilla attacks from there, with the aim of preventing the democratic faction from gaining control of the countryside and encouraging the rest of the citizens to demand a change of government. The Athenians continued to maintain contact with their allies in Corcyra and used the island as a staging point for their expeditions to Sicily.

In 410 the leaders of the pro-Athenian, democratic faction in Corcyra feared that their opponents were about to establish a new oligarchic constitution, with military backing from the Spartans. To forestall this they invited the Athenian general Konon to come from his base at Naupaktos and take control of the city. Konon brought with him a force of 600 Messenian exiles, hereditary enemies of the Spartans, who carried out a ruthless slaughter of many of the leading oligarchs in Corcyra and drove over 1,000 others out of the city. They were forced to take refuge on the mainland, opposite Corcyra. Konon and his force then withdrew, leaving the democratic faction in power. In an effort to preserve their numerical superiority they made many slaves and foreigners citizens of the *polis*, hoping that they would be staunch supporters of the democratic constitution. The remaining members of the oligarchic faction would not give in, however, and after the Athenians and Messenians had gone they occupied the market place in the centre of the city and encouraged their exiled comrades to return. After a day of bitter fighting in the city the survivors of both groups decided that their murderous quarrel had gone on long enough and agreed to put aside their differences and try to live together in harmony. The remaining citizens of Corcyra, realising how much death and destruction had been caused by allowing outsiders to become involved in their affairs, decided to keep out of the war and not to ally themselves with either Athens or Sparta.

Persia

The most significant royal power to become involved in the Peloponnesian War was the king of Persia. The king of Persia was known to the Greeks as the Great King. He ruled an enormous empire that stretched from Asia Minor and Egypt in the west to India and Afghanistan in the east. Most provinces of this empire paid an annual tribute of silver to the king's treasury in Persepolis. This tribute had been paid by many of the Greeks of western Asia Minor and the Aegean until 478, when they began making payments to the Delian League instead. But the wealth of the Persian Empire far exceeded that of all of the Greek states put together.

It is likely that both the Athenians and the Persians tried to persuade the Persian king to intervene on their side from the very start of the war. The Athenians had been making war on the territory of the Persian Empire since 478, but they made a peace treaty with the Persian king in 449 and were probably prepared to negotiate concessions

of territory or tribute in return for his aid against the Spartans. In 424 an Athenian naval patrol captured a Persian envoy called Artaphernes who was on his way to Sparta. The Persian king, Artaxerxes, was fed up with receiving contradictory requests and messages from successive Spartan envoys and he wanted Artaphernes to return with a definitive proposal. The Athenians tried to use the opportunity to put their own proposals to the Great King, but Artaxerxes died before their envoys reached his court. There was a brief but violent struggle over the succession, but eventually a new, strong king, Dareios II emerged and the Athenians were able to renew their peaceful relations with him.

In 414/413 Pissouthnes, one of the Persian king's governors or *satraps* in Asia Minor revolted. He obtained some Athenian assistance, but the Athenian general Lykon betrayed him to the Persian king. His illegitimate son, Amorges, continued the revolt and the Athenians helped him as well. As a result the Great King ordered another of his satraps, Tissaphernes, to make arrangements to aid the Spartans. In spite of their repeated claim to be fighting in order to liberate the Greeks, the Spartans negotiated a series of treaties with the representatives of King Dareios in which they agreed that those territories in Asia Minor which had formerly been under Persian domination should revert to his control. This included many Greek cities that had joined the Delian League under Athenian leadership in 478 and were now looking to Sparta to free them from Athenian domination. In return the king's men promised to help the Spartans with money, ships and men. This assistance was to prove decisive in bringing the war to an end.

Arts and culture in Athens

The period from the end of the Persian Wars to the end of the Peloponnesian War has often been called the Golden Age of Athens.

A gold coin of the Persian Empire from the fourth century. The design shows a Persian king carrying a bow and a spear, both traditional Persian weapons for war and hunting. Many Persian gold coins came to Greece as 'gifts' for those Greeks who were prepared to do the Great King's bidding. (AKG Berlin)

The city became one of the major cultural and artistic centres of the Classical Greek world. The most obvious manifestation of this was the magnificent temples and other public buildings which adorned the city. There is some evidence that the Athenians were criticised for spending money which, it was claimed, they had obtained from their subject allies to beautify their own city, which the critics compared to a woman decking herself out in expensive jewels. In response to such critics Perikles is said to have argued that it was not necessary to give an account of how all the money was spent. It was only fair, he claimed, if Athens used any surpluses that remained after the expenses of war were met to build works that would bring her glory for all time. He was certainly right in his prediction that such buildings would serve to perpetuate the fame of Athens well into the future. As Thucydides pointed out, in contrast to Athens Sparta had no magnificent public buildings and anyone comparing the remains of the two cities in future ages would find it hard to believe that they had been equally powerful.

This model reconstructs a temple on the Athenian Acropolis which was built between 447 and 438. It was dedicated to Athena the Maiden, or Athena *Parthenos* in Greek, hence it is called the Parthenon. It was designed by Pheidias and contained a statue covered in ivory and gold. In an emergency the god could be removed, melted down and turned into coins. (Ancient Art and Architecture)

It is not just for her buildings that fifth-century Athens has achieved lasting fame. The exquisite painted cups and vases produced by her master potters were exported across the Mediterranean, particularly to Italy and Sicily and are still considered to be among the great works of

art of the Western world. Athens was also a major centre for literature, rhetoric and philosophy. Many writers and philosophers from other Greek cities visited Athens, but probably the most famous literary figures of the Periklean age are the Athenian born writers of tragic and comic plays.

Euripides

Among the works of the great Athenian playwrights those of Euripides stand out as the most effective at conveying to modern audiences the emotions and passions of the time. This may be partly because his plays often focus on women as either the victims or avengers of violent acts. Many of his plays were written during the Peloponnesian War. In one of them, *The Trojan Women*, performed at the Great Festival of Dionysos in 415, Euripides offered his Athenian audience a chilling perspective on contemporary events. In the previous summer the Athenians had invaded the island of Melos in the Southern Aegean. The Melians were distantly related to the Spartans and had tried to maintain a position of neutrality, but the Athenians laid siege to their city and starved them into surrender. The citizen men were massacred and the women and children were sold into slavery. As was traditional for Athenian tragedies, Euripides based his play on an old, familiar story, the 10-year siege of Troy by the Greeks under their great king, Agamemnon. On this occasion, however, he chose to set the play in the immediate aftermath of the fall of Troy, when the Greeks had achieved their objective and recovered Helen, the stolen wife of Agamemnon's brother Menelaus, and were deciding what to do with the captured women of Troy and their children. This setting provided an opportunity for Euripides to present his audience with a view of how these women might feel as they contemplated a future as slaves of their conquerors.

We cannot be sure how the Athenians reacted to a play that invited them to sympathise with the helpless victims of war. Many of the men in the audience will have bought women or children from Melos as slaves. It has been suggested that the play failed to win first prize because it was so relevant to the current situation and its emotional impact was too painful for the Athenians to bear.

We know that Euripides' plays were famous across the whole of the Greek speaking world. Each new text was circulated among the Greek-speaking cities of the Mediterranean and many people learnt sections or even whole plays by heart. His verses were particularly popular among the Greeks of Sicily, whose delight in them was so great that Athenian prisoners captured and enslaved by the Syracusans in 413 were able to obtain better treatment by reciting extracts from the plays to their captors. Some were even said to have gained their freedom in return for teaching their masters all they could recall of Euripides' works. When they eventually returned home to Athens they visited Euripides to thank him in person. Euripides himself never seems to have been entirely at ease living in Athens. He was invited to Macedon towards the end of the Peloponnesian War and he remained there until he died in 407.

Euripides offers a woman's view
In this extract from Euripides' play, The Trojan Women, *Andromache, widow of the Trojan prince Hektor, who was slain by the Greek hero Achilles, learns that she is to be taken by Achilles' son, who wants her as his wife:*

'I will be enslaved in the household of my own people's killer, and if I put Hektor's love out of my mind and open my heart to this new husband I shall be seen to dishonour the dead. But the alternative is to hate and be hated by my own master. And yet they say that a single, sweet night removes the woman's dislike for her man's bed. I disown any woman who rejects her former husband to devote herself to a new love. Even a mare who has been uncoupled from her stable-companion does not readily take up the yoke. And yet dumb animals lack rational minds and are inferior to us by nature.' (ll. 659-671)

Hipparete, an Athenian citizen woman

Childhood in Athens

Although we have only limited evidence for the lives of non-combatants in the Peloponnesian War, it is possible to put together information from a variety of sources to present an account of how an individual's life might have been affected by the war. One such individual is Hipparete, the wife of the Athenian politician and general Alkibiades. Hipparete was born about 440. She was the daughter of a prominent Athenian citizen, Hipponikos, whose family owned a large amount of land in Attika and obtained considerable revenue from the silver mining industry. Indeed, he was reputed to be the richest man in Greece. Hipparete's mother, whose name is not known, had previously been married to the famous Perikles, but they were divorced in about 455 and she married Hipponikos soon after.

Hipparete's childhood was as comfortable and happy as was possible for the daughter of a citizen. Upper class Athenian girls led quiet, sheltered lives, surrounded by women and only occasionally venturing out of their homes to participate in religious festivals, particularly those associated with Athena, the patron goddess of the Athenians. In the words of one Athenian writer, Xenophon, the daughter of a wealthy citizen was expected to be raised, 'under careful supervision, so that she might see and hear and speak as little as possible.' Hipparete spent most of her childhood under the watchful eyes of her slave nurse and her mother, learning the skills considered appropriate for a young woman. These included cooking, spinning, weaving and caring for the sick. Since her family was wealthy she may even have learned to read and write, although such education was not considered necessary or even desirable for girls, whose upbringing was geared towards preparing them to be capable but subservient wives.

War and plague

The outbreak of the Peloponnesian War must have had a profound effect on Hipparete's life. The city in which she was growing up would have changed, both in appearance and in atmosphere. It was already becoming more densely populated, both in the main urban centre around the Acropolis, and the secondary area of Peiraieus. The increased prosperity which had accompanied Athens' expanding imperial power and flourishing maritime trade encouraged people from near and far to come and live there.

Perikles' strategy of avoiding pitched battles with the invading Peloponnesian armies resulted in many families having to abandon the countryside around Athens and move within the fortifications of the Long Walls. The narrow strips of land between the walls became home to many thousands of refugees, who built houses and cultivated the ground to try to compensate for the loss of their agricultural resources, which were at the mercy of the invaders. Their numbers were swelled by refugees from Plataia, who arrived in the city in the summer of 431, after an attack by the Thebans had demonstrated their city's vulnerability.

The crowded, unsanitary conditions, especially in the hot, dry summers, must have made the city a particularly unpleasant place for these refugees to live. In 430, when a deadly plague broke out in Athens, life there became much worse. The plague reached Athens from the East, having already

An Athenian painted vase from the mid-fifth century, showing a woman placing wreaths on a grave. This kind of small vase was commonly used for pouring libations at a graveside. The painting shows several similar vases on the steps of the grave monument, which probably marks a family burial plot. (Ancient Art and Architecture)

ravaged parts of the Persian Empire. The very maritime traders whose business was so vital to the city's economy also provided transport for the lethal bacteria. Initially the plague struck in the port of Peiraieus, where the first cases were reported in the summer, soon after the Peloponnesians had begun their second invasion of Athenian territory. From Peiraieus the epidemic spread rapidly to the main part of the city.

Hipparete was almost certainly infected by the plague, which did not discriminate between rich and poor in its devastating rampage though the city. Thucydides, who also survived the infection, describes its symptoms in vivid detail. They included a high fever, severe thirst, coughing, stomach pains, retching, uncontrollable diarrhoea and ulcers, both internal and external. Many modern experts have tried to identify the disease from his description, but they have not reached a firm conclusion. It was certainly very contagious and probably killed about one-third of the inhabitants of Athens over a period of about four years, with the worst casualties coming in the first year, when the lack of any acquired immunity made the population particularly vulnerable.

Thucydides tells us that so many people died of the plague, and so quickly, that proper funeral procedures were neglected. Normally Athenian funerals were marked by elaborate private and public rituals, especially in the case of the richer families, who liked to use such occasions to show off their wealth and social status. Preparing the body of the deceased was a duty for the women of the family, who would wash the corpse, anoint it with oil and garland it with flowers. It would be laid on a bier for a day and a night, allowing time for family and friends to mourn and pay their respects. The laws of Athens required the funeral to take place before dawn on the following day. A procession would leave the house of the deceased and go outside the walls of the city, to either a communal or a family cemetery, where the body would be buried or cremated. The men of the family would

lead the procession, with the women walking solemnly behind the corpse and singing a mourning song. When the plague was at its height, however, many bodies were left lying untended, at the mercy of dogs and carrion birds. Others were buried or cremated in haste, sometimes several together, without the proper rituals. Thucydides even describes people carrying corpses around looking for a recently dug grave to drop them in, or an already blazing pyre on which to throw them.

Hipparete was fortunate to have survived the disease, although some members of her father's household must certainly have died, possibly including her mother. We know that her father survived because he was in joint command of an Athenian expedition against the Boiotian city of Tanagra in 426. Her brother Kallias also lived through the infection, but the horrific effects of epidemic will certainly have left a lasting impression on the family. Young Hipparete had no choice but to remain in the city while all this was happening, whereas her father and many of the other men could leave the city on commercial or diplomatic missions, or as part of the military forces sent on raids against the Peloponnesians and their allies. We can be sure that it was a dark and troubled period of her life, as she longed for relief from the anxieties of war, like thousands of other women and girls in the city.

While people doubtless tried to carry on their lives as normally as possible during this period, for many the city must have felt like a living nightmare, comparable to the mythical Tartaros, where the souls of the wicked were subjected to eternal torments and punishments. Thucydides also blames the shattering impact of the plague for a general breakdown in the social structures and moral standards of the Athenians.

The general's wife

One example of the change in moral standards during the war may be the extravagant behaviour of Hipparete's husband, Alkibiades, whom she married in about 424, when she was aged no more than 16. Alkibiades was at least 10 years older than her, as was usual in Classical Athens. He came from one of a group of Athenian families known as the Eupatridai, or noble families. His father, Kleinias, had been killed in the battle of Koroneia in 446. His mother, Deinomache, was a relative by marriage of Perikles and for a time after his father's death Alkibiades lived in the household of Perikles, who, along with his brother Ariphron, was Alkibiades' guardian. Given the closeness of their respective families it is probable that Hipparete would have met her future husband before they were married, but she is unlikely to have spent much time in his company. Athenian marriages were normally arranged between the parents or guardians of the couple and it was not unusual for cousins or even siblings to arrange for their respective children to marry, renewing and strengthening their family ties. In this case it is very likely that there were strong financial considerations on Alkibiades' side, as Hipparete would have brought a substantial dowry to the marriage. There were also political advantages in the match, as her family connections were of the highest order. She would have been seen as the perfect wife for an ambitious young man.

The primary duty of an Athenian wife was to bear children for her husband, preferably a male child, who could inherit his father's property and continue the family line. Hipparete fulfilled this duty by providing her husband with a son, also called Alkibiades, and a daughter, whose name is not known. It is likely that she had another son, but he died in infancy, a common misfortune in ancient times, when medical knowledge was very limited.

In stark contrast to her husband, who participated in diplomatic missions and military campaigns as her father had done, once she was married Hipparete probably rarely travelled beyond the confines of her home. Nor is it likely that Hipparete would have been involved in any of Alkibiades'

activities. Citizen women participated in funerals and certain religious festivals, in some cases as the main celebrants, but otherwise they had no role in the public life of the cities. She will have heard about her husband's wartime adventures and, possibly, discussed them with him, but war and politics were seen as exclusively the concern of men. In a famous speech, which Thucydides puts into the mouth of Perikles, in honour of those who died in the early stages of the war, the only mention of women is a comment addressed to the widows of the fallen, that their greatest glory is not to be talked about by men, whether in praise or criticism.

Hipparete had been brought up to respect and obey the men in her life and she seems to have done all she could to be a good wife, but on at least one occasion her husband's behaviour drove her to attempt to end their marriage. While Athenian men expected their wives to be completely faithful, married men thought nothing of having intercourse with their female slaves, or with prostitutes, who might be slaves or free women from outside Athens. It was even considered acceptable for an unmarried man to keep a concubine in his home, but he would be expected to end such arrangements once he took a wife.

When the Athenians captured the island of Melos in 416 they killed the men and enslaved the women and children. Alkibiades bought one of these unfortunate women and kept her in his household as a concubine, eventually having a son by her. The effect of the Melian slave's presence upon Hipparete must have been devastating. Here was a woman whom her husband had purchased as booty, yet he preferred her to his own well-born wife as his sexual partner. We can imagine that Hipparete might have sympathised with the woman's plight, for if Athens were to be defeated in the war, then she too could expect to be enslaved by the victors. On the other hand, by installing another woman in their home Alkibiades was showing a lack of respect to Hipparete, even though she was the mother of his children and the daughter of a prominent Athenian citizen.

A young hoplite is shown saying goodbye to his family on this Athenian vase, painted around the start of the Peloponnesian War. Men over the age of 50 would not normally be expected to fight, unless there was a shortage of younger, fitter men. The wives and mothers of those who went off to war might have to wait months, or even years before they had news of their loved ones. (Ancient Art and Architecture)

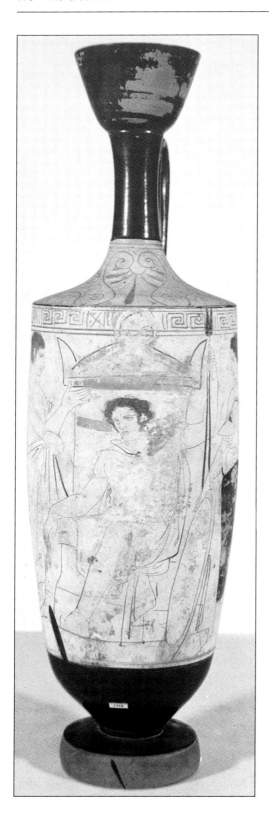

The Athenian white-ground oil jug was painted in the last quarter of the fifth century BC. The artist has chosen to portray a handsome man in front of what seems to be his own tomb, with a young woman and a young man standing on either side. The two spears in man's hand and the shield and helmet held by the woman suggest that he is a deceased hoplite whose wife and brother (or son) are mourning his death. (Ancient Art and Architecture)

It seems to have been this situation that finally induced Hipparete to leave her husband and return to her brother's house, her father having died by this time. An Athenian woman had the right to leave her husband's household if she was being mistreated, and to petition a magistrate to grant legal recognition of the divorce. When Hipparete approached the magistrate, however, Alkibiades himself was there. He dragged her back to his house, where she remained until her death, which occurred soon afterwards. Her life was a not a long one, but at least she did not live to see her husband tried for impiety and forced into exile in Sparta, his property auctioned, and her son threatened with banishment because of his father's political activities. Nor did she witness the bitter end to the war.

The fall of Athens

The defeat of the Athenian expedition to Sicily presented the Spartans and their allies with a golden opportunity to take the initiative in the war. They struck at Athens herself by establishing a permanent fort in Attika at Dekeleia, and they struck at the core of her maritime empire in the Aegean by assembling fleets and either persuading or forcing many of Athens' subject allies to desert her. For the Athenians this new phase of the war produced greater strains, both economic and political. They found it particularly difficult to fund their naval forces as their flow of tribute revenue was interrupted and their pool of naval manpower was diminished. Many of the non-Athenian oarsmen and sailors were attracted away by the higher and more regular pay available to those serving with the Spartans, who now enjoyed the enormous financial backing of the king of Persia. When they needed to assemble a fleet in 406 to rescue their admiral Konon who was blockaded at Mytilene the Athenians had to resort to offering freedom and citizenship to any slaves who would volunteer to row the ships.

One person who had changed sides in the other direction was the exiled Athenian leader Alkibiades. He had found it difficult to settle in at Sparta, where he was forced to swap the extravagant parties beloved of Athenian aristocrats for a tedious round of physical training and the more sombre religious gatherings of the elite Spartan citizens. He accompanied the early Spartan expedition to the Aegean, but as a defector from the enemy he was treated with suspicion, a situation that was not helped by the fact that he had an affair with King Agis' wife while in Sparta. Such suspicions restricted his opportunities for significant involvement in the war and provided no real outlet for his ambitious personality. In 411 he left the Spartan fleet and went to the one remaining centre of power and influence in the war, the Persians.

Oligarchic revolution in Athens

Tissaphernes the Persian satrap decided, possibly at the prompting of Alkibiades to adopt a new strategy in 411. Instead of helping the Spartans defeat the Athenians he would prolong the war between them and take advantage of their conflict to win back some of the Greek cities and islands that had once belonged to the Great King. Alkibiades for his part began plotting to obtain his own recall to Athens by engineering a change in the Athenian government to a more conservative, oligarchic one. He hoped to ingratiate himself with this new regime by offering to use his influence to bring Tissaphernes and the resources of the Persian Empire onto the side of the Athenians. Alkibiades persuaded several of the leading men in the Athenian fleet at Samos to bring about the change of government and in due course a programme of reforms was pushed through the Assembly with the help of a mixture of threats, political assassinations and promises of Persian support. The result was a new Council of 400, replacing the old democratic one of 500 and comprising men wealthy enough to afford their own hoplite equipment. They were charged with drawing up a list of no more than 5,000 Athenian citizens of similar status who would form the decision making body of the new constitution. The idea seems to have been that these men would be wealthy enough not to need payment for carrying out public offices. The 400 made peace overtures to Sparta. Meanwhile Tissaphernes made a new

The figures on the left and in the centre of this gravestone carved around 410 in Athens represent the deceased men Sosias and Kephisodoros. The figure on the right is bidding one of his fallen comrades farewell. As the war dragged on the large numbers of citizen casualties made many Athenians favour a peaceful settlement with Sparta. (AKG Berlin)

treaty with the Spartans, so the recall of Alkibiades ceased to be a worthwhile aim.

There was considerable resistance to these developments among the ordinary Athenians in the fleet at Samos. They met in their own version of the citizens' assembly, deposed their current generals and declared their opposition to the new regime. Alkibiades convinced them that he could bring Tissaphernes over to their side and was elected as a general. Back in Athens splits among the 400, a failure to produce the list of 5,000 elite citizens and the failure of negotiations with Sparta caused the regime to lose its credibility. A Spartan attack on Euboia, which prompted the cities there to revolt from Athens, hastened the collapse of the oligarchy. A meeting of an assembly which might be considered to comprise the 5,000 deposed the Council of 400 and voted to recall Alkibiades. Some of the leaders of the oligarchic revolution fled to Dekeleia, others were rounded up, put on trial and condemned to death.

There seems to have followed a brief period in which the Athenian assembly and official posts in the government were restricted to the members of the 5,000. In 410, however, a law was passed which allowed anyone who 'overthrows the democracy or holds any office after the democracy has been overthrown' to be killed without fear of reprisal and his property confiscated. A fund was set up to pay the holders of all public offices. In effect the old democratic constitution was restored.

The final conflicts

The period 410 to 406 was one of almost continuous naval activity in the Eastern Aegean and the Hellespontine region. The struggle for naval supremacy between the two sides eventually decided the outcome of the war. The northern Persian satrap, Pharnabazos, encouraged the Spartans to direct their attention to the Athenian controlled cities in the Hellespont, by offering them subsidies to pay the crews of their ships and troops to support their incursions on land. The city of Byzantion was won over in 410 by a Peloponnesian fleet led by the Spartan admiral Mindaros. Byzantion's position at the entrance to the Black Sea made it vital to Athenian interests. In addition to much other trade, each year a substantial fleet of ships carrying grain from the Black Sea sailed through the narrow Hellespontine channel that Byzantion protected. The Athenians took two years to recover the city and never managed to completely dislodge the Peloponnesians from the area for the rest of the war. There were several Athenian successes, notably at Kyzikos in 410, when almost the entire Peloponnesian fleet was lost and Mindaros was killed.

A major turning point occurred in 407, when two new leaders took up the struggle against the Athenians. One was a Spartan admiral called Lysandros, who improved the Spartan naval forces dramatically. The other was Kyros, the younger son of the Persian king, who was sent to the western satrapies of the Great King's empire with instructions to make sure that the Spartans won the war. Tissaphernes' strategy had evolved into a balancing act, attempting to keep the opposing Athenian and Peloponnesian forces roughly equal in strength, wearing each other down, until he could make a decisive intervention and drive both sides out of the western satrapies altogether. With the arrival of Kyros, however, this strategy was abandoned in favour of strong support for the Spartans and their allies.

The relationship between Kyros and Lysandros also made a significant difference to the course of the war in the Aegean. It may well be that they each recognised the ambitious streak in the other man and felt comfortable dealing with a kindred spirit. Kyros nurtured dreams of ruling the Persian Empire in place of his brother, Artaxerxes, who was the king's eldest son. Lysandros could not realistically aspire to the Spartan kingship, because he was not closely related to either of the royal families, but he seems to have felt that he could achieve even greater power and influence outside Sparta than the ambitious Spartan commanders Brasidas and Gylippos.

After the Athenian defeat at Aigospotamoi in 405 all their subject allies deserted them, except for the staunchly democratic island of Samos. The Athenians passed a decree giving them Athenian citizenship. It was reconfirmed in 403 when the Athenians and the Samians both overthrew pro-Spartan oligarchic regimes set up by Lysandros. The decree is inscribed here below figures of Athena and Hera, the patron goddesses of Athens and Samos. (Ancient Art and Architecture)

Alkibiades' influence on the war came to an end in 406 when he left the Athenian fleet at Notion and instead of putting one of the other generals in overall command he opted for his helmsman, Antiochos, who was an old friend. Antiochos unwisely tried to catch some of Lysandros' fleet in an ambush and suffered a serious defeat, losing 22 ships. Alkibiades was held responsible but, rather than return to Athens to face the wrath of the Assembly, he went off to some private fortresses he had established in the Hellespont. Lysandros was temporarily replaced by another Spartan admiral, Kallikratidas, who was killed in another Athenian naval victory at the Arginousai Islands in 406. The Athenians largely negated their success by condemning most of their generals to death for failing to do enough to rescue the crews of damaged ships. The Spartans, at Kyros' insistence, restored Lysandros to the command of their fleet. The final decisive battle was fought in the Hellespont late in 405. Lysandros' fleet was besieging the city of Lampsakos and the Athenians beached their ships on the opposite side of the Hellespont at Aigospotamoi. They sailed out for five successive days to try to draw Lysandros into a battle but he stayed put. When the Athenians had returned to their camp on the fifth evening, and their crews were dispersing to look for food, Lysandros attacked, catching them completely by surprise. All but a handful of the Athenian ships were captured. With this victory Lysandros effectively won the war for Sparta.

The Athenians realised that they could not continue their struggle without a strong fleet to give them access to their maritime empire. In the spring of 404 both Spartan kings led armies up to the walls of Athens and Lysandros moored his fleet outside the harbour at Peiraieus. The Athenians waited behind their walls during a tense period of negotiations between the Spartan ephors and an embassy headed by Theramenes. The embassy returned with the news that the Spartans had resisted pressure from her allies, led by Thebes and Corinth, to destroy the city and enslave the citizens. In return the Athenians were required to dismantle their fortifications, surrender all but 12 of their remaining ships and become allies of the Spartans. Lysandros and his fleet sailed into the harbour and immediately set to work demolishing sections of the walls to the accompaniment of flutes. The historian Xenophon, who witnessed this celebration of Spartan victory, wrote in his account: 'They believed this day to be the beginning of freedom for the Greeks.'

The Eastern Aegean and the Hellespont 411–404 BC

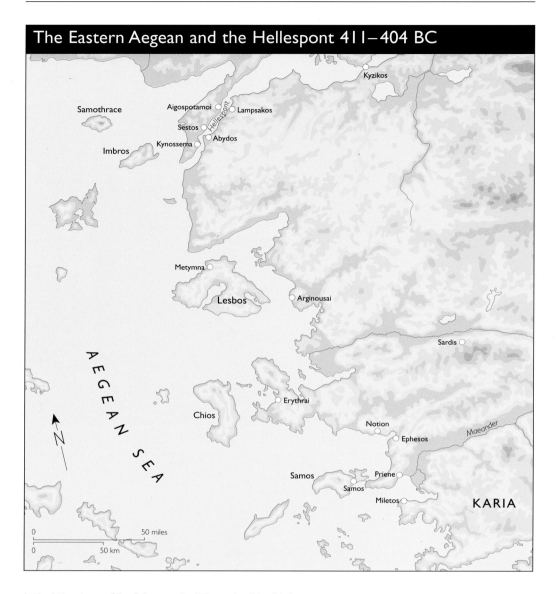

In the latter stages of the Peloponnesian War much of the fighting was concentrated on the cities and islands of the Eastern Aegean and the Hellespont. The Spartans, with Persian help, tried to detach as many places from the Athenian Empire as possible, especially the large islands of Chios, Samos and Lesbos. Control of the Hellespont was vitally important to Athenian maritime trade, particularly in grain; this is why the final, decisive sea battle was fought there.

The triumph of Sparta?

The defeat of Athens was to have far-reaching consequences for the balance of power between the Greek city-states. After their surrender to the Spartans in 404 the Athenians had to suffer the replacement of their democratic constitution by an oligarchy. This new regime consisted of a board of 30 men whose remit was to draw up a new long-term constitution for Athens. These so-called 'Thirty Tyrants' had the backing of Lysander and 700 hoplites sent by the Spartans. The oligarchs, many of whom had fled Athens after the failed revolution in 411, set about settling old scores and enriching themselves at the expense of both citizens and non-Athenian residents like the speech-writer Lysias and his brother Polemarchos, who were both

arrested on trumped up charges so that their property could be confiscated. Some of their victims fled, like Lysias, who escaped to Megara, but others, such as Polemarchos, were executed. Theramenes, one of the Thirty, tried to oppose this reign of terror, but he was denounced by his colleague Kritias and put to death.

Many of Athens' former enemies, such as Corinth, Megara and Thebes were upset that Sparta had refused their demands to punish the Athenians in the way that they had treated Melos and Skione, by executing their male citizens and enslaving the women and children. They also resented the fact that the Spartans plundered Athens but did not share the booty with their allies. The Thebans were particularly disillusioned with the way

An Athenian silver coin. The design features the owl as a symbol of Athena, goddess of wisdom and the letters ATHE. Lysandros entrusted most of the money plundered from Athens in 404 to Gylippos, who stole some of it and hid it under the tiles of his house. A Helot betrayed him to the ephors by saying that there were a lot of owls roosting under his roof. (Ancient Art and Architecture)

matters had turned out and their political leaders immediately embarked upon a policy of opposition to Sparta, which included offering assistance to the opponents of the Thirty who were trying to restore democracy in Athens.

The Spartans had won a resounding victory in 404, but the imposition of an oligarchy at Athens was just one of a series of insensitive, arrogant moves that served to alienate them from their former allies. Opinions were divided in Sparta as to how the victors should deal with the former Athenian Empire. Initially, at Lysander's prompting, the Spartans tried to create an empire of their own out of the Athenian one. They made alliances with prominent figures in many of the Greek cities that had been subject to Athens. They furnished garrisons commanded by Spartan governors, called 'harmosts', who extracted tribute from these cities in much the same way that the Athenians had done. In 403, however, a new board of Spartan ephors reversed this policy. In the same year a substantial democratic faction under the leadership of Thrasyboulos returned to Athens and occupied the Peiraieus. In the fighting that followed Kritias was killed and the Spartan king Pausanias intervened to stop further violence. The remaining oligarchs and their supporters were granted a refuge at Eleusis, on the borders of Attika and the Athenians gradually restored their full democracy.

A further problem that the Spartans did not immediately appreciate was the extent to which the end of the Peloponnesian War had removed the justification for their own power-base, the Peloponnesian League. Without their fear of the imperialist ambitions of the Athenians, the Peloponnesians had few reasons to continue to defer to the Spartans. Increasingly the Spartans came to rely upon brute force to maintain their dominant position. The city of Elis in the western Peloponnese tried to assert its independence by debarring Spartans from competing in the Olympic games, which the Eleans officiated over. In 402 the Spartans responded by ravaging the territory of Elis to enforce their will. As formal allies of Sparta, Thebes and Corinth were invited to contribute troops to this invasion, but declined. Some of the other Peloponnesians did participate in the invasion, however, seeing it as an opportunity to gain plunder at the expense of the Eleans.

The Spartans also got drawn into a war with Persia, partly over their failure to live up to their side of the agreement that had brought them Persian financial support against Athens, and partly as a result of the aid they gave to Kyros in his unsuccessful attempt to overthrow his brother Artaxerxes, who had become king on the death of Dareios in 405. The recruitment and deployment of a Spartan-led, Greek mercenary force by Kyros in 402–401 also involved the secession of many Ionian Greek cities from Persian control. Kyros' death and the disbandment of his mercenaries provided the perfect opportunity for King Artaxerxes' satrap Tissaphernes to launch attacks on these Greek cities, who in turn appealed to Sparta for assistance. In 396 the ambitious young Spartan king Agesilaos, son of Agis, resumed the imperialist policies of his mentor Lysander with a major expedition to the mainland of Asia Minor. He tried to present this venture as a second Trojan War by offering sacrifices to the gods at Aulis in Boiotia, the traditional departure point of King Agamemnon. The Boiotians broke up his ceremony, however, demonstrating that they understood his real motives.

While Agesilaos was busy with his Persian expedition Thebes, Corinth and Athens seized the opportunity provided by a dispute in Central Greece to embark on a war with Sparta. The pretext for the war was a quarrel between Phokis and Lokris over rights to pasture sheep on border lands, but it soon became a wide-ranging conflict, with much of the action centred around the Isthmus of Corinth, from which it gets the name 'Corinthian War'. Lysander was killed during a skirmish in Boiotia, but the Spartans avenged that defeat with a victory at Nemea in 394. The anti-Spartan alliance received both financial and naval support from the Persian king, whose fleet, commanded by the Athenian admiral Konon, sailed into Athens in 394 and restored the sections of the Long Walls that had been demolished in 404. Agesilaos and his army had to be recalled, and he led the Spartans to a narrow victory in a pitched battle at Koronea in Boiotia in 394. In 392 the Corinthians entered into a formal political union with neighbouring Argos, one of Sparta's oldest enemies, in an attempt to strengthen their anti-Spartan alliance. Peace negotiations in 392 came to nothing, however, and the conflict spread to the Aegean, where the Athenians began trying to revive their naval empire. In 389 they allied themselves with the would-be Pharoah Akoris, who was leading a revolt against Persian rule in Egypt. This rash move enabled a Spartan embassy led by Antalkidas to convince the Persians that Athens and her allies were their real enemies, allowing the Spartans to secure another treaty with the Great King in 387/6. This agreement, known as the King's Peace, proclaimed autonomy for all the Greeks, except those cities in Asia Minor that were supposed to have been returned to Persia under the terms of the treaty of 411 between Sparta and Persia. If anyone broke the terms of this common peace among the Greeks, then the Great King would make war on them. Thus the 'liberation' of the Greeks, that had been the rallying cry of the Peloponnesian War, was guaranteed not by the Spartans, but by the Persian king.

One of the stipulations of the King's Peace was that all the Greeks should be autonomous. This meant that Corinth and Argos had to dissolve their political union and that the Boiotian cities had to break up their Theban dominated federation. Consequently the Spartans, whose Peloponnesian League was a set of alliances, rather than a formal union, were able to continue their direction of the affairs of the Peloponnesian cities without serious opposition. Emboldened by the apparent success of their deal with the Persian king, some Spartans continued to look for opportunities to exercise power over other

Greeks. In 382 the Greek cities of Chalkidike appealed to Sparta for help against the growing power of Olynthos, a city which was on the verge of forming alliances with Athens and Thebes. A small army was despatched under the command of the new king Agesipolis, son of Pausanias. Later that year some pro-Spartan politicians in Thebes invited Phoibidas, a Spartan commander who was on his way north with reinforcements for Agesipolis, to take control of their city by seizing the acropolis. It was three years before the Spartans were forced out, by which time there was a growing feeling among many Greeks that the Spartans had become just as big a threat to their liberty as the Athenians had been in the fifth century.

A notable change in the nature of Greek warfare at this time was the increasing use of mercenaries. The financial support that the Persians had provided to the Spartans and their allies in the Peloponnesian War had mainly paid for the hire of rowers for their fleets of triremes. Kyros took this a stage further by hiring hoplites for his unsuccessful attempt to seize the Persian throne in 401. The Athenians had to keep a substantial army in the Isthmus of Corinth for five years during the Corinthian War. It was impossible to do this with ordinary citizen-soldiers, who would expect to return home at the end of the year's campaigning season, so they used mercenaries, partly paid for by money sent to Greece by the Persian king to subsidise the enemies of Sparta. It was not just the immense wealth of the Persians that encouraged the employment of mercenaries. When the Spartans decided to intervene in the affairs of the Greek cities in the northern Aegean their allies refused to send citizen-soldiers, preferring to contribute money for the Spartans to hire mercenaries. Thus the army that King Agesipolis led against Olynthos in 382 consisted of freed helots, perioikoi and mercenaries, mostly from Arkadia. In 378 the Spartan king Agesilaos, who was attacking Boiotia, took over the employment of mercenary forces from the small city of Klitor, which was

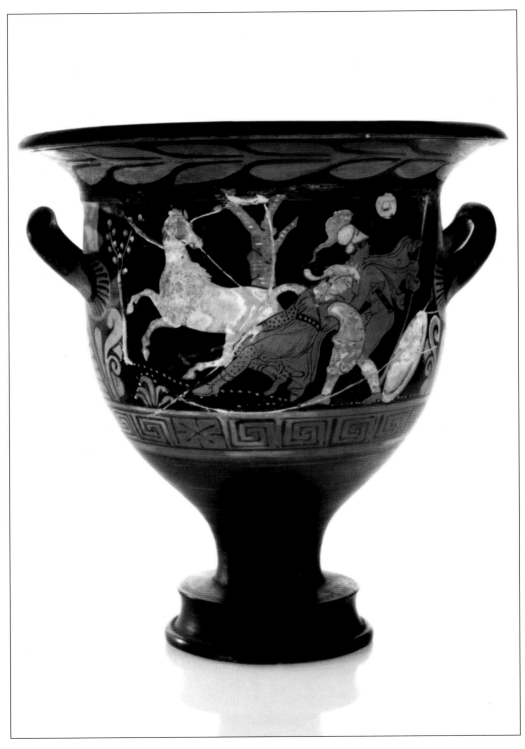

Campanian Bell Krater from the Classical Museum, University College, Dublin, 340–30BC by the Libation painer. The krater shows Achilles, wearing a Corinthian helmet, baldric and sword, supporting the Amazon queen, Penthesilea.

engaged in a minor war with the nearby city of Orchomenos in Arkadia. The fact that mercenaries were being employed even by the tiny polis of Klitor is a strong indication of how widespread their use had become by this time.

In 377 the Athenians started gathering allies among the islands and coastal cities of the Aegean, presenting this new League as a way of compelling the Spartans to allow the Greeks to be free. The Thebans forced the other Boiotians to form a new confederacy, destroying Plataia in 373 in order to encourage the others to join it. Diplomatic attempts to avert a full-scale confrontation failed and in 371 the Thebans and Spartans faced each other in a major hoplite battle at Leuktra, north-west of Plataia. The Theban general Epameinondas employed novel tactics, concentrating overwhelming strength on one wing of his army and using it to crush the enemy. Over half of the 700 full Spartan citizens who fought at Leuktra were killed. Because Spartan citizen numbers had been in decline for several generations this was a catastrophic defeat. Many of the Peloponnesian cities saw their chance to throw off the yoke of Sparta and took it. A Theban invasion of the Peloponnese brought about the liberation of Messenia

from the Spartans and the creation of a new federation in Arkadia, complete with a new capital called Megalopolis, 'the Great City'. But there were limits to what the Thebans could achieve. They lacked the financial resources to emulate the success of fifth-century Athens and their reserves of manpower, essentially drawn from citizen-farmers, were too small and too closely tied to their agricultural way of life for extended overseas campaigns. Fearful that they might try to imitate the Spartans, their former allies like Athens turned against them and an indecisive battle fought at Mantinea in the Peloponnese in 362 served only to make clear that no single Greek state was strong enough to dominate the others at this time. When a new dominant power did eventually emerge, it was in the northern region of Macedonia, where, after decades of weakness and anarchy, the young king Philip II managed to unite his kingdom under a strong, centralised monarchy in the 350s. The achievement of political stability enabled him to exploit the extensive mineral, agricultural and human resources at his disposal and turn Macedon into the leading Greek state. By doing so he prepared the way for his son Alexander to lead the Greeks in a spectacular invasion of the Persian Empire.

Marble head of Alexander. (Greek Ministry of Culture)

Part III
The Wars of Alexander the Great
336–323 BC

The decline of the city-states and the rise of Macedon

Decline of the Greek city-states

The victory of Sparta in the Peloponnesian War (431–404 BC) and the destruction of the Athenian Empire ended the balance of power in the Greek world. Sparta emerged as an oppressive and unimaginative master. Nevertheless, the price of victory had been great and domination of Greece made demands on Sparta that she could not easily meet. Sparta was notoriously short of manpower and the needs of empire – maintaining garrisons and fleets, and providing Spartiate officials abroad – strained her resources and undermined the simple but effective socio-economic basis of the state and its military power. Newly enfranchised helots (state slaves) performed garrison duty, and wealth infiltrated Spartan society; personal wealth and the use of gold and silver had been banned by the legendary lawgiver Lycurgus.

But the problems were not only domestic. Hostility to Spartan power, which was exercised in a ruthless and often corrupt manner, led to a coalition of Thebes, Corinth, Argos and a resurgent Athens against the new masters of Greece. Although Sparta withstood this initial test, which is referred to as the Corinthian War (394–387/386), the bitter confrontations of this war were the forerunners of a life-and-death struggle that would see the brief emergence of Thebes as the dominant hoplite power.

The famous Theban wedge began as a defensive measure in 394. Soon, however, it became clear that it had tremendous offensive potential and, as a result of the successful execution of Theban tactics by the renowned Sacred Band, Thebes replaced Sparta as the leader of Greece, at least on land. Sparta's defeat at Theban hands in the battle of Leuctra (371) was catastrophic and it was followed by Theban invasions of the Peloponnese, the foundation of Megalopolis as a check on Spartan activities in the south, and the liberation of Messenia, which had hitherto provided Sparta's helots and its economic underpinnings.

> *The Thebans' comment on the nature of Spartan imperialism*
> 'Now we are all aware, men of Athens, that you would like to get back the empire which you used to have. Surely this is more likely to happen if you go to the help of all victims of Spartan injustice … In the war with you [these states], at the urgent entreaties of Sparta, took their share in all the hardships and dangers and expense; but when the Spartans had achieved their object, did they ever get any share of the power or glory or money that was won? Far from it. The Spartans, now that things have gone well for them, think it perfectly proper to set up their own helots as governors, and meanwhile treat their free allies as though they were slaves … What they gave them was not freedom but a double measure of servitude.
>
> This arrogant dominion of Sparta is easier to destroy: … the Spartans, few in number themselves, are greedily dominating people who are many times as numerous as they and also just as well armed.'
> Xenophon, *Hellenica* 3.5.10–15 (Rex Warner trans., Penguin)

Greek encounters with Persia

These convulsions in central and southern Greece must be viewed against the

Monument commemorating the Theban victory over Sparta at Leuctra (371 BC). The victory was attributable to the Theban wedge and the courage of the Sacred Band. For Sparta the defeat was staggering, and the Theban general Epamonidas exploited Spartan weakness by invading Peloponnesus, establishing the city of Megalopolis and freeing the Messenians. Theban power came to an abrupt end at Chaeronea in 338 BC, and three years later the city was destroyed by Alexander. (Photo by the author)

ever-present backdrop of the Persian Empire. In the middle of the Peloponnesian War –

during an unstable period known, misleadingly, as the Peace of Nicias – the Athenians had suffered a devastating defeat in Sicily. For a state that was ringed with enemies, the collapse of the army in the west had much the same effect as Napoleon's and Hitler's disastrous Russian campaigns. For the subject states of the empire, it was the signal for rebellion, and defections occurred on a grand scale.

Economically battered and militarily shaken, Athens now resumed the war against

Sparta, which at the same time had found a paymaster in the Persian King. Although Athens had made peace with Artaxerxes I – the infamous and much disputed Peace of Callias (449) – this agreement needed to be renewed, and there had apparently not been a formal agreement with Artaxerxes' successor, Darius II (424–403). Darius at first allowed his satraps to distribute funds to Sparta and her allies in the hope of recovering the Greek coastal cities.

The compact with Persia that followed, while militarily expedient, was politically harmful to Sparta's reputation amongst the Greeks. For, in the struggle to defeat Athens, which had once espoused the liberty of the Hellenes, Sparta was agreeing to hand back Greek city-states in Asia Minor to Persia. In 407, Darius sent a younger son, Cyrus, to supply the Spartans with the resources to defeat their enemies. In the process, Cyrus developed a strong bond of friendship with the Spartan admiral Lysander. The latter had political ambitions at home, and the former was eager to bring about a Peloponnesian victory in the war so that he could, in the near future, draw upon their soldiery, which he regarded as the best in the ancient world.

The health of Darius II was clearly failing, and the heir to the throne was Cyrus's elder brother, Artaxerxes (II). He appears to have been a rather lethargic man, already approaching middle age. A faction at court, encouraged by the efforts of the queen mother, sought to win the kingship for Cyrus. But, in order to challenge his brother, Cyrus would need a military edge. And this, he believed, could be supplied by a Greek mercenary army. Darius died soon after the collapse of Athens, and in 402/401, Cyrus set in motion his scheme to overthrow Artaxerxes. A force of some 11,000 mercenaries – they were to become known (after some defections and casualties) as the 'Ten Thousand' – accompanied a vastly greater barbarian force from Lydia to Mesopotamia.

Not far from Babylon, at a place called Cunaxa, the armies of the feuding brothers met. Although the Greeks won an easy victory against the barbarians stationed opposite them, the effort was for naught, since Cyrus himself was killed in an attack on his brother in the centre of the line. Struck under the eye with a javelin, Cyrus fell, and with him collapsed the dream for the fulfilment of which an army had struggled against distance and difficult terrain, and ultimately a vastly more numerous enemy. But it was not entirely in vain, at least as a lesson to the Greeks: for the ease with which a relatively mobile and efficient army could strike at the heart of the empire exposed the weaknesses of Achaemenid Persia. One of the Greeks who participated in the campaign, Xenophon, wrote a colourful account of the adventure, which made delightful reading for Greek schoolboys. It was almost certainly read by Alexander in his youth, and its lessons did not elude him.

In the meantime, Athens too had attempted to revive its maritime power, creating the Second Athenian League. But this fell far short of the Delian League of the fifth century, for the member states were wary of Athenian imperialistic ambitions and

Xenophon's observations on the nature of the Persian Empire
'Generally speaking, it was obvious that Cyrus was pressing on all the way with no pause except when he halted for provisions or some other necessity. He thought that the quicker he arrived the more unprepared would be the King when he engaged him, and the slower he went, the greater would be the army that the King could get together. Indeed, an intelligent observer of the King's empire would form the following estimate: it is strong in respect of the extent of territory and numbers of inhabitants; but it is weak in respect of its lengthened communications and the dispersal of its forces, that is, if one can attack with speed.'
Xenophon, *Anabasis* 1.5.9 (Rex Warner trans., Penguin)

the Athenians themselves incapable of asserting their domination by force. In the event, it mattered little, since the debilitating wars of the city-states to the south had diverted Greek attention from the growing danger in the north.

The rise of Macedon

The northern kingdom of Macedon was benefiting from a union of the lower region that formed around the Axius river and the shoreline of the Thermaic Gulf with that of the mountain cantons of Upper Macedonia – Elimea, Orestis, Tymphaea and others.

During the Persian Wars, Macedon had been a vassal kingdom of the Persian Empire, and its king, Alexander Philhellene – despite his nickname, which means 'friend of the Greeks' – had acted primarily in his own interests. He had dissuaded a Greek expeditionary force from occupying the Vale of Tempe, which separated Macedonia from Thessaly, for he did not want Xerxes' large army bottled up in Macedonia, where it would be a drain on the kingdom's resources. Later he advised the Athenians to accept the reality of Persian power and surrender to Xerxes. This, of course, they decided not to do.

Alexander's son Perdiccas II ruled during the Peloponnesian War and maintained himself and the kingdom by vacillating between support of Sparta and Athens, according to the threat that each posed and the changing fortunes of the war. By the end of the century, Archelaus (the son of Perdiccas II) had begun to strengthen the kingdom: new roads were created and an effort was made to import Greek culture from the south. Indeed, the playwright Euripides died in Macedonia, where he had written his gruesome tragedy *The Bacchae*. But Archelaus did not live to fulfil his ambitions, succumbing as so many Macedonians did to an assassin's dagger.

The death of Archelaus was followed by a succession of ephemeral rulers until Amyntas III re-established a measure of stability. Nevertheless the kingdom was constantly threatened by the Illyrians to the west and the imperialistic (or, at least, hegemonic) tendencies of the Athenians and Thebans. By the queen Eurydice, Amyntas had three sons, all destined to rule. Alexander II held the throne only briefly (369–368) before he was murdered. A brother-in-law, Ptolemy of Alorus, then served as regent for the under-aged Perdiccas III, until he too was assassinated in 365. Perdiccas was now master of his own house and throne, but the kingdom continued to be threatened by the Illyrians to the west, and in 360/359 these destroyed the Macedonian army, leaving Perdiccas dead on the battlefield and only a child (Amyntas) as heir to the throne.

During the reign of his brothers, the youngest son, Philip, had spent some time as a hostage in Thebes, at that time the most powerful military state in Greece. Here he had witnessed the Theban infantry reforms and had given thought to applying the lessons to the Macedonian army. Hence, when the emergency created by the Illyrian disaster of 360/359 brought him to power, as regent for Amyntas IV, Philip knew not only what to do but how to do it. Indeed, he dealt with the crisis so effectively – combining military action with diplomacy, or even duplicity – that the claims of Amyntas were swept aside. It was Philip's reforms that made the army invincible: little did he realise that, while he was struggling to ensure Macedon's survival, he was training and organising an army of world conquerors.

Philip rapidly mastered northern Thessaly, with its chief town of Larisa, and sealed his political gains by marrying Philinna, a woman of the ruling family. The Phocians

A wonderful feat of surgery
'Critobulus enjoys great celebrity for having removed the arrow from Philip's eye and ensuring that the loss of the eye did not leave his face deformed.'
Pliny, *Natural History* 7.37 (J. C. Yardley trans.)

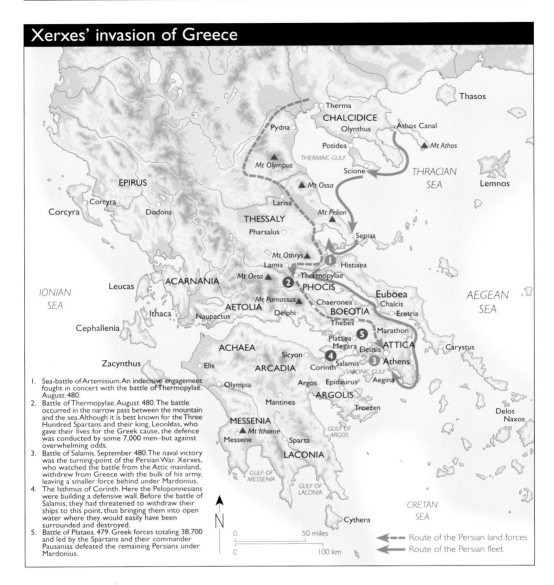

Xerxes' invasion of Greece

1. Sea-battle of Artemisium. An indecisive engagement fought in concert with the battle of Thermopylae. August 480.
2. Battle of Thermopylae. August 480. The battle occurred in the narrow pass between the mountain and the sea. Although it is best known for the Three Hundred Spartans and their king, Leonidas, who gave their lives for the Greek cause, the defence was conducted by some 7,000 men—but against overwhelming odds.
3. Battle of Salamis. September 480. The naval victory was the turning-point of the Persian War. Xerxes, who watched the battle from the Attic mainland, withdrew from Greece with the bulk of his army, leaving a smaller force behind under Mardonius.
4. The Isthmus of Corinth. Here the Peloponnesians were building a defensive wall. Before the battle of Salamis, they had threatened to withdraw their ships to this point, thus bringing them into open water where they would easily have been surrounded and destroyed.
5. Battle of Plataea. 479. Greek forces totaling 38,700 and led by the Spartans and their commander Pausanias defeated the remaining Persians under Mardonius.

Route of the Persian land forces
Route of the Persian fleet

had plundered the treasures of Delphi in order to buy mercenaries, and the inability of the Thessalians and the Thebans to deal with them cast Philip in the role of the god's champion. After his victory at the Crocus Field in 353, his men wore laurel wreaths on their heads, symbolising their service to Apollo. By 346, by the terms of the Peace of Philocrates, Philip had made himself master of northern Greece. He spoke for Thessaly and he held the deciding votes of the Amphictyonic Council that controlled Delphi.

For a while, Philip directed his attention to the north-east, to the Thraceward area and Byzantium. But in 338, he crushed the combined armies of Athens and Thebes at Chaeronea, and was able to impose a settlement on Greece, through the creation of the League of Corinth, which recognised him as its leader (*hegemon*). The foreign policy of the Greeks was securely in his hands, but Philip's greatest challenges were to come from his own kingdom; indeed, from his own household.

Alexander relates Philip's achievements

'Philip found you a tribe of impoverished vagabonds, most of you dressed in skins, feeding a few sheep on the hills and fighting, feebly enough, to keep them from your neighbours – Thracians, Triballians and Illyrians. He gave you cloaks to wear instead of skins; he brought you down from the hills into the plains; he taught you to fight on equal terms with the enemy on your borders, till you knew that your safety lay not, as once, in your mountain strongholds, but in your own valour. He made you city-dwellers; he brought you law; he civilized you … Thessaly, so long your bugbear and your dread, he subjected to your rule, and by humbling the Phocians he made the narrow and difficult path into Greece a broad and easy road. The men of Athens and Thebes, who for years had kept watching for their moment to strike us down, he brought so low – and by this time I myself was working at my father's side – that they who once exacted from us either our money or our obedience, now, in their turn, looked to us as the means of their salvation.'
Arrian 7.9 (A. de Sélincourt trans., Penguin)

Medallion showing the head of Philip II. The fact that the left side of his face is shown may be significant: Philip was struck by an arrow in the right eye during the siege of Methone in 354 BC. (Archaeological Museum of Thessaloniki)

Remains of the Temple of Apollo at Delphi. The Pythia,
the priestess of the god, declared that Alexander would
be invincible. (Author's collection)

The lion of Chaeronea, a monument to the Greeks
who fell at Chaeronea in 338 BC fighting Philip II.
(Author's collection)

The Persians, the Macedonians and allied troops

The Persians

From the time of Darius I (521–486), the Persian Empire was divided administratively into 20 provinces known as satrapies, each governed by a satrap – at least, such was the Greek approximation of *khshathrapavan*, a word that is Median in origin and appears to have meant 'protector of the realm'. These satrapies were assessed an annual tribute that ranged from a low of 170 talents of Euboean silver paid by the dwellers of the Hindu Kush region to a staggering 4,680 talents from the neighbouring Indians. (It is pointless to attempt a conversion of ancient into modern values, but it is worth noting that in the late stages of the Peloponnesian War, i.e. about 80 years before Alexander's invasion, 1 talent was sufficient to maintain a trireme, with its complement of 200 men, for a month.) Sums collected in excess of these amounts were presumably for the satraps' personal use.

In addition to the satraps of these 20 provinces, there were rulers of smaller administrative units known to the Greeks as hyparchs (*hyparchoi*), but the use of terminology is often inconsistent in Greek sources and the titles 'satrap' and 'hyparch' are sometimes used interchangeably. Both can be found commanding regionally recruited troops.

The Persian army was composed primarily of satrapal levies, each of the Achaemenid provinces providing troops in accordance with wealth and population. These troops were then divided into units based on tens. Herodotus and Xenophon speak regularly of myriads and chiliarchies, units of 10,000 and 1,000, which the Persians themselves called *baivaraba* and *hazaraba*. Each *baivarabam* had its *baivarpatish* ('myriarch'); and there was a *hazarapatish* ('chiliarch') for every *hazarabam*,

which in turn was subdivided into ten groups of 100 (*sataba*), and these into ten units of ten (*dathaba*). These were, in reality, only nominal strengths, and thus we can explain, at least in part, the wildly exaggerated numbers of Persians in the Greek sources, especially in Herodotus' account of the Persian Wars.

One unit, however, did maintain its full strength of 10,000 and hence was known as the 'Immortals'. This unit formed the elite – men selected for their physical excellence and their valour – and appears to have included a contingent of 1,000 spear-bearers, who followed the King's chariot. In addition to these came the King's special guard of spearmen, known from the golden apples that constituted their spearbutts as *melophoroi* or 'apple-bearers'. These also numbered 1,000 and preceded the King's chariot in the royal procession. Similarly, the King was accompanied by units of 1,000 and 10,000 cavalry.

When Alexander crossed to Asia, Darius III had only recently become king as a result of the convulsions at the Achaemenid court. The ruthless Artaxerxes III Ochus had elevated to positions of great power at the court – he was *hazarapatish* or chiliarch – and in the army, a eunuch by the name of Bagoas. In 338 BC, however, Bagoas murdered first Ochus, and then his sons. Hence, the kingship devolved upon a certain

The Persian Immortals were the elite troops. Their name derives from the fact that their numbers were never allowed to dip below 10,000, Nineteenth - century chromolithograph of the frieze at Susa. (ARPL)

Artashata, whom Greek writers (for reasons that are unclear to us) called Codomannus, and who took the dynastic name Darius (III). Unlike the sons of Ochus, Darius was a mature individual, already in his early forties, and an experienced warrior – he had defeated a Cadusian champion in single combat – who was wise to the machinations of Bagoas and forced him to drink his own poison. When he turned his attention to the Macedonian invaders, he had only just returned from suppressing a fresh uprising in Egypt.

The Royal Procession of the Persians
' ... in front, on silver altars, was carried the fire which the Persians called sacred and eternal. Next came the Magi, singing the traditional hymn, and they were followed by 365 young men in scarlet cloaks, their number equalling the days of the year. Then came the chariot consecrated to Jupiter [Ahura-Mazda], drawn by white horses, followed by a horse of extraordinary size, which the Persians called "the Sun's horse". Those driving the horses were equipped with golden whips and white robes ... and these were followed by the cavalry of 12 nations of different cultures, variously armed. Next in line were the soldiers whom the Persians called the "Immortals", 10,000 in number ... After a short interval came the 15,000 men known as "the King's kinsmen" ... The column next to these comprised the so-called *Doryphoroe*, ... and these preceded the royal chariot on which rode the King himself ... 10,000 spearmen carrying lances chased with silver and tipped with gold followed the King's chariot, and to the right and left he was attended by some 200 of his most noble relatives. At the end of the column came 30,000 foot-soldiers followed by 400 of the King's horses.'
Quintus Curtius Rufus, *The History of Alexander* 3.3.9–21

The Macedonians

Macedon, by contrast, was the product of a union of Upper and Lower Macedonia, which had been completed in the time of Philip II and to which were added new cities containing new – that is, naturalised – citizens. Several of Alexander's closest friends (*hetairoi*) belonged to the latter group: Nearchus and the sons of Larichus, Laomedon and Erigyius, in particular. Generally speaking, the country was not highly urbanised and most were herdsmen; the state did not have the material for a citizen hoplite army, since most lacked the resources from which to supply themselves with hoplite armour. But Macedonia had a large and robust population, which, if it could be armed cheaply and effectively, could prove too much for its neighbours.

Originally, the core of the Macedonian military was the cavalry, particularly the nobility that formed the king's guard and rode into battle with him as his *comitatus*. Here we first encounter the term *hetairoi*, 'companions' (or 'friends'). Philip appears to have formed an élite battalion of infantry, which he named his 'foot-companions' (*pezhetairoi*). Later the name came to mean the Macedonian infantry in general – that is, the territorial levies, many of them from the Upper Macedonian cantons of Elimeia, Lyncus, Orestis and Tymphaea. The élite foot-guard now became known as the *hypaspistai* or 'shield-bearers', and even these were separate from a group of noble guards described variously as the 'royal hypaspists' or the *agema*.

In the army that followed Alexander to Asia there were 9,000 *pezhetairoi*, dispersed among six brigades (*taxeis*) – each *taxis* comprised 1,500 men – and 3,000 hypaspists. Although some have regarded the hypaspists as more lightly armed than the *pezhetairoi*, the truth is that they were identically armed and only the basis of recruitment was different.

The weapon that distinguished the Macedonian infantryman or phalangite was known as the *sarissa*, a hardwood lance

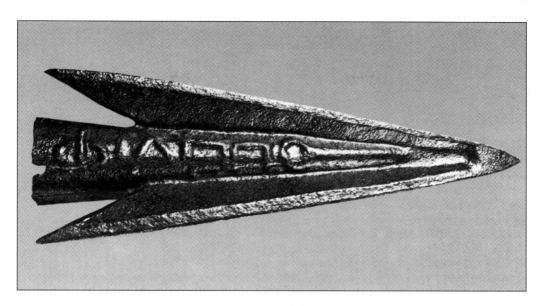

Arrowhead. This one bears the name of Philip.
(Archaeological Museum of Thessaloniki)

(often cornel wood) with a metal point and
butt-spike. This ranged in length from 15 to
18ft (4.5–5.5m), though longer ones seem to
have come into use, and weighed about 14lb
(6kg). Since it required two hands to wield,
the shield, about 2ft (0.6m) in diameter,
was either suspended from the neck, thus
rendering the breastplate virtually
superfluous, or else attached by means of a
sling to the upper arm. The helmet was
that of the 'Phrygian' style, worn also by
cavalrymen, though the latter are often
depicted sporting the so-called
Boeotian helmet.

The Macedonian cavalry, known as the
Companion Cavalry, was subdivided into
squadrons called *ilai*. The strength of an *ile* was
probably about 200, though the Royal
Squadron (*ile basilike*) comprised 300 men.
Eight *ile* of Companions were supplemented by
four *ilai* of scouts (*prodromoi*) or sarissa-bearers
(*sarissophoroi*) and one of Paeonians. Whereas
the Companions were generally armed with
the cavalryman's spear (*xyston*), the
sarissophoroi, as their name implies, wielded the
cavalry *sarissa*, a shorter version of the
infantryman's lance, probably in the 12–14ft
(3.5–4.25m) range, weighing about 4½lb (2kg).

Allied troops

Both Macedonians and Persians made
extensive use of Greek hoplites, while the
Macedonians also employed Greek cavalry.
But the numbers of Greeks in the Persian
army were substantially larger – an
embarrassing statistic for Alexander, whose
propaganda had attempted to sell his
campaign as a Panhellenic war, fought for
the good and the pride of all Greeks against
a hated enemy.

In Alexander's army, the Thessalian cavalry
equalled in strength the Macedonian
Companions (1,800–2,000) and fought on the
left wing under the general command of
Parmenion; but since Thessaly belonged to the
political orbit of Macedon and Alexander was
the *archon* of the Thessalian League, these
troops must be regarded as distinct from those
of the 'allies'. Nevertheless, it is worth noting
that, once the Panhellenic phase of the
conquest was declared over, the Thessalians
were allowed to return home, though they
sold their horses and returned on foot.

Other allied horsemen are attested,
including Peloponnesian horse, Thracians
and mercenary cavalry. An inscription from
Orchomenus records the names of local
cavalrymen who served with Alexander. In
334, Alexander led 7,000 allies and

The extent of Macedonia

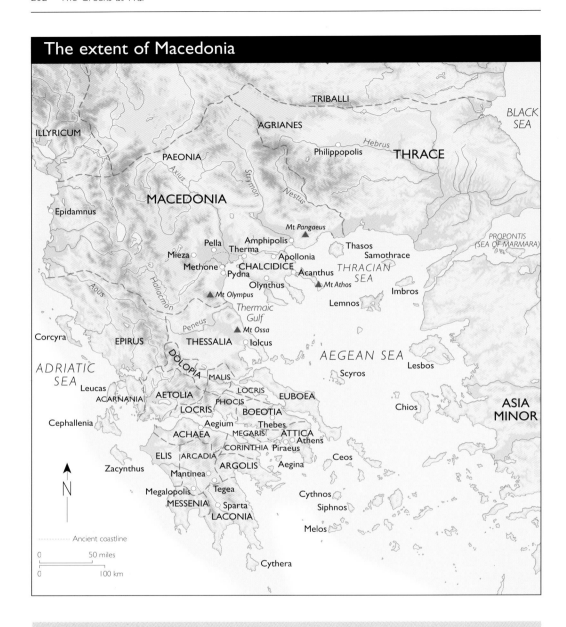

Surrender of the Greek mercenaries

'To the envoys of the Greeks, who begged him to grant them terms for the whole mercenary force, Alexander replied that he would make no compact with them whatever; men who fought with the barbarians against Greece against the decrees of the Greeks were guilty of grave wrongs. He ordered them to come in a body and surrender, leaving it to him to do what he would with them; if not, they must take what steps they could for their own safety. They replied that they placed themselves and the rest in Alexander's hands, and urged him to send an officer to lead them under safe conduct to his camp.'

Arrian 3.23.8–9 (P. A. Brunt trans., Loeb Classical Library)

Bronze greaves from Tomb II at Vergina, believed by many scholars to have belonged to Philip II, the father of Alexander the Great. Note the mismatched pair. (Archaeological Museum of Thessaloniki)

5,000 mercenary infantry to Asia, and there was a steady flow of reinforcements throughout the campaign, but also large numbers of Greeks deposited throughout the empire as garrison troops. At the time of Alexander's death, some 10,000 in the Upper Satrapies were planning to abandon their posts and return to Greece, something they had previously attempted upon hearing the false news of the King's death in 325.

The Persians, of course, employed large numbers of Greek mercenaries: 20,000 are attested at the Granicus, and 30,000 at Issus. Captured Greeks were, however, sent by Alexander to hard-labour camps, and it was only with difficulty that their countrymen secured their release. Even when Darius was fleeing south of the Caspian, shortly before his murder at the hands of Nabarzanes and Bessus, significant numbers of Greek mercenaries remained with him, commanded by Patron the Phocian and Glaucus of Aetolia. Eventually these orphaned mercenaries were forced to place themselves at Alexander's mercy.

Alexander's rise to power

The assassination of Philip

The outbreak of the Macedonian war of conquest was in fact a two-part process, the first arrested by the assassination of its initiator, Philip II. Once he had crushed Greek resistance at Chaeronea in late summer 338, Philip forged an alliance of city-states, known, after the place where its council met, as the League of Corinth. This convened for the first time in spring 337, elected Philip as its military leader (*hegemon*) and laid the foundations for a Panhellenic expedition against Persia.

What Philip's exact aims were, in terms of territorial acquisition, are not clear. Many suppose that he would have contented himself, initially at least, with the liberation of Asia Minor. This would certainly have been in keeping with Philip's practices in the past. From the time that he overcame internal opposition and secured his borders against barbarian incursions, Philip expanded slowly and cautiously over a period of almost 20 years. Unlike Alexander, whose practice it was to conquer first and consolidate later – and, indeed, 'later' never came in some cases – Philip was content to acquire territory systematically, without overextending Macedonian power.

But Philip's conquests were pre-empted by assassination, and the stability of the kingdom was disrupted by an ill-advised marriage. Macedonian kings, at least from the time of Persian influence in the region (after 513), were polygamous, and Philip married for the seventh time in October 337. The bride was a teenager of aristocratic Macedonian background – most of Philip's brides had, in fact, been foreigners – but the union was the result of a love affair rather than politics. Indeed, Philip was experiencing what we would call a 'mid-life

crisis', and the attractions of the young Cleopatra were a pleasant diversion from the affairs of state and the demands of his shrewish queen, Olympias, the mother of Alexander the Great. Philip's infatuation blinded him to both the political expectations of his new wife's family and the resentment of his son and heir.

At the wedding-feast, Cleopatra's uncle, Attalus, had toasted the marriage with the tactless prayer that it should produce 'legitimate' heirs to the Macedonian throne. Alexander (understandably) took issue with this remark, and hurled his drinking cup at Attalus. Philip, in turn, besotted with love and wine, drew his sword and lunged at his son. But he stumbled and fell amid the couches of the banquet, impaired by drink and an old war injury.

When the groom awoke the next morning to the sobering reality, Alexander was already on his way to Epirus, the ancestral home of his mother, who accompanied him. From there he meant to journey to the kingdom of the Illyrians, the traditional enemy of Macedon, intending to reassert his birthright with their aid. But this right had never really been challenged by Philip, at least not intentionally, and diplomacy served eventually to bring about the son's return and a reconciliation.

The abrasive Attalus had, in the interval, been sent with Parmenion and an army to establish a beachhead in Asia Minor. But there were nevertheless in Macedonia those who resented Attalus and feared the fulfilment of his prayer. Many looked to Philip's nephew, Amyntas son of Perdiccas, who had ruled briefly as a minor, but had been forced to yield the kingship to his uncle. Instead of eliminating him as a potential rival, Philip allowed him to live as a private citizen and married him to one of his

Cleopatra

The name Cleopatra is commonly associated with Egypt: virtually everyone is familiar with Cleopatra VII, the mistress of Julius Caesar and Mark Antony, who died in 30 BC. But the name occurs already in Homer's *Iliad* and was popular in ancient Macedonia. Archelaus I's queen, Philip's seventh wife and Alexander the Great's sister were all Cleopatras. It was actually the daughter of the Seleucid king Antiochus III who became the first Cleopatra to rule Egypt, when in 194/3 she married the young king Ptolemy V Epiphanes.

daughters, Cynnane. Now in 337/336 he became the focus of a dissident group, an unwilling candidate for the throne, supported by a faction from Upper Macedonia that planned the assassination of Philip.

This at least was the official version that followed the deed; the version promulgated by Alexander, perhaps with the aim of diverting attention from the true culprits – for

Medallion with the head of Alexander's mother Olympias, from a series of medallions commissioned by the Roman Emperor Caracalla (AD 212–17). This queen, one of Philip's seven wives, had a profound influence on her son's character and also created considerable political mischief in Macedonia during Alexander's absence in Asia. (ISI)

Philip's marriages

'In the twenty years of his rule Philip married the Illyrian Audata, by whom he had a daughter, Cynnane, and he also married Phila, sister of Derdas and Machatas. Then, since he wished to extend his realm to include the Thessalian nation, he had children by two Thessalian women, Nicesipolis of Pherae, who bore him Thessalonice, and Philinna of Larissa, by whom he produced Arrhidaeus. In addition, he took possession of the Molossian kingdom by marrying Olympias, by whom he had Alexander and Cleopatra, and when he took Thrace the Thracian king Cothelas came to him with his daughter Meda and many gifts. After marrying Meda, Philip also took her home to be a second wife along with Olympias. In addition to all these wives he also married Cleopatra, with whom he was in love; she was the daughter of Hippostratus and niece of Attalus. By bringing her home as another wife alongside Olympias he made a total shambles of his life. For straightaway, right at the wedding ceremony, Attalus made the remark "Well, now we shall certainly see royalty born who are legitimate and not bastards". Hearing this, Alexander hurled the cup he had in his hands at Attalus, who in turn hurled his goblet at Alexander.

After that Olympias took refuge with the Molossians and Alexander with the Illyrians, and Cleopatra presented Philip with a daughter who was called Europa.' Athenaeus 13.557 (J. C. Yardley trans.)

there were many who held Alexander himself responsible, or, failing that, the jilted queen, his mother. It was an act in keeping with her character, and certainly she voiced no public disapproval, though we may doubt that she crowned the assassin, Pausanias of Orestis, who had been killed as he tried to escape and whose body was subsequently impaled.

The assassination of Philip II

'In the meantime, as the auxiliary troops from Greece were assembling, Philip celebrated the marriage of his daughter Cleopatra to that Alexander whom he had made King of Epirus. The day was remarkable for its sumptuous preparations, which befitted the greatness of the two kings, the one giving away a daughter and the other taking a wife. There were also splendid games. Philip was hurrying to see these, flanked by the two Alexanders, his son and his son-in-law, without bodyguards, when Pausanias, a young Macedonian nobleman whom nobody suspected, took up a position in a narrow alleyway and cut Philip down as he went by, thus polluting with funereal sorrow a day set aside for rejoicing ... It is thought that Olympias and her son ... incited Pausanias to proceed to so heinous a crime ... At all events, Olympias had horses ready for the assassin's getaway. Afterwards, when she heard of the King's murder, she came quickly to the funeral, ostensibly doing her duty; and on the night of her arrival she set a golden crown on Pausanias' head while he still hung on the cross, something which no one else but she could have done while Philip's son was still alive. A few days later, she had the murderer's body taken down and cremated it over the remains of her husband; she then erected a tomb for him in the same place and, by inspiring superstition in the people, saw to it that funerary offerings were made to him every year. After this she forced Cleopatra, for whom Philip had divorced her, to hang herself, having first murdered her daughter in the mother's arms, and it was from the sight of her rival hanging there that Olympias gained the vengeance she had accelerated by murder. Finally she consecrated to Apollo the sword with which the King was stabbed, doing so under the name Myrtale, which was the name that Olympias bore as a little girl. All this was done so openly that she appears to have been afraid that the crime might not be clearly demonstrated as her work.'

Justin 9.6.1–4, 7.8–14 (J. C. Yardley, trans.)

Marble bust believed to be Aristotle. As a boy, Alexander had been educated by Leonidas and Lysimachus, tutors selected by his mother. In 343 BC, Aristotle, whose father Nicomachus had been a physician at the court of Philip's father, Amyntas III, was summoned to Macedonia from Asia Minor and taught Alexander at Mieza. His attitudes towards barbarians (non-Greeks) whom he regarded as inferior and worthy of being slaves of the Greeks, did not rub off on his pupil. (Ann Ronan Picture Library)

Alexander was quick to mete out punishment, freeing himself at the same time of rivals for the throne. Antipater, who had in the past served as regent of Macedon in Philip's absence, supported Alexander's claims, and it was an easy matter to round up and execute rivals on charges of conspiracy. Attalus too was found to have been corresponding with the Athenians – an unlikely scenario – and executed on the new king's orders by his colleague, Parmenion. A bloody purge masqueraded as filial piety, and those who could saved themselves by accommodation with the new king or by flight. Both types would resurface during the campaign, having delayed rather than averted the extreme penalty.

Alexander, the worthy heir

Philip's abortive expedition thus represented a false start. But Alexander acceded to more than just the throne of Macedon; he also inherited his father's Persian campaign. He was doubtless eager to depart, for we are told that as an adolescent he complained to his father that he was leaving little for him to conquer.

Things did not, however, proceed as planned. The accession of Alexander incited rebellion amongst the subject states and the barbarian kingdoms that bordered on Macedonia. And the new king was forced to prove himself, especially in the south, where the Athenian orator Demosthenes, the implacable enemy of Philip II, was deriding Alexander as a child and a fool.

Resistance to the new king in Thessaly was crushed by speed and daring, as steps (known as 'Alexander's Ladder') cut into the side of Mt Ossa allowed the Macedonians to turn the Thessalians' position. They responded with gestures of contrition and recognised Alexander as *archon* of the Thessalian League, a position previously held by his father. An initial uprising by Thebans, Athenians and Spartans was stifled by Alexander's timely arrival in Greece, where he summoned a meeting of the League of Corinth, the very existence of which was symbolic of Macedonian power. The meeting elected him *hegemon* and Philip's successor as *strategos* ('general') of the Panhellenic crusade.

Bust of Demosthenes. The Athenian orator was a bitter opponent of Macedon and of Philip II in particular. At the time of Alexander's accession he mocked him as 'a child' and compared him with the simpleton, Margites. But Demosthenes soon discovered his mistake. Copy of the original by Polyeuktos produced c. 280 BC, Copenhagen. (Ann Ronan Picture Library)

Sparta, however, refused to join the League or make public recognition of Macedonian suzerainty, for they claimed that they could not follow another, since it was their prerogative to lead. Spartan intransigence was to flare into open rebellion in 331, when Agis III attacked Macedonian troops in the Peloponnese, only to be defeated and killed at Megalopolis. For the time being, however, Alexander was content to ignore them, as they bore their military impotence with ill grace.

Nevertheless, the Greek city-states were not yet ready to renounce all claims to independence and leadership. Alexander clearly thought that he had cowed them into submission with the mere show of force, and

The remains of Pella, birthplace of Alexander the Great. (Greek Ministry of Culture)

he now turned to deal with the border tribes of the Illyrians and Triballians before turning his attentions to Asia. Both were subdued in short order, though in each case the training and discipline of the Macedonian troops made the task seem easier than it was. It was an efficient fighting machine that Philip had left to his son, and Macedonian dominion in the east was built on the foundations of Philip's military reforms.

But Alexander's activities in the north gave rise to rumours – false, but deliberately spread – that the King had been killed in Illyria. In spring 335 the Thebans threw off the Macedonian yoke, besieging the garrison that Philip had planted on their acropolis (the Cadmea) after Chaeronea and claiming

Alexander's response was quick and brutal: within two weeks he was before the gates of Thebes. Athens and Demosthenes proved that they were more capable of inciting others to mischief than of supporting the causes they had so nobly espoused. Through their inaction, they saved themselves and stood by as Alexander dealt most harshly with Thebes, which would now become an example to the other Greek *poleis*: Alexander would tolerate no rebellion in his absence, and he would regard those who preferred the barbarian cause to that of their fellow Greeks as Medisers and traitors to the common cause. Indeed, the city had a long history of Medism, and there was a

to champion the Hellenic cause. The cornerstone of Macedonian propaganda had been the claim that Philip had unified the Greeks for the purpose of attacking Persia, the 'common enemy of Greece', and avenging past wrongs. In this he was merely borrowing the sentiments of Isocrates and other Panhellenists. But the Thebans now proposed to use Persian funds to liberate Greece from the true oppressor, Macedon.

Panhellenism and anti-Persian sentiment
'I maintain that you [Philip] should be the benefactor of Greece, and King of Macedon, and gain to the greatest possible extent the empire of the non-Greek world. If you accomplish this, you will win universal gratitude: from the Greeks for the benefits they gain, from Macedonia if your rule is kingly and not tyrannical, and from the rest of the world if it is through you that they are liberated from Persian despotism and exchange it for Greek protection.'
Isocrates, *Philip* 153 (A. N. W. Saunders trans., Penguin).

A contrary view
'For, personally, I am not in agreement with the Corinthian Demaratus who claimed that the Greeks missed a very pleasurable experience in not seeing Alexander seated on Darius' throne. Actually, I think they might have had more reason to shed tears at the realisation that the men who left this honour to Alexander were those who sacrificed the armies of the Greeks at Leuctra, Coronea, and Corinth and in Arcadia.'
Plutarch, *Agesilaus* 15.3–4 (J. C. Yardley trans.)

Ivory portrait head of Alexander. (Archaeological Museum of Thessaloniki)

tradition that the allied Greeks, at the time of Xerxes' invasion, had sworn the 'Oath of Plataea', which called for the destruction of the city.

Officially, the razing of Thebes could be presented as the initial act of the war of vengeance. (Gryneum in Asia Minor would suffer a similar fate, with the same justification.) Terror would prove more effective than any garrison. To avert the charge of senseless brutality, Alexander portrayed the decision to destroy the city and enslave its population as the work of the Phocians and disaffected Boeotians, for even in those days, inveterate hatred knew no respect for human life.

Persuaded by Demades, the Athenians sent an embassy to congratulate Alexander on his victories in the north and to beg forgiveness for their own recent indiscretions. The King demanded that they surrender the worst trouble-makers, ten prominent orators and generals, including Demosthenes, Lycurgus and Hyperides, but in the event only one, Charidemus, was offered up, and he promptly fled to the court of Darius III.

Alexander conquers an empire

Asia Minor

The Macedonian advance forces under
Parmenion and Attalus encountered stubborn
resistance in Asia Minor after landing there in
spring 336. Although they captured Cyzicus,
and thus threatened Dascylium, the capital of
Hellespontine Phrygia, their push southward
was thwarted by Memnon the Rhodian, a
son-in-law of the Persian Artabazus and brother
of the mercenary captain who had helped
Artaxerxes III recapture Egypt in the 340s.
Memnon's successes were followed by the
arrest and execution of Attalus, which probably
did nothing to raise the morale of the army.
Parmenion did, however, take Gryneum,
sacking the town and enslaving its inhabitants,
for the city had a history of 'Medism'.
Elsewhere, another colleague of Parmenion,
Callas son of Harpalus, who had perhaps come
out as Attalus's replacement, was confined to
the coastline. All in all, the expeditionary force
had not made a good beginning.

The advent of Alexander, with an army
of about 40,000, altered the situation
dramatically. The satraps of Asia Minor led
their territorial levies into Hellespontine
Phrygia and held a council of war at Zeleia.
Here they rejected Memnon's proposal that
they adopt a 'scorched earth' policy, opting
instead to challenge the Macedonian army
at the nearby Granicus river.

Asia Minor was no stranger to Greek
invasion. In the 390s, Tissaphernes and
Pharnabazus, the satraps of Sardis and
Dascylium, proved adequate to deal with
forces dispatched by Sparta and, in fact,
played each other false for the sake of minor
gains. The Macedonian invasion was on a
different scale, with much greater avowed
intentions, for the Persians were not
ignorant of the creation of the League of
Corinth, or of its mandate to wage war

against them. Some sources, and possibly
Alexander himself (for official purposes),
charged the Persian King with trying to
pre-empt the expedition by engineering
Philip's assassination. If there was any truth
to the charge, the act itself had little effect.
Indeed, it replaced a more cautious
commander with a daring and ambitious
one. The reality of Alexander's presence on
Asian soil demanded immediate and
concerted action.

The Persians continued to hire large
numbers of Greek mercenaries, who for once
were fighting for more than pay. Like many

The composition of Alexander's army
'It was found that, of infantry, there
were 12,000 Macedonians, 7,000 allies
and 5,000 mercenaries. These were all
under the command of Parmenion. The
Odrysians, Triballians and Illyrians
accompanying him numbered 7,000,
and there were a thousand archers and
so-called Agrianes, so that the infantry
totalled 32,000. Cavalry numbers were
as follows: 1,800 Macedonians,
commanded by Parmenion's son
Philotas; 1,800 Thessalians, commanded
by Callas, the son of Harpalus; from
the rest of Greece a total of 600,
commanded by Erigyius; and
900 Thracian guides and Paeonians,
with Cassander as their commander.
This made a total of 4,500 cavalry.

Such was the strength of the army
that crossed to Asia with Alexander. The
number of soldiers left behind in
Europe, who were under Antipater's
command, totalled 12,000 infantry and
15,000 cavalry.'
Diodorus 17.17.3–5 (J. C. Yardley trans.)

of their compatriots at home, they doubtless regarded Persia as the lesser evil, and Alexander for his part treated captured mercenaries harshly, as traitors rather than defeated enemies. The Persian commanders, however, failed to appreciate the personal motivations of the Greek mercenaries and their leaders: distrustful of the very men who had nothing to gain by surrendering, they viewed Memnon with suspicion and negated the effectiveness of the mercenary infantry. At any rate, they stationed their cavalry on the eastern bank of the Granicus river and kept the Greek infantry in reserve. Before these saw action, the battle had been lost.

The Persian cavalry proved to be no match, in tactics or hand-to-hand combat, for the European horsemen. Two would-be champions were felled by Alexander's *sarissa*, a third was in the act of striking the King

when slain. Most of the prominent Persian leaders were among the dead; Arsites escaped the battlefield, only to die by his own hand; Arsames fled to Cilicia, to fight again at Issus.

Upon receiving the news of the Persian disaster at the Granicus, Mithrenes, the commandant of Sardis, chose to surrender to Alexander despite the city's strong natural defences. His judgement proved sound, for Alexander kept him in his entourage and treated him with respect, eventually entrusting him with the governorship of Armenia. But the Greek cities of the coast continued to resist, in part because history had taught them that the Persian yoke was lighter than that of previous 'liberators', but also because Memnon's army and the Persian fleet limited their options.

The cities of Miletus and Halicarnassus both offered fierce resistance. The former

Alexander at the Granicus

'Alexander plunged into the river with 13 cavalry squadrons. He was now driving into enemy projectiles towards an area that was sheer and protected by armed men and cavalry, and negotiating a current that swept his men off their feet and pulled them under. His leadership seemed madcap and senseless rather than prudent. Even so, he persisted with the crossing and, after great effort and hardship, made it to the targeted area, which was wet and slippery with mud. He was immediately forced into a disorganised battle and to engage, man against man, the enemies who came bearing down on them, before the troops making the crossing could get into some sort of formation.

The Persians came charging at these with a shout. They lined up their horses against those of their enemy and fought with their lances and then, when the lances were shattered, with their swords. A large number closed in on the King, who stood out because of his shield and the crest on his helmet, on each side of

which there was plume striking for its whiteness and its size. Alexander received a spear in the joint of his cuirass, but was not wounded. Then the Persian generals Rhoesaces and Spithridates came at him together. Sidestepping the latter, Alexander managed to strike Rhoesaces, who was wearing a cuirass, with his spear, but when he shattered this he resorted to his sword. While the two were engaged hand-to-hand, Spithridates brought his horse to a halt beside them and, swiftly pulling himself up from the animal, dealt the King a blow with the barbarian battle-axe. He broke off Alexander's crest, along with one of the plumes, and the helmet only just held out against the blow, the blade of the axe actually touching the top of the King's hair. Spithridates then began to raise the axe for a second blow but Cleitus (the Black) got there first, running him through with his spear. At the same moment Rhosaeces also fell, struck down by a sword-blow from Alexander. Plutarch, *Alexander* 16.3–11 (J. C. Yardley trans.)

could count on support from the Persian fleet until the occupation of Mycale by Philotas deprived it of a base. At Halicarnassus, daring sallies were made against Alexander's siege equipment, but eventually the city was betrayed by the commanders of the army, Orontopates and Memnon, who abandoned it to the Macedonians. Alexander restored to the throne Ada, the widow of the previous ruler, who had been supplanted by Orontopates, and allowed her to become his adoptive mother – in effect, reserving for himself the hereditary claim to Caria. (Philip had taught his son that not all power was gained by the sword.) By winter 334/333, Alexander had made considerable headway in the conquest of Asia Minor, but he had yet to face Darius III and the weight of the Persian army.

For Darius, the necessity of taking the field in person was less than welcome, since the Great King had had only a brief respite from the chaos that attended his accession. In spite of the débâcle at the Granicus, the Persian situation was far from critical: a counter-offensive in the Aegean was beginning to enjoy some success, with the anti-Macedonian forces regaining ground on Lesbos and at Halicarnassus. But Memnon died suddenly from illness. To replace him Darius appointed Pharnabazus, who assigned the naval command to Datames and met with the Spartan King, Agis, near Siphnos in the hope of encouraging an uprising in the Peloponnese.

At Gordium Alexander had fulfilled – or, perhaps, cheated – the prophecy that gave dominion over Asia to anyone who could undo the Gordian knot. Frustrated by the intricacies of the knot, he cut it with his sword. Some of the Macedonians were far from convinced that a venture deeper into the heart of the empire would be successful: Harpalus, his personal friend and treasurer, fled shortly before the battle of Issus. The official story was that he had been up to some mischief with a scoundrel named Tauriscus, but Harpalus may have had serious misgivings about his king's chances. To complicate matters further, Alexander had

Harpalus, the Imperial Treasurer

Harpalus, son of Machatas, belonged to one of the royal houses of Upper Macedonia, that of Elimea. Afflicted by a physical ailment that left him unfit for military service, he nevertheless served Alexander in other ways. In the 330s he served as one of Alexander's *hetairoi*, in this case, probably one of the Crown Prince's advisers; he was exiled by Philip for encouraging Alexander to offer himself as a prospective husband of the Carian princess Ada, whom Philip had planned to marry off to his half-witted son, Arrhidaeus. Harpalus was appointed treasurer early in the campaign, but he became involved with an unscrupulous individual named Tauriscus, who persuaded him to flee from Alexander's camp – no doubt he absconded with a sum of the King's money. Alexander, however, forgave and recalled him, reinstating him as treasurer.

Later in the campaign, when the King had gone to India and Harpalus remained in Babylon, the latter enjoyed a life of extravagance and debauchery, importing delicacies for his table and courtesans for his bed. When news arrived that Alexander was returning from the east, he fled to Athens, taking with him vast sums of money, and attempted to induce the Athenians to go to war. Rebuffed by the Athenians – at least, on an official level – he sailed away to Crete, where he was murdered by one of his followers, a certain Pausanias.

been struck down by fever – probably a bout of malaria – after bathing in the Cydnus river, and it was not at all certain that he would survive.

Darius, for his part, had attracted to his cause the largest force of Greek mercenaries employed by a Persian king in the history of Achaemenid rule – 30,000 Greeks, according to the official historian, Callisthenes. Amongst these was Amyntas, son of

Antiochus, who had been a supporter of Alexander's cousin and rival, Amyntas IV, and who fled Macedonia soon after Philip's assassination. Another leader of mercenaries was Charidemus, a longstanding enemy of Macedon. Charidemus, as it turned out, fell victim to court intrigue, but Amyntas gave a good account of himself before escaping from the battlefield with some 4,000 mercenaries, only to find adventure and death in Egypt.

Darius's army, which the Alexander historians (Curtius, Justin, Diodorus and Arrian) estimated at between 312,000 and 600,000, moved from Babylon to Sochi, where it encamped at the beginning of autumn 333. Alexander, meanwhile, reached the coastal plain of Cilicia and the Pillar of Jonah – the so-called 'Syrian' or 'Assyrian' Gates – south of modern Iskenderun, which gave access to Syria. In fact, it was in order to avoid the Belen Pass that the Persians entered Cilicia via the Amanic Gates (the Bahçe Pass) and reached Issus through Toprakkale. To Alexander's surprise, the positions of the two armies were now reversed, with Darius situated north of the Pinarus river and astride the Macedonian lines of communication. By the same token, there was nothing to prevent Alexander from marching into Syria except the danger to his rear.

But if the protagonists were to meet, it was advantageous for Alexander to fight in the restricted terrain of Cilicia, where the mountains and sea reduced the mobility of the enemy's troops and negated his numerical superiority. Even Alexander, who seized the narrows to the south on the night before the engagement, had to march his smaller army considerably forward into the widening coastal plain before he could deploy his infantry in a line and leave sufficient room for the cavalry to protect the flanks. He positioned himself with the Companion Cavalry on the right wing, hard against the hills that restricted movement.

Darius sent a force south of the Pinarus in order to buy time for the deployment of his own troops. Now that it was clear that the

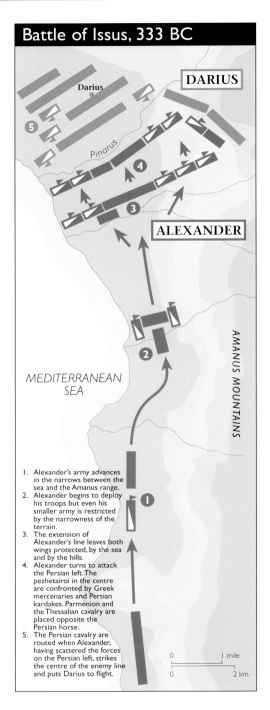

Battle of Issus, 333 BC

1. Alexander's army advances in the narrows between the sea and the Amanus range.
2. Alexander begins to deploy his troops but even his smaller army is restricted by the narrowness of the terrain.
3. The extension of Alexander's line leaves both wings protected, by the sea and by the hills.
4. Alexander turns to attack the Persian left. The pezhetairoi in the centre are confronted by Greek mercenaries and Persian kardakes. Parmenion and the Thessalian cavalry are placed opposite the Persian horse.
5. The Persian cavalry are routed when Alexander, having scattered the forces on the Persian left, strikes the centre of the enemy line and puts Darius to flight.

DARIUS

Darius

Pinarus

ALEXANDER

MEDITERRANEAN SEA

AMANUS MOUNTAINS

0   1 mile
0   2 km

Macedonians would not be overawed by Persian numbers, he took a defensive position, using the banks of the Pinarus as

Relief of Persian guards from Persepolis. (TRIP)

an added impediment; where the riverbanks gave insufficient protection, he erected palisades. A bid to move forces behind the Macedonian position, in the hills, proved ineffective, and Alexander drove them to seek refuge in higher ground by using the Agrianes and the archers; in the event, they were not a factor in the battle of Issus.

That Alexander, in imitation of the younger Cyrus at Cunaxa, charged directly at the Persian centre, where Darius himself was positioned, may be more than mere fiction. There was something in the mentality of the age that required leaders to seek each other out. (One is reminded of Alexander's apocryphal remark that he would participate in the Olympic games but only if he competed with princes!) But, if the story is true, this must have occurred in the second phase of the battle, when Alexander turned to deal with the Greek infantry that were exploiting a breach in the Macedonian phalanx.

The Greek infantry occupied the centre of the line and were most encumbered by the terrain. While Alexander routed the Persian left, which shattered on the initial assault, the heavy infantry in the centre surged forward, losing its cohesiveness. (The pattern would repeat itself at Gaugamela, with more dangerous results.) Here, opposite them, Darius had stationed his 30,000 Greek infantry, supported by 60,000 picked infantrymen whom the Persians called

Kardakes, half on each side. Against these troops the vaunted Macedonian *pezhetairoi* found it difficult to advance, and here they suffered the majority of their casualties, including the taxiarch Ptolemy, son of Seleucus.

Having put the Persian left to flight, Alexander now wheeled to his own left, slamming into the Greek mercenaries and destroying their formation. Before he could come to grips with the Great King, the Persian ranks broke and Darius fled in his chariot. Hampered in his flight by the rough terrain, he abandoned his chariot and mounted a horse to make good his escape; as an added precaution he removed his royal insignia and eluded the enemy under the cover of darkness.

Some 100,000 Persian infantry were either killed or captured at Issus, along with 10,000 horsemen, for the armoured horse, which had fought gallantly, dispersed when it learned of Darius's flight, only to suffer more grievously in their bid for safety. Among the captives were found the mother,

Detail from the Alexander Mosaic at Pompeii. Darius III prepares to flee the battlefield. (Ann Ronan Picture Library)

Alexander's alleged encounter with Darius
'In this action he received a sword wound in the thigh: according to Chares this was given him by Darius, with whom he engaged in hand-to-hand combat. Alexander sent a letter to Antipater describing the battle, but made no mention in it of who had given him the wound: he said no more than that he had been stabbed in the thigh with a dagger and that the wound was not a dangerous one.'
Plutarch, *Alexander* 20 (I. Scott-Kilvert trans., Penguin)

The Alexander Mosaic. Darius and the Persians under attack by Alexander. (Ann Ronan Picture Library)

wife and children of Darius himself. By contrast, Alexander's losses were slight. But we have only Macedonian propaganda to go by, and figures, like the sensational stories of Alexander struggling with Darius in person, must be treated with caution.

After the staggering defeat at Issus, Damascus fell into the hands of Parmenion. The amount of treasure and the importance of the individuals captured there reveal that the city was not merely a convenient place to deposit the treasures and non-combatants, but that Darius had intended to move his base of operations forward. He clearly did not expect to be routed in a single

Antigonus the One-Eyed

An officer of Philip II's generation, Antigonus was already approaching 60 when he accompanied Alexander to Asia. In the spring of 333 he was left behind as the governor (*satrap*) of Phrygia, which had its administrative centre at Celaenae. There he remained for the duration of the war, attended by his wife Stratonice and his sons, one of whom, Demetrius, was to become the famous *Poliorcetes* ('the Besieger'). After Alexander's death, Antigonus emerged as one of the leading Successors and, together with his son, made a bid for supreme power. He died, however, on the battlefield of Ipsus in 301, and Demetrius, who experienced his share of victories and defeats, proved to possess more showmanship than generalship. But ultimately his son, named after his paternal grandfather, was to establish the Antigonid dynasty in Macedonia.

Detail of Alexander from the Alexander Mosaic, now at Pompeii. Alexander is intent upon attacking Darius in person. (Ann Ronan Picture Library)

Sisygambis, mother of Darius III, mistakes Hephaestion for Alexander the Great after the Persian defeat at Issus in 333 BC. Painting by Francisco de Mura (1696–1782). (Ann Ronan Picture Library)

engagement and forced to seek refuge in the centre of the empire.

For Alexander the victory – particularly in the aftermath of Memnon's death – provided the opportunity of pushing ahead himself with the conquest and leaving his newly appointed satraps to deal with the continued resistance in Asia Minor. Antigonus the One-Eyed, a certain Ptolemy (perhaps even a kinsman of Antigonus) and Balacrus dealt effectively with what Persian forces remained behind.

Phoenicia and Egypt

In Phoenicia, meanwhile, the news of Issus led to defection on a large scale. Representatives of the coastal cities brought Alexander crowns of gold that symbolised their surrender: Aradus, Marathus and Byblus submitted in short order. And, although the cities themselves received good treatment from the conqueror, there were some rulers, like Straton (Abd-astart) of Sidon, who despite their surrender were deposed. It appears that the Sidonians, who now welcomed Alexander as a 'liberator' – for Artaxerxes III had put down an insurrection in the city with the utmost brutality – were not inclined to retain in power a man with a lengthy record of collaboration with the Persians. According to the tradition, Alexander allowed his best friend, Hephaestion, to select a new king: he found a scion of the royal house, Abdalonymus, reduced by poverty to working as a gardener, and upon him he bestowed the crown.

The capture of Phoenicia added a new dimension to Alexander's campaign, one that must not be downplayed. The area was critical for the survival of the Persian fleet, which was, in turn, Darius's chief hope of defeating Alexander if he could not do so on the battlefields of the east. Alexander had abandoned all attempts at defeating the Persian navy at sea and had disbanded the Macedonian fleet: it was numerically inferior, just as its ships and sailors were of inferior quality; and, to make matters worse, the Greek naval powers, especially the Athenians, could not be fully trusted. It was better to deprive the Persian navy of its bases and thereby reduce its power, without running the risk of a military disaster at sea that might turn the tide of the war but would almost certainly tarnish Alexander's reputation as an invincible foe.

Alexander's naval strategy worked. As the inhabitants and governments of each region surrendered to him, their naval contingents too abandoned the Persian cause. The Phoenicians found themselves in an awkward position, since large numbers of their citizens, including many of their local dynasts, served with the Persian fleet. These rulers especially found it preferable to surrender to Alexander in the hope of retaining their power rather than remain

Hephaestion, Alexander's alter ego

Hephaestion, son of Amyntor, had been a close friend of the King since boyhood. He had been with Alexander as a teenager at Mieza, when the Crown Prince was educated by Aristotle. Romanticised accounts compared the two with Achilles and Patroclus. Whether they were lovers, as many modern writers like to assert, is not entirely clear. But Alexander certainly promoted Hephaestion's career despite the fact that he seems to have possessed poor leadership qualities and little military skill. He was nevertheless a gifted organiser and Alexander left many matters of logistics – supply, transport of equipment, bridge-building and the founding of settlements – to him.

By the time the army reached India, Hephaestion's promotion had brought about friction with other officers, especially the fine soldier Craterus. At one point the two came to blows in front of their respective troops and Alexander had to intervene. Although he chided Hephaestion because he failed to recognise that 'without Alexander he would be nothing', he remained devoted to his lifelong friend. In October 324, Hephaestion died of illness, and the King was inconsolable.

loyal to Darius. By contrast, the inland Syrians were more inclined to stay with Darius, and we find them joining their former satrap, Mazaeus, in the army that faced Alexander again in 331 at Gaugamela.

Darius meanwhile resorted to diplomacy, for his family had fallen into the victor's hands when the Persian camp was taken after the King's flight from Issus. Letters were sent to Alexander offering money and territory in exchange for Darius's kinfolk. But the exchanges between the two kings demonstrated merely the Persian King's refusal to recognise the gravity of the danger to the empire. Furthermore, Darius persisted

ΓΝΛΕΙΣ ΕΠΟΗΣΕΝ

Relief showing a hunting scene. Hephaestion is the figure with the raised sword. He was Alexander's boyhood friend and alter ego. In 324 BC he married the younger daughter of Darius III, and thus became the brother-in-law of one of Alexander's own Persian brides, the princess Stateira. In October of the same year he died of an illness at Ecbatana. (Greek Ministry of Culture)

in treating Alexander as an upstart, an inferior who could, as he thought, be bought off with the cession of Asia Minor and 10,000 talents.

But Alexander held the trump cards and was not prepared to fold, when diplomacy offered less than he had obtained by conquest. Negotiations continued for almost two years, with an escalation of the terms – Darius was eventually to offer Asia west of the Euphrates, 30,000 talents and the hand of his daughter in marriage – but Persian concessions failed to keep pace with Macedonian conquests. Darius no longer had the authority to dispose of Alexander's 'spear-won land'.

Whereas the northern Phoenician cities had capitulated on the news of Alexander's approach, Tyre resisted the King's request to make sacrifices to Hercules (Melqart) within their city. This was, of course, a transparent ploy to gain control of the place. But the Tyrians could afford to be defiant, or at least so they thought, for about half a mile (0.8km) of sea separated them from the Macedonian army, and the city fathers responded that Alexander was welcome to

A modern Greek coin depicting Alexander wearing the diadem and the Horns of Amun, the Egyptian deity whom the Greeks regarded as a ram-headed Zeus. The inscription on top reads 'megas Alexandros' (Alexander the Great). On his own coinage and in his own time this epithet was never used. (TRIP)

Macedonians and burning their towers to the ground. Here the ancient sources diverge on the matter of the causeway, and it is not certain whether Alexander began a new one, approaching the city from a different angle, or merely widened the existing one. In the event, the mole did not prove to be the decisive factor, since the city walls, which rose 160ft (50m) above the point of attack, were most heavily fortified at that very point and could not be shaken by battering rams.

Instead the critical support came from the Cypriotes and Phoenicians, many of whom had abandoned the Persian fleet of Autophradates once they received news that their cities had surrendered. These ships gave Alexander the advantage on the sea and the Tyrians were content to block their harbour entrances – when they did sail out, it was with heavy losses. Using the fleet to assail the walls, Alexander found that the south side of the city had the weakest

sacrifice to Hercules at 'Old Tyre', which was situated on the mainland. Furthermore, there was the expectation – vain, as it turned out – of aid from their North African colony, Carthage. Neither grand strategy nor Alexander's reputation, however, could allow the young king to bypass the city.

Alexander realised that the siege of an island city would be no easy matter, and that a lengthy siege would buy valuable time for his enemy. Hence, he sent heralds into the city in the hope of persuading the Tyrians to surrender. But the diplomatic approaches were rebuffed, and the heralds executed and thrown into the sea. Work began immediately upon the building of a causeway from the mainland to the island.

In the early stages the work went well and quickly, because the water was shallower near the mainland and out of range of Tyrian missiles. As the mole approached the city, however, ships began to harass the workers, and Alexander erected two towers, with hides and canvases to shield the workers and with turrets from which to shower missiles upon the enemy. To this the Tyrians responded by sending a fire-ship against the end of the mole, driving off the

The importance of Tyre
'Friends and fellow soldiers, I do not see how we can safely advance upon Egypt, so long as Persia controls the sea; and to pursue Darius with the neutral city of Tyre in our rear and Egypt and Cyprus still in enemy hands would be a serious risk, especially in view of the situation in Greece. With our army on the track of Darius, far inland in the direction of Babylon, the Persians might well regain control of the coast, and thus be enabled with more power behind them to transfer the war to Greece, where Sparta is already openly hostile to us, and Athens, at the moment, is but an unwilling ally; fear, not friendliness, keeping her on our side. But with Tyre destroyed, all Phoenicia would be ours, and the Phoenician fleet, which both in numbers and quality is the predominant element in the sea-power of Persia, would very like come over to us.'
Arrian 2.18 (A. de Sélincourt trans., Penguin)

The Libyan oasis of Siwah, where Alexander was acknowledged by the priests as the 'Son of Amun', hence legitimate pharaoh of Egypt. (TRIP)

fortifications, and these he assaulted until a breach occurred. Once the walls had given way, the defenders were virtually helpless, but they fought desperately. The citizens paid for their defiance in the slaughter that ensued, though many Sidonians helped to save their fellow Phoenicians from the enemy's rage.

Gaza, too, resisted Alexander, but the city fell after only two months. By contrast, Egypt, which now lay open, welcomed the Macedonians as liberators. Thus ended the last period of Persian occupation and the brief reign of the Thirty-First Dynasty. Alexander's legitimacy as Egyptian pharaoh was proclaimed in Memphis and given divine sanction at the Libyan oasis of Siwah, where the conqueror was greeted as the 'son of Amun'.

Uprising in Greece

When Alexander returned to Tyre, after his lengthy sojourn in Egypt, he learned of serious unrest in the Peloponnese. There the Spartan King, Agis III, who had begun his dealings with the Persian leaders in the Aegean very soon after Alexander's departure from Europe, openly resisted Macedonian power. In a bold move he defeated the army of Corrhagus, thus forcing Antipater himself to lead an army to the south. Nor was Agis's force inconsequential: he had collected 22,000 men from the neighbouring states of Elis, Arcadia and Achaea, and with these he now laid siege to Megalopolis. (This was the city that the Theban general Epaminondas had founded when he invaded the Peloponnese and ended Sparta's hegemony there.)

Antipater was, however, preoccupied with affairs in Thrace, where the *strategos* (military governor) of the region, Memnon, was in open rebellion. This was clearly not done by prearrangement with Agis and the anti-Macedonian forces in the south, for Memnon quickly came to terms with Antipater and thus freed him to deal with the Greek insurrection. Furthermore, the fact that Memnon later brought reinforcements to Alexander in the east suggests that the King did not regard his actions as treasonous.

The Macedonian army confronted Agis at Megalopolis in the summer of 331 – certainly the entire rebellion had been suppressed before the battle of Gaugamela was fought. The contest was a renewal of the bitter struggle between Macedon and the Greeks, who had still not accepted the suzerainty of the former. Although he fell on

> **Alexander makes light of Antipater's victory over Agis III at Megalopolis**
> 'Alexander even added a joke when he was told of the war waged by Antipater against Agis. "Men," he said, "it appears that while we were in the process of vanquishing Darius, there was a battle of mice over there in Arcadia.'
> Plutarch, *Life of Agesilaus* 15 (J. C. Yardley trans.)

the battlefield, Agis did not sell his life cheaply; nor did the 5,300 other Greeks who perished in the battle. Alexander, when he learned of the engagement, dismissed it as insignificant. But the contest had left 3,500 Macedonians dead, and until it had been decided his activities in the east were suspended in uncertainty.

The final clash with Darius

While Alexander directed his attentions to Phoenicia and Egypt, Darius, once his attempts to win a negotiated settlement had failed, marshalled another army. If there was anything that the empire had in abundance, it was manpower; though, as Darius would learn, mere numbers of men would not suffice against a brilliant tactician like Alexander. Nevertheless, the barbarian army at Gaugamela contained several contingents that had faced the Macedonians before. Syrians, defeated at Issus but steadfast in their loyalty to Persia, stood shoulder to shoulder with Persians, Babylonians and Medes, who formed the nucleus of the Great King's strength.

Nevertheless, the composition of Darius's army was radically different from that which had been routed at Issus, for it included the fine horsemen from the Upper Satrapies (Central Asia) – not just the Arians, Arachosians and Bactrians, but the Scythian cavalry of the Dahae, Sacae and Massagetae – which Darius had either been unable to mobilise or considered superfluous in 333.

Not restricted by the terrain as they had been at Issus, the Persians were more confident of victory on the expansive plains of northern Mesopotamia. And here too they would bring to bear the terrifying spectacle of scythed chariots and elephants.

As he had done at Issus, Darius prepared the battlefield, which was littered with obstacles and traps for the unsuspecting enemy, though these were revealed by deserters and their effectiveness negated. But primarily the Persians relied on vastly superior numbers and the luxury of deploying them as they chose on the plains beyond the Tigris. Darius expected to outflank and envelop the Macedonian army, which was pitifully small by comparison. The scythed chariots, making a frontal charge, proved ineffectual: Alexander's javelin-men simply parted ranks upon their approach and shot down their drivers or their teams. The chariot had become a symbol of oriental vanity, for its effectiveness had already been challenged by infantrymen at the end of the Bronze Age, and it remained a splendid anachronism, but no match for cool minds and brave hearts.

Some aspects of the battle of Gaugamela are reminiscent of Issus – not surprisingly, since Alexander's method was to drive hard at the Persian left while the infantry held the centre. This time, however, his infantry did not attack the centre head-on, as the Macedonians had tackled the Greeks and Kardakes in the first engagement. Instead it advanced obliquely, the hypaspists following closely the cavalry attack, and the remainder of the *pezhetairoi* surging to keep up with the hypaspists. And, just as had happened at Issus, a gap occurred as the phalanx rushed forward, which was again exploited by the enemy. This time, however, Alexander did not turn immediately to aid the phalanx, but instead rode on in pursuit of the Persian left. His thinking was surely that he did not want Darius to escape him a second time.

Nor was the infantry challenged by troops of similar quality to those at Issus. Rather it was the Scythian and Indian cavalry that broke through the line, only to turn their attention to plundering the Macedonian baggage camp. More disciplined were the horsemen stationed on the Persian right. Here Mazaeus's squadrons were exerting pressure on the Macedonian left, under the command of Parmenion. Although the old general eventually overcame his opponents, he had been forced to send riders to

Excavated ruins of Babylon. (TRIP)

summon Alexander to return. It was the proper thing to do, but it was also to harm his reputation, for the official history questioned Parmenion's competence and blamed him for spoiling an otherwise total victory. In truth, it was the steadfastness of Parmenion and Craterus on the left, combined with the rapacity of the barbarian allied horse – who stopped to plunder instead of coming to Mazaeus's aid – that secured the victory at Gaugamela.

Although Darius had again escaped from the battlefield, Gaugamela proved fatal for the Persian Empire. The Great King fled in the direction of Arbela, which he reached by midnight. Other contingents dispersed to their territories, as was the custom amongst the barbarians. Those who commanded the garrisons and guarded the treasures in the empire's capitals made formal surrender to Alexander. One man, Mazaeus, the Persian hero of Gaugamela, surrendered Babylon, together with the *gazophylax* ('guardian of the treasures'), Bagophanes. Alexander entered in great ceremony the ancient city, which now publicly turned its resources over to the new king, as it were.

What the Alexander historians depict as a spontaneous welcome was in fact ritual surrender, enacted so many times in the

past – in ceremony for the legitimate heir to the throne, as well as in earnest for a conquering king. In return, Alexander appointed Mazaeus satrap of Babylon, though he installed a garrison in the city and military overseers (*strategoi*) to ensure the loyalty of the new governor and the population.

Despite Gaugamela's ranking as one of the 'decisive' battles of world history, the fact is that it was only decisive for the Persian side. For Darius it was, one might say, the final nail in the coffin; Alexander, on the other hand, could have survived defeat in northern Mesopotamia and still held the

Babylon surrenders to the Macedonian conqueror

'A large number of the Babylonians had taken up a position on the walls, eager to have a view of their new king, but most went out to meet him, including the man in charge of the citadel and royal treasury, Bagophanes. Not to be outdone by Mazaeus in paying his respects to Alexander, Bagophanes had carpeted the whole road with flowers and garlands and set up at intervals on both sides silver altars heaped not just with frankincense but with all manner of perfumes. Following him were his gifts – herds of cattle and horses, and lions, too, and leopards, carried along in cages. Next came the Magi chanting a song in their native fashion, and behind them were the Chaldaeans, then the Babylonians, represented not only by priests but also by musicians equipped with their national instrument. (The role of the latter was to sing the praises of the Persian kings, that of the Chaldaeans to reveal astronomical movements and regular seasonal changes.) At the rear came the Babylonian cavalry, their equipment and that of their horses suggesting extravagance rather than majesty.

Surrounded by an armed guard, the king instructed the townspeople to follow at the rear of his infantry; then he entered the city on a chariot and went to the palace.'

Curtius Rufus, *The History of Alexander* 5.1.19–23 (J. C. Yardley trans., Penguin)

western portion of the empire. Victory, however, belonged to the Macedonians, and the might of Persia was shattered. Babylon had no hope of resisting, and Susa, too, avoided pillage by embracing the conqueror.

The entry of Alexander the Great into Babylon. Painting by Johann Georg Platzer (1704–61). (Ann Ronan Picture Library)

Reconstruction of the Ishtar Gate of Nebuchadrezzar.
(AKG Berlin)

Again the defecting satrap, Aboulites, was
retained and once more a Macedonian
garrison was imposed.

The blueprint had been established:
Alexander would regularly combine a show
of native rule with the fetters of military
occupation. But, with Darius still at large,
Alexander introduced military reforms to
strengthen the army and the command

structures. Reinforcements continued to
arrive, even though the avenging army
moved ever closer to its ultimate goal, that
most hated of all cities: Persepolis.

The satrap of Persis, Ariobarzanes,
had mustered a sizeable force: with
25,000 defenders he blocked the so-called
'Persian' or 'Susidan' Gates in an attempt to
stall the Macedonians until the city's
treasures could be removed. If this was not
his aim, it was certainly Alexander's fear.
Dividing his force in two, Alexander led the

more mobile contingents through the mountains to the rear of the pass, leaving Craterus to fix the enemy's attention on what he perceived as the stalled army. In

Reconstruction of Babylon showing the Ishtar Gate. (TRIP)

fact, Ariobarzanes was delaying only a portion of the Macedonian force: the slowest

elements and the baggage-train were following the wagon road into Persis under the command of Parmenion. The satrap's position was circumvented by Alexander, whose men braved the perils of terrain and winter snow, led by captive guides. Ariobarzanes' troops were slaughtered in the pass and it was now a relatively simple matter to bridge the Araxes, whereupon Tiridates surrendered both city and treasure to the Macedonians.

Its symbolic importance – the very meaning of the Greek form of the name Persepolis, 'City of the Persians', enhanced its actual associations with Xerxes and the great invasion – dictated its fate: pillage, rape and massacre ensued. The palace too fell victim to the victor's wrath, but only after the treasures had been removed and shipped to Ecbatana. Then, whether by design or through a spontaneous urge for revenge, it was put to the torch. One version attributed

the burning to an Athenian courtesan, Thaïs, who was to become the mistress of Ptolemy, the later King of Egypt.

The destruction of Persepolis was symbolic rather than total, for it continued as the capital of the province during the age of the Successors. It did, however, illuminate the difficulties faced by the conqueror. For one thing, it could be taken to signify the completion of the war of vengeance, the attainment of the stated goal of the

Battle of Gaugamela, 331 BC, commonly but inaccurately referred to as the battle of Arbela. The town of Arbela was actually some distance from the battlefield, and Darius in his flight did not reach it until after midnight. From the studio of Charles Le Brun (1619–90). (AKG Berlin)

expedition, and the allied troops would naturally assume that it warranted their demobilisation. Still, Alexander could remind them that as long as Darius lived, the mission had not been completed.

Conversely, the destruction of the palace and the maltreatment of the citizens undermined Alexander's propaganda, which had at an early stage sought to portray him as the legitimate successor of the Great King.

Rightly had Parmenion advised against such action, reminding Alexander that he should not destroy what was now his own property. Nevertheless, what may have caused resentment in Persia could well have been received with a degree of satisfaction in Babylon and Susa, even Ecbatana, all of which had been overshadowed by the advent of the Achaemenids and the establishment of Persepolis.

Ruins of Persepolis. The palace was put to the torch by Alexander, as an act of policy since the city symbolised past atrocities by Persians against Greeks, but most of the city remained untouched and continued to function during the Hellenistic period. (TRIP)

Columns of the ancient audience hall at Persepolis. (TRIP)

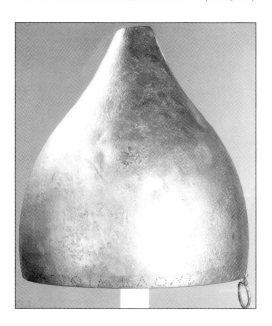

Persian helmet from Olympia in Greece. (AKG Berlin)

Advance into Central Asia

At the beginning of 330, Darius retained only one of the four capitals of the empire, Ecbatana (modern Hamadan). It was a convenient location, from which he could receive reports of Alexander's activities in Persia and at the same time summon reinforcements from the Upper Satrapies. Furthermore, it lay astride the Silk Road, the great east–west corridor that ran south of the Elburz mountains and the Caspian and north of the Great Salt Desert. Unfortunately, many of the King's paladins advised against awaiting Alexander in that place, and they urged Darius to withdraw in the direction of Bactria, which lay beyond the Merv oasis, just north-west of modern Afghanistan.

This plan was adopted by Darius, but only when it was too late to elude Alexander, who resumed hostilities once the mountain passes were free of snow. The Great King's column was much too cumbersome: the royal equipment that offered the necessary comforts, and the covered wagons that sheltered the concubines on the journey, made slow progress through the Sar-i-Darreh or Caspian Gates, even though they had been sent in advance of the army. Only 40,000 native troops and 4,000 Greeks remained with Darius, and deserters – many of them prominent men – drifted back towards the Macedonian force that was, every day, shortening the distance between the two armies.

In the remote village of Thara, the chiliarch, Nabarzanes, and Bessus, one of the King's kinsmen, challenged Darius's leadership. Aided by other prominent figures, they arrested the King, only to murder him soon afterwards. His body was left by the side of the road in the hope that when Alexander encountered it he might break off the pursuit. Nabarzanes himself attempted to rally support in Hyrcania and Parthia; Bessus continued towards Bactria and Sogdiana, accompanied by 600 horsemen. With Darius dead, he himself assumed the upright tiara, the sign of kingship, and styled himself Artaxerxes, the fifth of that name.

For Alexander, the time had come to call a halt. He had covered some 450 miles (720km) in three weeks: with a larger force he had pushed east from Ecbatana to Rhagae (that is, from Hamadan to Rey, on the edge of modern Teheran), a march of roughly

Alexander comes upon the dead Persian King. (ISI)

250 miles (400km), in 11 days; after a five-day rest, he had taken a much smaller, mounted force another 200 miles (320km), coming upon Darius's body late on the sixth day of pursuit. Bessus himself had, for the present, eluded him, but the Macedonian army had scattered in the chase and the daily arrival of high-ranking Persian deserters made it necessary to take stock before turning to deal with the usurper.

Some Persians were installed as satraps – Phrataphernes in Parthia, Autophradates amongst the Tapurians – while others remained in the King's entourage, awaiting suitable employment and reward. Two dangerous men were pardoned, Nabarzanes and Satibarzanes. The former ought to have considered himself lucky to escape execution, but instead contrived to regain control of Parthia and Hyrcania; ultimately, however, he was arrested and killed. The latter was reinstated in his old satrapy of Aria (in the Herat region of Afghanistan), though a detachment of 40 javelin-men under Anaxippus was sent with him to his capital of Artacoana. Satibarzanes promptly murdered his escort and openly rebelled, encouraged perhaps by reports of Bessus's usurpation.

Only two days after learning of Satibarzanes' treachery, Alexander was in Artacoana, from which the rebellious satrap had fled. But when Alexander replaced him with another native ruler, Arsaces, and moved on to subdue Afghanistan, Satibarzanes returned with the aim of reimposing his rule. In this he failed, and he was killed in single combat by the Macedonian cavalry officer Erigyius.

Alexander, meanwhile, moved south and came upon the Ariaspians, who lived near Lake Seistan. These supplied his army, just as 200 years earlier they had aided Cyrus the Great of Persia and earned the title *Euergetai* ('Benefactors'). From there the Macedonians followed the Helmand river valley, the course of which took them in the direction of Arachosia. A new settlement was established at Alexandria-in-Arachosia (near modern Kandahar), one of many such foundations in the area.

The death of Satibarzanes
'The deserter Satibarzanes commanded the barbarians. When he saw the battle flagging, with both sides equally matched in strength, he rode up to the front ranks, removed his helmet ... and challenged anyone willing to fight him in single combat, adding that he would remain bare-headed in the fight. Erigyius found the barbarian general's display of bravado intolerable. Though well advanced in age, Erigyius was not to be ranked second to any of the younger men in courage and agility. He took off his helmet and revealed his white hair ... One might have thought that an order to cease fighting had been given on both sides. At all events they immediately fell back, leaving an open space, eager to see how matters would turn out ...

The barbarian threw his spear first. Moving his head slightly to the side, Erigyius avoided it. Then, spurring on his horse, he brought up his lance and ran it straight through the barbarian's gullet, so that it projected through the back of his neck. The barbarian was thrown from his mount, but still fought on. Erigyius drew the spear from the wound and drove it again into his face. Satibarzanes grabbed it with his hand, aiding his enemy's stroke to hasten his own death.
Quintus Curtius Rufus, *History of Alexander* 7.4.33–37

In 329, Alexander again turned to deal with Bessus in Bactria, crossing the Hindu Kush via the Khawak Pass and reaching Qunduz. On his approach, the barbarians sent word that they were prepared to hand over to him the usurper Bessus; stripped naked, in chains and wearing a dog-collar, Bessus was left by the roadway to be picked up by Alexander's agent, Ptolemy. But those who had betrayed him fled, wary of submitting to Alexander and determined to maintain their independence in one of the most remote regions of the empire.

Bessus was sent to Ecbatana to be tortured and executed, the traditional punishment for traitors. He had done more than simply murder Darius; he had challenged Alexander's claims to the kingship. Claims to legitimacy have little force, however, unless backed by military action, as Darius's illustrious forefather and namesake had discovered in the years from 522 to 519. That king's imperial propaganda, inscribed in three languages on the rock face of Bisutun, proclaims how he became king through the will of Ahura-Mazda; but it took the might of his armies and the public execution of his opponents to confirm the god's will.

And so too Alexander was forced to fight on. Seven towns along the Iaxartes (Syr-Darya) offered stubborn resistance but fell to the conquerors, and at Cyropolis,

founded by Cyrus the Great at the northern limit of his empire, the King was wounded in the neck. A new frontier settlement nearby – this one called Alexandria-Eschate ('Alexandria the Farthest', modern Khojend) – served to restrict the flow of the Scythian horsemen who were aiding the Bactrian rebels, but it threatened the patterns of life in Sogdiana and only incited further insurrections. A guerrilla war ensued, with the rebels entrusting their families and property to the numerous strongholds in the region.

One of the local barons, Sisimithres (known officially as Chorienes), took refuge on Koh-i-nor, which the ancients called simply the Rock of Chorienes. Although his mother pressed him to resist the invader, Sisimithres was persuaded to surrender. Alexander had sent to him another prominent Sogdianian named Oxyartes, who may well have reported how the rebel Arimazes had been captured with relative ease, despite the natural defences of his fortress, and punished with crucifixion.

Over the winter of 328/327 Sisimithres supplied Alexander's army with pack

Modern Khojend. The city began as a settlement (Alexandria-Eschate) to protect the crossing of the Iaxartes river (Syr-Darya). In this vicinity Cyrus the Great had also established a frontier outpost. (TRIP)

Alexander and Roxane

'Writers give the height of the rock of Sisimithres as 15 stades, with 80 stades as its circumference. On top, it is reportedly flat and contains good soil, which can support 500 men, and on it Alexander is said to have been sumptuously entertained and to have married Roxane, the daughter of Oxyartes.'
Strabo, *Geography* 11.11.4

animals, sheep and cattle, as well as 2,000 camels. Alexander returned the favour when spring approached, plundering the territory of the Sacae and returning to Sisimithres with 30,000 head of cattle. This gesture, too, was matched by the barbarian, who entertained him on the Rock. Here it was that Alexander met Oxyartes' daughter, Roxane, whom he subsequently married. It is depicted as a love-match, which may be true, but the political implications did not escape Alexander either. By means of a wedding ceremony, the Macedonian King terminated

Tension between Alexander and his Macedonians

Ever since the death of Darius, Alexander had become increasingly orientalised. He had begun to adopt certain elements of Persian dress; his belief in his divine parentage was also regarded as an eastern pretension. Furthermore, he had become more autocratic. In summer 328 Alexander killed Cleitus the Black, the man who had saved his life at the Granicus, in a drunken quarrel in Samarkand. In the following spring, several pages along with Hermolaus conspired to murder the King, but their plot was revealed and the conspirators were executed. Callisthenes, the tutor of the pages, was suspected of complicity and put to death as well. And, in these years, the King had begun to drink more heavily than before.

the lengthy guerrilla war that he had been unable to bring to an end militarily. Philip II had used political marriage to great advantage in his time; after seven years of campaigning, Alexander too had come to appreciate its usefulness.

It is difficult to determine how much the marriage to Roxane influenced Alexander's thinking about the benefits of intermarriage with the barbarians. Some ancient writers mention other marriages between Macedonians and barbarian women at this time, but these may anticipate the great mass-marriage ceremony at Susa in 324. It is certain, however, that soon after marrying Roxane Alexander attempted to introduce the Persian custom of obeisance (*proskynesis*) at his court. This met with fierce resistance on the part of his Macedonian generals and courtiers, and the King reluctantly abandoned the scheme.

Invasion of India

The political marriage of Alexander and Roxane had brought the guerrilla war in Bactria and Sogdiana to an end, but the fighting was to continue. The Macedonian army now turned its attention to the last corner of the Achaemenid Empire. Here three provinces remained: Parapamisadae, which lay beyond the passes of the Hindu Kush as one marched east from the city of Bactra (Balkh, near Masar-e-sharif); Gandhara (now part of northern Pakistan); and Hindush (Sindh), the valley of the Indus. Once through the Hindu Kush, Alexander advanced into the Bajaur and Swat regions, moving relentlessly towards the Indus, where an advance force under Hephaestion and Perdiccas had constructed a boat-bridge across the river, leading into the territory of the Taxiles.

On the march, Alexander had encountered fierce resistance from the Aspasians and Assacenians. The chief city of the latter was Massaga, located in the Katgala Pass and defended by a woman, Cleophis, the mother (or possibly widow) of the local

The wedding of Alexander and Roxane. Painting by Il Sodoma, based on an ancient account of the painting by Aetion. (AKG Berlin)

Perdiccas, son of Orontes

Perdiccas was another of the young and talented officers of Alexander, one of several who would struggle for power after the death of the King. In 336, he was a member of Philip II's hypaspist bodyguard: it was unfortunate that the King's assassination occurred 'on his shift', to use modern parlance. Alexander promoted him to the rank of taxiarch and as such he led one of the brigades of the *pezhetairoi*. Probably in 330, he became a member of the seven-man Bodyguard (*Somatophylakes*) and soon afterwards he commanded a hipparchy of the Companion Cavalry. He appears to have worked well with Alexander's closest friend, Hephaestion, but others found him difficult to deal with.

After Hephaestion's death, he was undoubtedly the most influential of the King's officers, and after Alexander's own death Perdiccas was the logical person to assume control of affairs in Babylon. Nevertheless, he had made too many enemies and his ambition made him the object of suspicion and hatred. In 320 BC his invasion of Egypt failed and he was murdered by his own officers.

dynast, Assacenus. He had died only shortly before Alexander's arrival at the city, probably in an earlier attempt to stop the Macedonians *en route*. It was Assacenus's brother, Amminais, who conducted the actual defence, with the help of 9,000 mercenaries, but legend chooses instead to focus on the Queen, who negotiated the surrender of the city and retained her throne

Queen Cleophis of Massaga

'From there he headed for … the realm of Queen Cleophis. She surrendered to Alexander but subsequently regained her throne, which she ransomed by sleeping with him, attaining by sexual favours what she could not by force of arms. The child fathered by the king she named Alexander, and he later rose to sovereignty over the Indians. Because she had thus degraded herself Queen Cleophis was from that time called the "royal whore" by the Indians.'
Justin 12.7.9–11 (J. C. Yardley trans., Clarendon Ancient History series)

Samarkand today. The old city of Maracanda occupied the mound behind the city. It was here that Alexander killed his friend and general Cleitus in a drunken brawl. (TRIP)

by dazzling Alexander with her beauty. Her story must be read with caution, since her name and conduct are reminiscent of the famous Egyptian queen, Cleopatra VII. The first historian to mention her may, indeed, have written in the Augustan age, when Cleopatra herself had gained notoriety.

Some of the Assacenians fled to a seemingly impregnable mountain known to the ancients as Aornus (probably Pir-sar, though some have suggested Mt Ilam). Here, just as he had done in his siege of Arimazes, Alexander overcame the rugged terrain, this time herding many of the terrified natives to their deaths as they attempted to descend the steep embankment overhanging the Indus. By capturing the place, the King could claim to have outdone his mythical ancestor, Hercules, who had been driven off by an earthquake.

The King now crossed into the territory of Ambhi (officially 'Taxiles'), who ruled the region between the Indus and Hydaspes (Jhelum) rivers and gave Alexander a lavish reception in his capital at Taxila (near modern Islamabad). He was at the time hard pressed by his enemies – Abisares to the north (in the Kashmir) and Porus, Rajah of the Paurava, to the west. In exchange for support, he accepted a Macedonian garrison and an overseer, Philip, son of Machatas. But Ambhi remained nominal head of the territory.

Porus meanwhile had urged Abisares to lend aid against Taxiles and the Macedonian invader. Instead, he made (token?) submission to Alexander, content to await the outcome of events. And when Porus went down to defeat, Abisares sent money and elephants, but argued that he could not come in person on account of illness. It is an old trick of rulers who are confronted by those more powerful, and it was attempted later by Montezuma when Cortés approached Tenochtitlán.

Porus himself determined to face the invader and his arch-enemy, Taxiles, at the Hydaspes river, guarding the crossing near modern Haranpur. There would be no repeat of the charge at the Granicus. The Hydaspes was a much greater river, the banks steeper, and the effect of the elephants stationed upon them decisive. It was necessary to make the crossing elsewhere, and to do so unopposed.

At first, Alexander resorted to a series of feints – or, more precisely, to a repetition of the same feint, as he marched a detachment

The battle between Alexander and Porus. In the battle at the Hydaspes river, Alexander and Porus did not actually meet each other in combat, although the Macedonian King met the Indian rajah after he had suffered numerous wounds. (Ann Ronan Picture Library)

A digression on boat-bridges

The historian Arrian can find no evidence for how Alexander bridged the Indus, but he comments: 'The quickest way of bridging I know is the Roman use of boats ... Their boats are at a signal allowed to float downstream, yet not bows on, but as if backing. The stream naturally carries them down, but a rowing skiff holds them up till it manoeuvres them into the appointed place and at that point wicker crates of pyramid shape full of unhewn stones are let down from the bows of each ship to hold it against the stream. No sooner has one ship thus been made fast than another, just at the right interval to carry the superstructure safely, is anchored upstream and from both boats timbers are accurately and smartly laid and planks crosswise to bind them together. The work goes on in this way for all the boats needed ... On either side of the bridge gangways are laid and fastened down, so that the passage may be safer for horses and baggage animals, and also to bind the bridge together.' Arrian 5.7.3–5 (P. A. Brunt trans., Loeb Classical Library)

of the army to a position upstream and returned again to the main camp, while Porus's forces on the opposite bank mirrored his actions. Soon he positioned a contingent under Meleager several miles to the north; but Porus too had taken precautions against encirclement by instructing his brother, Spitaces, to keep watch upstream.

Craterus, with the heavy infantry, was left to face the main Indian army at the original crossing-point, and Alexander eventually, under the cover of night, heavy rain and thunder, marched some 17½ miles (28km) upriver (near modern Jalalpur) and made a crossing just where the heavily wooded island of Admana sits in a bend of the river. Here he reached the opposite side before Spitaces was able to challenge him. Indeed, the island had proved to be such an effective screen that Alexander himself landed his men there, mistaking it for the opposite bank of the Hydaspes. Consequently, Porus had to abandon his original position and turn to meet the encircling force, while Craterus began to lead the rest of the army across the river.

The engagement that followed was decided primarily by the cavalry, even though the heavy rains had reduced the battlefield to mud and swamp. The elephants, interspersed between units of infantry, proved once again to be a greater liability than advantage to Porus's army. In the end, the Macedonians were victorious. Porus had fought gallantly and received many wounds.

The valiant enemy earned Alexander's respect, and was allowed to retain his kingdom. It had not always been so: Alexander had often been less than generous in his treatment of stubborn adversaries. (Witness the case of Batis of Gaza, whom Alexander dragged behind his chariot in imitation of Achilles' treatment of Hector.) The greater challenge lay, however, in the attempt to bring about lasting peace between the Indian rivals. Curtius claims that an alliance between Taxiles and Poros was sealed by marriage, the common currency in such transactions. But the arrangement was never entirely satisfactory. Though Taxiles was perhaps more to be trusted than Poros, Alexander needed the latter for his upcoming campaigns in the Punjab.

Porus and Alexander

Alexander was the first to speak. 'What,' he said, 'do you wish that I should do with you?'

'Treat me as a king ought,' Porus is said to have replied.

'For my part,' said Alexander, pleased by the answer, 'your request shall be granted. But is there not something you would wish for yourself? Ask it.'

'Everything,' said Porus, 'is contained in this one request.'

Arrian 5.19 (A. de Sélincourt trans., Penguin)

The limits of conquest

Victorious over the army of Porus, the Macedonians had moved eastward across the Punjab, coming inevitably to the Hyphasis (Beas) river. Beyond this lay the populous and little-known subcontinent of India proper. (It should be noted that Alexander never crossed the boundaries of what is modern India.) Here it was that the war-weary Macedonians, battered by the elements, their uniforms literally rotting off their bodies, called a halt. Alexander yearned for further adventure and conquest, this time in the valley of the Ganges. The soldiers, however, conducted a strike (*secessio*) and even the bravest and most loyal of Alexander's officers spoke on their behalf. The King sulked in his tent, but the men remained obdurate. There was nothing to do but turn back.

This is the traditionally accepted view of the end of Alexander's eastward march. But did it really happen in this way? Why, one asks, would an experienced and shrewd military leader like Alexander allow reports of extraordinary dangers, or numerous enemies and exotic places, to come to the attention of soldiers who, as he knew perfectly well, were demoralised and tired? The skilful leader tells his troops what he wants them to know, which is virtually always less than the whole truth. If the fantastic report of India beyond the Hyphasis was 'leaked' to the Macedonian soldiery, it was because he wanted them to hear it. If it was merely a case of rumour taking hold, then Alexander handled the matter badly. In his speech to the men, in which he claims to be debunking the rumours, he nevertheless reports them in vivid detail; then he changes his tack and argues that, even if the stories are true, there is no need to be concerned.

This was not the time for the truth, much less for exaggeration. It was a face-saving gesture by a king who was just as tired as his men, for whom it would have been unheroic to decline further challenges. Instead the responsibility for ending this glorious march into the unknown was placed squarely on the shoulders of the common soldier. His

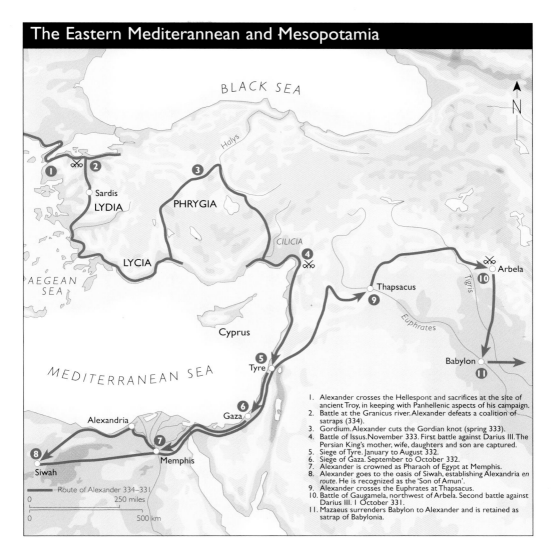

The Eastern Mediterannean and Mesopotamia

BLACK SEA

Halys

PHRYGIA

LYDIA

Sardis

LYCIA

AEGEAN SEA

CILICIA

Thapsacus

Cyprus

Euphrates

Tigris

Arbela

Babylon

MEDITERRANEAN SEA

Tyre

Gaza

Alexandria

Memphis

Siwah

1. Alexander crosses the Hellespont and sacrifices at the site of ancient Troy, in keeping with Panhellenic aspects of his campaign.
2. Battle at the Granicus river. Alexander defeats a coalition of satraps (334).
3. Gordium. Alexander cuts the Gordian knot (spring 333).
4. Battle of Issus. November 333. First battle against Darius III. The Persian King's mother, wife, daughters and son are captured.
5. Siege of Tyre. January to August 332.
6. Siege of Gaza. September to October 332.
7. Alexander is crowned as Pharaoh of Egypt at Memphis.
8. Alexander goes to the oasis of Siwah, establishing Alexandria *en route*. He is recognized as the 'Son of Amun'.
9. Alexander crosses the Euphrates at Thapsacus.
10. Battle of Gaugamela, northwest of Arbela. Second battle against Darius III. 1 October 331.
11. Mazaeus surrenders Babylon to Alexander and is retained as satrap of Babylonia.

Route of Alexander 334–331
0   250 miles
0   500 km

stubbornness alone robbed Alexander of further glory. This was the propaganda line, and this is how it has come down to us. Further evidence of Alexander's duplicity can be found in the fact that he ordered the men to build a camp of abnormal size, containing artefacts that were larger than life, in order to cheat posterity into thinking that the expeditionary force had been superhuman.

Return to the west

The army was returning to the west – but not directly. It was not necessary to cross the Hyphasis in the quest for ocean. Alexander knew full well that the Indus river system would lead him there, and he had transported boats in sections for the very purpose of following the river to its mouth. On the way, he subdued warlike tribes, troublesome neighbours for his new vassal, Porus. Among these were the Mallians, in whose town Alexander would have a close brush with death.

Disregarding his own safety and forgetting that the Macedonians' enthusiasm for war was no longer what it had been, Alexander was the first to scale the city walls and jump inside. Only a few bodyguards accompanied

Deception at the limits of Alexander's march
'Two days were devoted to his anger
and on the third Alexander emerged
from his tent to issue instructions for
twelve altars of square-cut stone to be
erected to commemorate his expedition.
He further ordered the camp
fortifications to be extended, and
couches on a larger scale than their size
required to be left behind, his intention
being to make everything appear greater
than it was, for he was preparing to
leave to posterity a fraudulent wonder.'
Quintus Curtius Rufus, *The History of
Alexander* 9.3.19 (J. C. Yardley
trans., Penguin)

him. When the troops saw that their King
was trapped, they scrambled up the ladders,
overloading and breaking them. Inside the
walls, the King was showered with arrows:
one protector at least perished in his
defence, while others were as gravely
wounded as Alexander himself. Once the
troops poured over the battlements, the
slaughter began, but their King had an arrow
lodged deep in his chest, just below the ribs.

Miraculously, Alexander survived, though
for a good portion of the journey downriver
he was all but incapacitated. By the time he
reached the Indus delta, he had recovered,
and from here he sailed out into the Indian
Ocean and conducted sacrifices at the limits
of his empire, just as he had done at the
Hellespont in 334.

Nevertheless, the return of the Macedonian
army can hardly be depicted as triumphant.
One portion sailed along the coast, eventually
passing through the Straits of Hormuz and
entering the Persian Gulf: it was a journey
fraught with hardship, deprivation and
danger. Another, led by Alexander himself,
struggled through the Gedrosian desert,
suffering staggering losses on account of the
elements and the malfeasance of the
neighbouring satraps. Although Alexander

stood up to the hardships as well as any man,
and indeed it was on this march that he
displayed some of his most noble qualities,
the march was an unmitigated disaster. Those
modern writers who delight in blackening his
reputation have gone so far as to suggest that
Alexander exposed his men to the perils of
the Gedrosian wasteland in order to pay them
back for their refusal to proceed beyond
the Hyphasis.

When Alexander returned to the west, he
celebrated mixed marriages on a grand scale
at Susa (324 BC). Alexander himself married
Stateira, daughter of Darius III, and Parysatis,
whose father, Artaxerxes III, had ruled
shortly before. Another of Darius's daughters,
Drypetis, married Hephaestion, and nearly a
hundred other noble Persian women were
given as brides to Macedonian officers. Even
larger numbers of common soldiers took
barbarian wives, but this was probably just a
way of legitimising common-law unions that
had existed for some time. The marriages
appear to have been unpopular with the
aristocracy, and after Alexander's death
most appear to have repudiated their
Persian wives.

On the other hand, it was the integration
of large numbers of barbarian troops into the
Macedonian army that gave offence to the
soldiery. Not long afterwards, at Opis on the
Tigris, the army mutinied, complaining that

Alexander wearing the elephant headdress. (AKG Berlin)

Craterus, Alexander's most trusted commander

Craterus began the expedition as a taxiarch, a commander of *pezhetairoi*. He served as the second-in-command on the left wing, under the direct authority of Parmenion, whom he was being groomed to replace. Craterus was an officer of unswerving loyalty to the King. The saying went that Hephaestion was 'fond of Alexander' (*philalexandros*) but Craterus was 'fond of the king' (*philobasileus*). Not surprisingly, these two young commanders would become rivals and their disagreements would lead to an open confrontation that threatened to involve their respective units. But Craterus's promotion was based on ability, whereas in Hephaestion's case there was at least a suspicion of nepotism – even if no one said so publicly.

As the campaign progressed, Craterus exercised more frequent independent commands. When Alexander returned through the Gedrosian desert, Craterus led the slower troops and the invalids through the Bolan Pass towards modern Kandahar. *En route* he apprehended rebels, whom he brought to the King for execution. In 324 he was sent to replace Antipater as viceroy of Macedon. This order would be pre-empted by Alexander's death and the outbreak of the Lamian War. In 321/320 Craterus returned to Asia and did battle with Eumenes near the Hellespont. He was, however, thrown from his horse and trampled beneath its hoofs. It was an ignominious end for one of Alexander's greatest generals.

they were being supplanted by foreigners. These complaints Alexander countered with soothing words, but the ringleaders of the mutiny were seized, chained and thrown into the Tigris. Ten thousand veterans, many of them injured, were sent back to Macedonia under the command of Craterus, who was himself in poor health. Some of them would indeed reach their homeland, but only to fight some more. Others would not advance beyond Cilicia before becoming embroiled in the wars of the Successors.

Battle of the Hydaspes

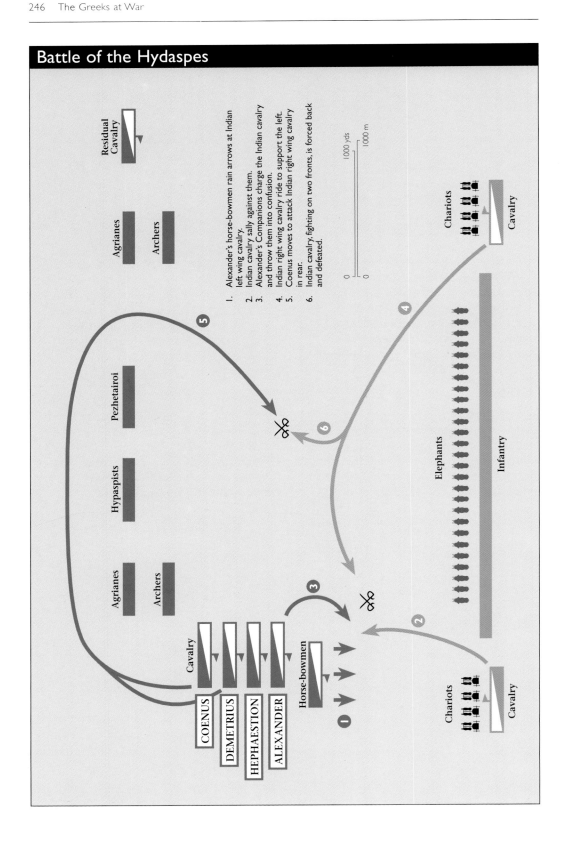

1. Alexander's horse-bowmen rain arrows at Indian left wing cavalry.
2. Indian cavalry sally against them.
3. Alexander's Companions charge the Indian cavalry and throw them into confusion.
4. Indian right wing cavalry ride to support the left.
5. Coenus moves to attack Indian right wing cavalry in rear.
6. Indian cavalry, fighting on two fronts, is forced back and defeated.

Alexander's campaigns

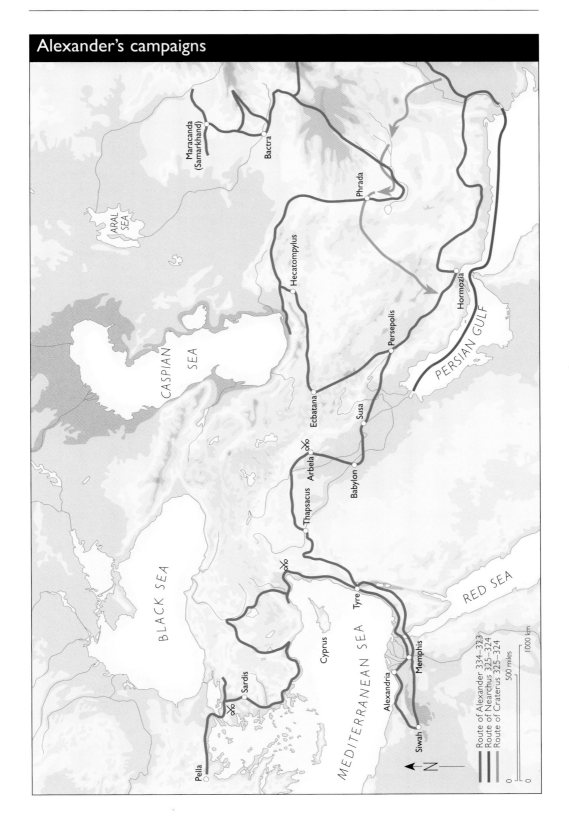

Route of Alexander 334–323
Route of Nearchus 325–324
Route of Craterus 325–324

Two generals and a satrap

Parmenion and Philotas

When Alexander ascended the Macedonian throne, two powerful generals of Philip II exercised considerable influence at the court and in the army. Only one, Antipater, was in Macedonia at the time. The other, Parmenion, had been sent by Philip to command the advance force in Asia Minor. He was an experienced and well-loved leader of men. In the year of Alexander's birth, 356 BC, Parmenion had defeated the Illyrian ruler Grabus, while Philip himself was besieging Potidaea. Twenty years later, he was the senior officer in the army and his sons, Philotas and Nicanor, commanded the Companion Cavalry and the hypaspists respectively. These were amongst the finest troops in the Macedonian army.

Parmenion's contributions were, however, a source of embarrassment to the young king, who believed that the success of others detracted somehow from his own glory. And he was particularly annoyed when he learned that in Egypt Parmenion's son, Philotas, was boasting that all the King's successes were due to his father's generalship.

The information had come to Alexander in an unusual way. Amongst the spoils taken at Damascus was a woman named Antigone. This woman was of Macedonian origin, from the town of Pydna, but had been captured by the Persian admiral Autophradates while travelling by sea to celebrate the mysteries of Samothrace. (It was at this festival, many years earlier, that Philip had met the young Olympias, the future mother of Alexander.) Antigone had thus become the mistress or concubine of a Persian notable and had been deposited at Damascus before the battle of Issus.

When Parmenion captured the city and the spoils were divided, Antigone became Philotas's mistress. What he told her, by way of bragging about his own family's achievements or disparaging those of the King, she repeated to others, until the talk was reported to Craterus, a faithful friend and officer of Alexander. Craterus disliked Philotas personally – and in this he was not alone, for Philotas had many enemies who were at the same time close friends of the King. Craterus therefore gathered incriminating evidence from Antigone and brought this to Alexander's attention. But, at that time, with the outcome of the war against Darius still undecided, the King chose to overlook the indiscretion.

Things changed, however, when Alexander found himself master of the Persian capitals. Parmenion had suddenly become expendable, and he was left at Ecbatana when Alexander pushed on in pursuit of Darius and Bessus. At first, it was to be a temporary measure, but Darius's murder altered the complexion of the campaign. The Thessalian cavalry, which had served on Parmenion's wing, was now dismissed and sent back to Europe. And Craterus, who had been groomed as Parmenion's replacement – at both Issus and Gaugamela he was the old general's second-in-command – had proved himself more than capable; furthermore, he was younger, more energetic and, what was most important, unswervingly loyal to the King. These circumstances, and the fact that Parmenion's elimination required justification, gave rise to stories that Parmenion's advice was timid or unsound and that his performance at Gaugamela was substandard.

Separated from his influential father, Philotas became more vulnerable to the intrigues of his enemies. And this vulnerability was increased when, during the march through Aria, Philotas's brother

The 'official' historian criticises Parmenion
'There is general criticism of a
lacklustre and apathetic performance on
Parmenion's part in that battle, either
because age was by now to some extent
sapping his courage or because, as
Callisthenes has it, he was embittered
and envious of the officious and
self-important way in which Alexander
was wielding his authority. In any case,
Alexander was annoyed by Parmenion's
call for help, but did not tell his men the
truth about it. Instead, he gave the
signal to fall back on the ground that he
was calling a halt to the slaughter and
that night was coming on.'
Plutarch, *Alexander* 38.11 (J. C.
Yardley trans.)

Nicanor died of illness. Indeed, not only was
the family itself weakened, but also many
who had served with Parmenion were no
longer with the army. Hence, when Philotas
was implicated in a conspiracy at Phrada
(modern Farah) in Afghanistan in late 330,
there were few to defend or protect him.

The crime itself was one of negligence rather
than overt treason. A young Macedonian – he
is described as one of the *hetairoi*, and hence
not insignificant – by the name of Dimnus had
divulged the details of a conspiracy to which
he was a party (though he was clearly not its
instigator), to his lover, Nicomachus. The latter,
fearing for his life if the conspiracy should fail
and he be implicated, told everything he knew
to his brother, Cebalinus, who promptly went
to report the matter to Alexander.

Unable to gain access to the King,
Cebalinus informed Philotas and urged him
to deal with the matter. But on the following
day, when he approached Philotas again,
Cebalinus discovered that the latter had not
spoken to the King concerning the
conspiracy because, as he claimed, it had not
seemed to him a matter of great importance.
Cebalinus therefore devised other means of
revealing the plot, mentioning also Philotas's
suspicious behaviour.

Alexander thus called a meeting of his
advisers – excluding Philotas, who might
otherwise have been summoned – and asked
for their candid opinions. These were freely
given and unanimous: Philotas would not
have suppressed the information unless he
were either party to the plot or at least
favoured it. Such negligence could not be
excused when it involved the life and safety
of the King. And so Atarrhias with a
detachment of hypaspists – in effect, these
were the Macedonian military police – was
sent to arrest Philotas.

Confronted with the facts, Philotas
confessed that he had indeed learned of the
conspiracy, but that he had not taken it
seriously. If this was the truth – we shall
never know what went through Philotas's
mind – he may have reflected on an earlier
episode, when his father had sent an urgent
letter to Alexander, alleging that Philip of
Acarnania, the King's personal physician, had
been bribed to poison him in Cilicia. In the
event, the report proved false and
Parmenion's reputation was tarnished.

On the other hand, in the shadowy world
of the Macedonian court, where kings had
often been murdered for merely slighting a
man's honour, anything was possible and
everything potentially dangerous. Philotas's
trustworthiness was called into question: had
he not been guilty of disloyal talk in the past?
As a young man, he had been raised at the
court of Philip as a companion of Amyntas,
son of Perdiccas, whom Alexander had
executed on suspicion of aspiring to regain
his throne. Furthermore, his sister had been
married briefly to the King's bitter enemy
Attalus.

When questioned under torture, Philotas
admitted also that another adherent of
Attalus, a certain squadron commander
(*ilarches*) named Hegelochus had suggested
to Parmenion and his sons that they murder
the King; but the plan was rejected as too
dangerous in the circumstances of 331. At any
rate, it seems that the topic of Alexander's
removal from power had certainly come up.

The younger commanders urged the King
not to forgive Philotas a second time, for he

Alexander, as portrayed on the Alexander Sarcophagus, which shows his victory at Issus. (AKG Berlin)

would continue to be a danger to him. Their professed concern for Alexander's safety masked, only slightly, their hatred for Philotas and their desire for military advancement; this could best be achieved by eliminating him and members of his faction. For Alexander, although he concurred with their opinion, it was nevertheless a difficult decision. How would Parmenion react to his son's execution? He remained in Ecbatana, astride the lines of communication and at the head of a substantial army. If Philotas were to be executed for treason, then the charge must be extended to include his father. The army, which tried Philotas and found him guilty, accepted also the guilt of his father. The Macedonians were realists and recognised that expediency must triumph over legal niceties.

Philotas was publicly executed; his father in Ecbatana was presented with a letter outlining the charges against him and struck down as he read them.

Mazaeus, servant of three kings

Mazaeus is known from both historical sources and coin legends to have been satrap of Cilicia, and later of Syria and Mesopotamia (Abarnahara, 'the land beyond the river') in the time of King Artaxerxes III. Under Darius III he had doubtless fought at Issus, although there is no mention of him. In 331, he had been ordered to prevent Alexander's crossing of the Euphrates at Thapsacus, but had insufficient numbers to do more than harass the bridge-builders. Upon Alexander's arrival, Mazaeus withdrew and rejoined Darius, who was now following the course of the Tigris northward.

At Gaugamela Mazaeus commanded the Persian cavalry on the right wing and led a charge of dense squadrons together with the scythe-chariots, inflicting heavy casualties. He then sent a squadron of Scythian horsemen to capture the Macedonian camp, while he himself exerted pressure on Parmenion and the Thessalian cavalry on the Macedonian left. Parmenion, in turn, was forced to send riders to recall Alexander, who

A missed opportunity

'The [Macedonian] army could have been annihilated if anyone had had the courage to seize victory at this juncture, but the King's unceasing good fortune kept the enemy at bay ... If Mazaeus had attacked the Macedonians as they crossed [the Tigris], he would no doubt have defeated them while they were in disorder, but he began to ride towards them only when they were on the bank and already under arms. He had sent only 1,000 cavalry ahead, and so Alexander, discovering and then scorning their small numbers, ordered Ariston, the commander of the Paeonian cavalry, to charge them at full gallop.' Quintus Curtius Rufus, *The History of Alexander* 4.9.22–24

had gone off in pursuit of Darius. Eventually Mazaeus was overcome by the tenacity of the Thessalians and the demoralising news of Darius's flight.

It is highly likely that the great battle-scene on the so-called Alexander Sarcophagus from Sidon – now in the Istanbul Museum – depicts Mazaeus's valour. If this is so, then, contrary to the accepted modern scholarly view, the sarcophagus itself would have been commissioned for the former satrap of Syria (and resident of Sidon) rather than the undistinguished Abdalonymus, whom Hephaestion had elevated to the kingship in 332.

Mazaeus fled from the battlefield to Babylon, which he promptly surrendered to the Macedonians. In return he was installed as its satrap, the first Persian to be so honoured by Alexander. (Mithrenes had been in Alexander's entourage since 334, but his appointment as satrap of Armenia did not occur until 330.) The Alexander Sarcophagus also depicts a notable Persian engaged in a lion hunt together with Alexander and other Macedonians – one of the Macedonian riders may be Hephaestion. If this depicts a historical event, then it could not have occurred before late 331, and the most likely Persian with whom Alexander hunted is once again Mazaeus.

When Alexander pursued Darius in his final days, Mazaeus's son, Brochubelus or Antibelus, defected to him. Mazaeus himself remained in office and served his new master loyally until his death in late 328, whereupon he was replaced by another barbarian: Arrian calls the successor 'Stamenes' and Quintus Curtius Rufus writes, 'Ditamenes', but neither form is convincing.

Rome, Carthage and India

Emergence of Rome

The fourth century BC, which is treated by Greek historians as a period of decline after the so-called 'Golden Age of Athens', was for the Roman world a time of rebirth. The city which, according to its historical traditions, was founded in 753 BC – that is, 244 years before the establishment of the Republic in 509 – had experienced a period of growth in the fifth century that was arrested, indeed shattered, by the irruption of Gauls in 390 or 386. Despite face-saving propaganda that saw Camillus snatch victory from the grasp of the Gauls after they had defeated the Romans at the river Allia, the truth is that the Romans paid the marauders in order to be rid of them. The conquest of the Italian peninsula had to be started anew, if indeed much of it had been subject to Rome before the Gallic sack.

At about the same time as Alexander crossed into Asia, his uncle and brother-in-law, Alexander I of Epirus, crossed the Adriatic in order to champion the cause of the Greeks in southern Italy, who were being hard pressed by the Lucanians and Bruttians. Roman historians later commented on the Epirote King's failure, noting that 'whereas Alexander the Great had been fighting *women* in Asia, the other Alexander had encountered *men*'. This unflattering remark was typical of Roman attitudes towards Alexander the Great, for it was a popular topic of debate whether Alexander would have been able to conquer the Romans.

Later Hellenistic kings, like Philip V, Antiochus III and Perseus, proved to be unworthy of Alexander's reputation, and the Romans themselves, or at least those who were honest with themselves, knew that these were pale reflections of a bygone era.

Indeed, Pyrrhus, a second cousin of the conqueror, was destined to give the Romans a fright some 43 years after Alexander's death. And his was but a small army, with limited goals.

Alexander of Epirus, however, suffered the fate of all champions summoned by the Italian Greeks: rather than joining him in the struggle against their enemies, they were content to sit back and let him do the fighting for them. Ultimately, he was killed – the victim of a prophesied fate that he had gone to Italy to avoid. The oracle of Dodona had foretold that he would die by the Acheron river. Since there was a river of this name in Epirus, Alexander decided to move on to Italy, only to discover as he was struck down in an Italian stream that it too was known as the Acheron.

Such at least is the legend and the bitter lesson that those who seek to avert fortune must learn. But the important fact is that, as Alexander the Great was subduing the east, his namesake was engaged in a struggle between the inhabitants of the western peninsula who had not yet fallen under the power of Rome. But this was soon to come. In the years that followed, the Romans defeated the Samnites in three bitter wars, and by 265, seven years after the death of Pyrrhus, they were confronting the Carthaginians across the straits of Messina. When Alexander the Great died in Babylon, the First Punic War was only two generations in the future (see *The Punic Wars* in this series).

Carthage

Carthage, the North African city near modern Tunis, was founded according to tradition in 814/813 by settlers from Tyre: the name Kart-Hadasht is Phoenician for 'New Town'.

Although archaeological evidence has yet to confirm the traditional date, it certainly existed by the late eighth century and soon developed as the most important Phoenician settlement in the western Mediterranean. Its proximity to Sicily, where numerous Phoenician trading posts (*emporia*) had been established, made it a natural protector of the Punic peoples against the Greeks of the island.

By Alexander's time, Carthaginian power had been restricted to western Sicily, but it was to become a serious threat to the city of Syracuse by the last decade of the fourth century. Not much later Carthage became embroiled in a struggle with Rome, as a result of an appeal to both parties by a group of lawless mercenaries, the Mamartines (or 'Sons of Mars'), who had taken over Messana, across from the toe of Italy.

That incident led to the First Punic War (264–241), which forced the Romans to develop a real navy for the first time in their history – along with the effective but ephemeral device known as the *corvus* or

The fate of Alexander of Epirus

'Alexander, king of Epirus, had been invited into Italy when the people of Tarentum petitioned his aid against the Bruttii. He had embarked on the expedition enthusiastically, as though a partition of the world had been made, the East being allotted to Alexander, son of his sister Olympias, and the West to himself, and believing he would have no less scope to prove himself in Italy, Africa and Sicily than Alexander was going to have in Asia and Persia. There was a further consideration. Just as the Delphic Oracle had forewarned Alexander the Great of a plot against him in Macedonia, so an oracular response from Jupiter at Dodona had warned this Alexander against the city of Pandosia and the Acherusian River; and since both were in Epirus – and he was unaware that identically-named places existed in Italy – he had been all the more eager to opt for a campaign abroad, in order to avoid the perils of destiny … He commenced hostilities with both the Bruttii and the Lucanians, capturing many of their cities, and he concluded treaties and alliances with the Metapontines, the Poediculi and the Romans. The Bruttii and the Lucanians, however, gathered auxiliary forces from their neighbours and resumed their war with increased fervour. During this campaign the king was killed in the vicinity of Pandosia and the River Acheron. He did not discover the name of the fateful region until he fell, and only when he was dying did he realize that the death which had led him to flee his native land had not threatened him there after all. The people of Thurii ransomed and buried his body at public expense.' Justin 12.2.1–5, 12–15 (J.C. Yardley trans., Clarendon Ancient History series)

Bronze head of Alexander from the third century BC. (Madrid, Prado)

Persian illustration of Alexander talking to wise men. (Ann
Ronan Picture Library)

Dionysus on a leopard. Mosaic from Pella, 4th century BC. When Alexander reached India he began to emulate Dionysus as well as Heracles, the paternal ancestor he had venerated since the beginning of his reign. (Archaeological Museum of Thessaloniki)

korax, a beaked grappling device attached to a boarding platform. It also led them to acquire their first provinces outside Italy. But it was the first of a series of life-and-death struggles between the two dominant states of

Alexander learns of the Nanda rulers
'Porus … added that their ruler was not merely a commoner but a man from the lowest class. His father had been a barber whose regular employment barely kept starvation at bay, but by his good looks he had won the heart of the queen. By her he had been brought into a comparatively close friendship with the king of the time, whom he then treacherously murdered, seizing the throne ostensibly as protector of the king's children. He then killed the children and sired this present ruler, who had earned the hatred and contempt of the people by behaviour more in keeping with his father's station in life than his own.'
Curtius 9.2.6–7 (J. C. Yardley trans., Penguin)

the west. This would see the emergence of a general who was, in many ways, the equal of Alexander: Hannibal, the avowed 'enemy of Rome'. But when Alexander was conquering the east, the bitter Punic Wars and the brilliance of Hannibal and Scipio were still in the unforeseen future.

India and the Mauryan dynasty

In the east, meanwhile, in the valley of the Ganges, the Nanda dynasty was nearing its end. Rumour held that the ruling king, whom the Greeks called Xandrames, was the son of a lowly barber who had murdered his sovereign and married the Queen. Plutarch, in his *Life of Alexander*, comments that when the Macedonians reached the Punjab they were seen by a young man named Sandracottus, who was destined to be the founder of the Mauryan dynasty and was known to the Indians as Chandragupta. He would later force Alexander's successor in the east, Seleucus Nicator, to cede the satrapies adjacent to the Indus in return for 500 elephants. But in the mid-320s, much of India was ripe for the picking.

The Galatians

Far to the north and the west of Greece, another group, the Celts or Gauls, were beginning a steady migration eastward that would lead them down the Balkan river valleys towards Macedonia. In the years that followed 280, they would throw Macedonia and northern Greece into turmoil. One column would advance as far as Delphi, only to be driven off (seemingly with the aid of Apollo) by the Aetolians, who were hailed as saviours of Greece. According to their own tradition, they were beaten by their own drunkenness and lack of discipline. Eventually, they were transported across the Bosporus and came to settle in north-central Anatolia in the region that bears their name, Galatia. For the next century they would be the scourge of Asia Minor.

A historian, athletes and courtesans

Callisthenes the historian

Callisthenes of Olynthus was, according to some accounts, the nephew of the philosopher Aristotle, and although he is often depicted as a philosopher himself, he was little more than an amateur. He joined Alexander's expedition as the official historian and, if – as appears to be the case – he sent his history back to European Greece in instalments, he was at the same time historian, propagandist and war correspondent.

His travels with Alexander took him to exotic places and he was able to speculate on natural phenomena as well as describe the course of the war, for he appears to have theorised about the source of the Nile. It was his literary training that led him to depict Alexander as a latter-day Achilles, and it would not be wrong to class him with the numerous flatterers who swelled the King's ego and entourage. But, although he likened the receding sea near Mt Climax in Pamphylia to a courtier doing obeisance (*proskynesis*) to the Great King, he nevertheless resisted Alexander's attempt to introduce the Persian court protocol in 328/327. For this reason, he fell out with the King and when, some time later, a conspiracy was uncovered involving the royal pages, Callisthenes was easily implicated.

It was one of his functions at the court to tutor the young men of the Macedonian aristocracy – just as in the 340s Aristotle had tutored Alexander and several of his coeval friends (*syntrophoi*) at Mieza. Abrupt and austere in manner, Callisthenes had made few friends, though some like Lysimachus the Bodyguard may have enjoyed exchanging philosophical ideas with him. These two 'serious types' may have 'bonded', as modern jargon would have it, for Lysimachus's personality can hardly be termed effervescent.

Convicted of complicity in the conspiracy of the pages, Callisthenes was apparently incarcerated and died some months later of obesity and a disease of lice. The Peripatetic philosophers, the followers of Aristotle, never forgave Alexander.

Callisthenes defies Alexander
Alexander sent around a loving cup of gold, first to those with whom he had made an agreement about obeisance (*proskynesis*); the first who drank from it rose, did obeisance, and received a kiss from Alexander, and this went round all in turn. But when the pledge came to Callisthenes, he rose, drank from the cup, went up to Alexander and made to kiss him without having done obeisance. At that moment Alexander was talking to Hephaestion and therefore was not attending to see whether the ceremony of obeisance was carried out ... But as Callisthenes approached to kiss Alexander, Demetrius, son of Pythonax, one of the Companions, remarked that he was coming without having done obeisance. Alexander did not permit Callisthenes to kiss him; and Callisthenes remarked: 'I shall go away short one kiss.'
Arrian 4.12.4–5 (P. A. Brunt trans., Loeb Classical Library, slightly modified)

Flatterers and professional athletes

The entourage of the Macedonian King included a wide variety of non-combatants. Actors and musicians, poets and dancers, jugglers and ball-players can all be found in Alexander's camp, though many of them made only brief stops with the army as they toured the Greek cities of the Near East. Actors were particularly useful: because they travelled and because they spoke so eloquently, they were often used as envoys to the court of some king or dynast; sometimes they merely brought news of events in another part of the empire. Thus Alexander received news of the defection of his treasurer Harpalus from Cissus and Ephialtes, two comic actors who are attested as winners in dramatic competitions in Athens.

Some actors were clearly present at the Hydaspes river, for it was there that the troops were entertained with a production of the comic play *Agen*, written by a certain Python – possibly of Sicilian origin. Another actor, Thersippus, carried Alexander's letter to Darius, rejecting the King's offer to ransom the members of his family, whom Alexander had captured at Issus. And, at the drinking party in Maracanda (Samarkand) there were bards who sang of a Macedonian battle in the region. We are not told what it was they sang about, except that it was a Macedonian defeat. One scholar has plausibly suggested that they had produced a mock heroic epic that recounted the valour of one of their own, the harpist Aristonicus, who fought valiantly and died when barbarian horsemen attacked a small contingent of Macedonians, including pages and non-combatants.

Athletes are also attested in the camp. A young man named Serapion appears to have served no useful purpose other than to play ball with the King. But most famous of the athletes was an Athenian boxer, Dioxippus, who is named also as one of the King's flatterers. The confrontation in India between a Macedonian soldier, Corrhagus, and the Greek athlete reveals not only the ethnic tension that existed in the army between Greeks and Macedonians, but also the typical disdain of the veteran soldier for the professional athlete. Both men had imbibed excessively and, after they had exchanged insults, the Macedonian challenged the Athenian to a duel. This was fought on the

A Greek boxer in Alexander's entourage: a warrior's opinion of a professional athlete

'One person present at the banquet was the Athenian Dioxippus, a former boxer whose superlative strength had rendered him well known and well liked by Alexander. Jealous and spiteful men would make cutting remarks about him, partly in jest, partly in earnest, saying that they had along with them a useless, bloated animal and that, while they went into battle, he was dripping with oil and preparing his belly for a banquet. Now at this feast the Macedonian Horratas, who was already drunk, began to make the same type of insulting comment to Dioxippus and to challenge him, if he were a man, to fight a duel with him with swords the next day. Only then, said Horratas, would Alexander be able to decide whether he was reckless or Dioxippus a coward.'
Q. Curtius Rufus, *The History of Alexander* 9.7.16–17 (J. C Yardley trans., Penguin)

following day, with the athlete getting the better of the soldier. But Dioxippus's success did not endear him to the King, and soon afterwards he was framed by certain courtiers, who planted a drinking cup in his quarters and claimed that he had stolen it from one of the King's parties. Dishonoured by this trick, Dioxippus committed suicide, the victim of two forms of prejudice.

Courtesans: Thaïs, Pythionice and Glycera

The presence of prostitutes has been a feature of armies since the earliest time. Even the Crusader armies, motivated by the most righteous intentions, had no shortage of them. Alexander himself certainly had the occasional liaison with such women: Pancaste had been the mistress of Alexander before he gave her to the painter Apelles, who had fallen in love with her.

Whether the Athenian courtesan Thaïs was originally Alexander's mistress before she took up with Ptolemy is unclear. The popular account of Alexander (the so-called Vulgate) portrays her as the one who, when revelling with the King in Persepolis, induced him to put the torch to the royal palace. But she is not some fictitious character, invented to discredit the King. At some point she became the mistress of Ptolemy and bore him three children – Lagus, Leontiscus and Eirene – the first named after Ptolemy's father, the last destined to become the bride of Eunostus, the King of Soli on Cyprus.

Most notorious, however, were the Athenian courtesans Pythionice and Glycera. They were in succession the mistresses of the treasurer Harpalus, who grieved excessively at the death of the former, and who allegedly built monuments for her, in Babylon and Athens, which surpassed those of great politicians and generals. The latter, Glycera, was treated by Harpalus as if she were a queen. He erected statues of himself and Glycera in Syria, and according to a hostile tradition made the people perform *proskynesis* in front of her.

Theopompus denounces Harpalus to Alexander

'Theopompus says, in his treatise *On the Chian Letter*, that after the death of Pythionice Harpalus summoned Glycera from Athens; on her arrival she took up her residence in the palace at Tarsus and had obeisance done to her by the populace, being hailed as queen; further, all persons were forbidden to honour Harpalus with a crown unless they also gave a crown to Glycera. In Rhossus they even went so far as to set up an image of her in bronze beside his own. The like is recorded by Cleitarchus in his *History of Alexander*.'

Athenaeus 13.586c (C. B. Gulick trans., Loeb Classical Library)

The death of Alexander

The war against the barbarians of the east had, in fact, several different endings. The Panhellenic crusade, which was the pretext for going to war in the first place and the justification for the recruitment of allied Greek troops, came to an end in 330 BC, with the symbolic destruction of Persepolis and, later in Hyrcania, with the death of Darius. Those allied soldiers who wished to return home were dismissed from Hecatompylus. But the war itself was not yet finished. First, there was the matter of Bessus, who had usurped the throne: he wore the tiara upright, in the style of the Great King, and called himself Artaxerxes V. Secondly, there was the matter of annexing the remainder of the Persian Empire, which required Alexander to campaign as far north as the Syr-Darya (the Iaxartes river) and as far east as the Indus. And, when all this had been done, there was the task of consolidating his conquests.

But one thing had the effect of bringing Alexander's wars to an abrupt and permanent end: his premature death in Babylon. Those stories about seers warning him to avoid Babylon and omens of others occupying his throne are all inventions after the fact. Even the cause of his death was debated in ancient times and continues to be today. Was it typhoid, cholera or malaria? A good case has recently been made for the last one. Did he die of poison, the victim of a conspiracy by a number of his generals? This too gains support from the occasional modern historian, though the story of his murder was clearly a fabrication of the propaganda wars of his successors. Or was he the victim of depression and alcoholism? This is the most difficult to prove, since we cannot psychoanalyse him or determine to what extent his drinking affected his health. The Macedonians were notoriously heavy drinkers, by ancient standards at least, and there are tales of drinking contests in which the winner does not live long enough to enjoy the prize. In fact, the stories of alcoholism are suspect as well: they were invented, or at least embellished, by writers like Ephippus of Olynthus with the aim of discrediting the King.

This is what we do know. After sailing on the marshes of the Euphrates waterway near Babylon, a region where malaria was endemic, the King returned to the city. One evening he was invited to a drinking party at the home of Medius of Larisa. While drinking, he suddenly experienced a pain in his chest, 'as if he had been pierced by an arrow or a spear'. He soon returned to his own quarters and his health deteriorated steadily. Nevertheless, he slept, bathed and continued drinking, at least for a while. He developed a fever, which became more severe, and not long afterwards he began to lose the ability to speak. By the time the men had learned of his predicament, he was not longer able to address them, but could only make physical gestures of recognition. On 10 or 11 June 323, he was dead. He had not yet reached his thirty-third birthday.

The loss of a dearly loved king was bad enough, but the uncertainty of the future was increased by the fact that no provisions had been made for the succession and numerous controversial policies had been set in motion – the proclamation of the Exiles' Decree, which had a disruptive effect on the politics of the Greek world, and the orders that Craterus should relieve Antipater of his command in Europe. Grandiose and expensive plans had also been laid, both for the erection of monuments (e.g. the massive funeral pyre for Hephaestion) and for military expeditions. It soon became clear that, although the conquests had come to an end, the war was about to be prolonged; for the struggles between Alexander's marshals were destined to be more bitter and more destructive than those against the Persian enemy.

The Persian Queen Mother learns of Alexander's death

'The news quickly reached Darius' mother too. She ripped off the clothes she wore and assumed the dress of mourning; she tore her hair and flung herself to the ground. Next to her sat one of her granddaughters who was in mourning after the recent loss of her husband, Hephaestion, and the general anguish reminded her of her personal grief. But Sisygambis alone felt the woes that engulfed her entire family: she wept for her own plight and that of her granddaughters. The fresh pain had also reminded her of the past. One might have thought that Darius was recently lost and that at the same time the poor woman had to bury two sons. She wept simultaneously for the living and the dead. Who would look after her girls, she wondered? Who would be another Alexander? This meant a second captivity, a second loss of royal status. On the death of Darius they had found a protector, but after Alexander they would certainly not find someone to guard their interests.

... Finally, she surrendered to her sorrow. She covered her head, turned away from her granddaughter and grandson, who fell at her knees to plead with her, and withdrew simultaneously from nourishment and daylight. Five days after deciding on death, she expired.'
Quintus Curtius Rufus, *The History of Alexander* 10.5.19–22, 24 (J. C. Yardley trans., Penguin)

The Wars of the Successors (323–301 BC)

Alexander's death in Babylon caught the Macedonians off guard. In the army, the problem of the succession was foremost in the mind of commander and common soldier alike, but the difficulties were immense. Alexander had not designated an heir, nor were the troops clear on who should ascend the throne. Dynastic struggles were nothing new to the Macedonian state, but the situation in 323 was unique: there were no competent male adherents of the Argead house, and the marshals in Babylon were used to sharing the king's power but not to serving one another. The days that followed the king's death were thus consumed by the question of how to accommodate the aspirations of the marshals to the needs and stability of the new Empire. Alexander's widow, Roxane, was six to eight months pregnant, but the conservative soldiers were in no mood to await the birth or to acknowledge a king of mixed blood. For the same reason, they rejected Hercules, an illegitimate son of Alexander and Barsine, now in his fifth year and living in Pergamum. Only the king's half-brother, Arridaeus was untainted by barbarian blood, but he was afflicted with an incurable mental disorder. Therefore, it quickly became clear that whoever was chosen would need a guardian and the regency would have to be assumed by one of Alexander's marshals.

The matter was complicated by the fact that, for the first time, the Macedonians ruled an empire as opposed to a single kingdom. Hence, it was necessary to grapple with the consequences of Alexander's stunning success. Were the imperial head-quarters to remain in Pella, which many of the conquerors had not seen in over 12 years? Or would the new king reside in a more central location? Babylon, perhaps? Would distinctions be made between the administration of Europe and that of Asia? Indeed, what would be the role of the League of Corinth in relation to Alexander's spear-won empire?

An immediate concern was the position of Antipater in Europe. In 324 Alexander had sent Craterus with 10,000 discharged veterans to replace him as regent and to enforce the terms of the 'Exiles' Decree', which demanded of the Greek states that they restore the citizenship rights of their political exiles. However, at the time of Alexander's death Craterus had not advanced beyond Cilicia and the Greek states, threatened by the 'Exiles' Decree', were poised to make a bid for independence. Word of Alexander's death spread like wild-fire and the Greeks commenced hostilities by occupying the strategically vital pass of Thermopylae. Antipater, who hurried south to deal with the problem, found himself besieged in the Thessalian town of Lamia, with insufficient troops to suppress the uprising. Hence, he was compelled to summon reinforcements from Asia, where compromise solutions to the succession problem had been pre-empted by Perdiccas' usurpation.

Perdiccas' bid for power

The settlement at Babylon had recognised Arridaeus, who was renamed Philip III, as king and assigned the guardianship (prostasia) to Craterus. A concession was, however, made for Roxane's unborn child, which if male would be accepted as co-ruler (symbasileus). Now because Craterus was absent — from Cilicia he had eventually answered Antipater's call and returned to Macedonia – Perdiccas had little difficulty in assuming the regency for both Philip III and the infant Alexander IV. In the name of Philip III he assigned the administration of the satrapies of the empire to the most powerful generals and gained a free hand to consolidate his own power. With the royal army he moved into Cappadocia, which Alexander had left unconquered, defeating and crucifying its king, Ariarathes. His successes in the field were, however, blunted by the ineptitude of his policies. In an attempt to legitimize his power, Perdiccas sought the hand of Alexander's sister Cleopatra. She had married Alexander of Epirus in 336 but had now been a widow for some eight years. In order to bring about this union, he was forced to renege upon an earlier agreement to marry Nicaea, daughter of Antipater. Also, he had tried to conceal his duplicity until he could return to Macedonia, bringing with him the living members of Alexander's family and the very corpse of Alexander himself, destined for burial in the royal graveyard at Vergina.

Perdiccas' plans were, however, exposed by Antigonus the One-Eyed and thwarted by Ptolemy. The latter arranged for the funeral carriage to be escorted to Egypt, where the body of the conqueror would be taken to the oracle of Amun at Siwah, in accordance with Alexander's own dying wish. Antigonus, for his part, left his satrapy of Phrygia and sailed to Europe to inform Craterus and Antipater of Perdiccas' schemes. These two had only recently subdued the Greek states, with whom they had made peace individually; only the Aetolians remained, and it was from the protracted campaign against them that they were called away to Asia. Perdiccas had left Eumenes of Cardia with an army to guard against this eventuality while he himself marched on Egypt. Ostensibly, Ptolemy was guilty of executing Cleomenes of Naucratis, who had been designated as his lieutenant (hyparchos) in Egypt, but the true motive for the invasion was clear enough.

Ptolemy took refuge on the outskirts of Memphis, at a place called Kamelon Teichos (the Camels' Fort). In order to assail this place Perdiccas would need to ford a branch of the Nile, but the current was swift and the bottom treacherous; futhermore, the river was infested with crocodiles. Crossing with heavy losses the Perdiccan troops were insufficient to storm the walls and forced to retrace their steps. Demoralised and hostile to a leader whose arrogance seemed now to be balanced by incompetence, the leading men, including the future king, Seleucus, and Antigenes, commander of the Silver Shields (Argyraspids), murdered Perdiccas during the night.

Near the Hellespont, Eumenes conducted a more successful campaign: in successive battles he defeated and killed Neoptolemus (a former hypaspist commander) and Craterus. Antipater, with a portion of the army had slipped away in the direction of Cilicia. Eventually, he was united with the remnants of the royal army in northern Syria and a new distribution of power took place at Triparadeisus. However, the decisions made here simply provided the blueprint for another series of deadly encounters that ultimately weakened the empire.

The struggle between Antigonus and Eumenes

At Triparadeisus the army and its new leaders outlawed the Perdiccan faction, particularly Eumenes and Perdiccas' brother Alcetas, and entrusted military affairs to Antigonus the One-Eyed, now in his 60th year. At first, Antigonus managed to shut up Eumenes in the mountain fortress of Nora in Asia Minor while he himself turned his attention to Alcetas, whose army awaited him in Pisidia. At Cretopolis Antigonus won an overwhelming victory, capturing many of the Perdiccan officers; Alcetas himself escaped but soon committed suicide. As if to crown his victory, news reached Antigonus that Antipater had died of old age and entrusted the regency to Polyperchon, another of Alexander's generals. Polyperchon's authority was, however, challenged by Antipater's son, Cassander, and the struggle for power in Europe spilled over into Asia.

Cassander's sisters had married Lysimachus of Thrace, Ptolemy of Egypt and Demetrius, son of Antigonus. These marriage bonds formed the basis of a pact against Polyperchon in Macedonia and Eumenes in Asia. Polyperchon countered by lifting the death sentence on Eumenes and giving him authority to defend the interests of the 'Kings' in Asia. For this purpose, Eumenes was to enlist the services of the Silver Shields.

The Silver Shields had been crack infantrymen from the very beginning, serving as Alexander's hypaspists, soldiers chosen for their strength and courage rather than regional levies. Their officers too were selected on the basis of valour and the unit's name was changed in India to reflect the decoration of its arms and its untarnished record of service. By 318 they had been reduced to guard and escort duty, little knowing that their moment of fame, or rather infamy, was yet to come.

With the Silver Shields, Eumenes and the eastern satraps (with the notable exception of Seleucus and Peithon) withdrew toward the Iranian plateau. There followed in 317 two successive battles, at Paraitacene and Gabiene, that brought together roughly 70,000 men. Although neither could be termed decisive, at least not on the battlefield, the capture of the baggage train at Gabiene led to negotiations between the Silver Shields and Antigonus. The 'fighting seniors' had lost their families and their accumulated savings, as it were, and they were prepared to surrender their commander to win them back. Betrayed by his own men, Eumenes was led captive to the enemy camp where, some time later, he was strangled by his captors. The Silver Shields themselves were not unanimous in their action. Their leader, Antigenes, appears to have opposed the treachery, as did some of his men (who later paid a heavy price), and for this he was burned alive by the victor. His colleague, Teutamus, the architect of the treachery, was apparently rewarded by Antigonus but he too vanishes from the historical record.

In Europe, Cassander overcame the forces of Polyperchon and captured the surviving members of the royal family, including the ageing queen, Olympias, who was promptly

> *Fate of the Silver Shields*
> "Antigonus summoned from Arachosia Sibyrtius, who was well disposed towards him. He allowed him to keep his satrapy and assigned to him the most troublesome of the Silver Shields, in theory, so that they would be of use in war but, in reality, for the sake of their destruction; privately he instructed him to send a few of them at a time into such operations where they were bound to be killed."
> (Diodorus of Sicily 19.48.3)

murdered. In 315, he married Thessalonice, Alexander's half-sister, and set out on his own path to kingship. The coalition of Antigonus and Cassander appeared to have prevailed.

Failure of the Antigonids

The victory over Eumenes left Antigonus virtually unchallenged in Asia. The satraps of the Achaemenid heartland were deposed, executed or driven into exile. When they reappeared on the shores of the Mediterranean, Antigonus and his son Demetrius, who was beginning his military apprenticeship, were all but irresistible. However, success breeds fear and envy, and a new coalition of weaker players emerged as Cassander, Lysimachus, Ptolemy and Seleucus prepared to tackle the Antigonid juggernaut. Ptolemy indeed defeated the inexperienced Demetrius in the battle of Gaza in 312 and thus opened the door for Seleucus' recovery of Babylonia. However, in 307, Demetrius captured Athens when his fleet was mistaken for that of the friendly Ptolemy and, in the following year, the Ptolemaic navy was destroyed by the same fleet off the shores of Cyprus and the town of Salamis. With a well-coordinated spontaneity, the supporters of the Antigonids now proclaimed father and son 'kings'; for of the Macedonian royal house no male adherents remained. Philip III had been killed in 317, and Alexander IV and the illegitimate Heracles were murdered in 310 and 309 respectively. The regal aspirations of Antigonus and his son were thus fulfilled, but the empire of Alexander was not destined to be theirs. Instead, the move merely inspired others to follow suit. The disintegration of the empire into Hellenistic kingdoms had thus been formally inaugurated.

Demetrius now set his sights on Rhodes, where he conducted a spectacular siege in 305–304, thus gaining through failure the epithet that was to remain his for all time: the Besieger (Poliorketes). The size and ingenuity of his siege equipment was such that it elicited wonder, but in Demetrius there was often more showmanship than generalship. The failure of the Rhodian siege was the first of a series of setbacks that culminated in the battle of Ipsus in 301 BC. Here the forces of Lysimachus and Seleucus met the Antigonid army in a life-and-death struggle. Demetrius, commanding the cavalry, pushed too eagerly and too far in pursuit of his defeated opposite, Antiochus son of Seleucus, leaving the heavy infantry to be overwhelmed by the enemy. Antigonus died there, vainly expecting his son's return. For Demetrius it was a lesson in tactics and generalship, but for the Antigonid cause and for the integrity of Alexander's empire, it was fatal.

Late 4th-century Macedonian silver tetradrachm showing
Alexander the Great dressed as the Greek hero
Heracles. He is portrayed wearing Heracles' lion skin.
(Ashmolean Museum, Oxford)

Conclusion and consequences

The wars of Alexander had resulted in the conquest of an empire and the imposition of a Graeco-Macedonian ruling class upon a diverse population that had hitherto been united under Persian control. Greek was now to replace Aramaic as the official written language of the east, although local tongues would endure – just as regional culture and religion would not be wiped out by the mere change of rulers. However, the success of the expedition must be measured by the effectiveness of the process of consolidation rather than the speed of conquest. In fact, the Macedonian conquest was far from complete, as some areas were only partially subdued and others bypassed intentionally in a bid to come to grips with the Persian king and to strike at the nerve-centres of the Achaemenid empire. Pockets of independent or recalcitrant states remained throughout the east. Pisidia, Cappadocia, Armenia are notable examples from the northwestern region and the Uxians, who had collected payment from the Persians who crossed their territories – like the hongo demanded by African tribes of European explorers and Arab caravans – and who had been chased from the invasion route by Alexander, were again asserting their independence in the age of the Successors.

Hence the Diadochoi, starting from a position of disadvantage and weakness, could scarcely be expected to succeed. Posterity remembers them as lesser men who jeopardized the whole for the sake of individual gain, whose pettiness and personal rivalries squandered all that Alexander had won and sacrificed countless lives in the process. This verdict is unfair. Premature death had saved Alexander's reputation, ensuring his greatness. His generals were left to clean up the mess, to attempt to consolidate the conquered empire, without

enjoying any of the authority of the man who had created it.

Perdiccas, Antigonus, Demetrius and even Ptolemy had at various times made bids for greater power, but the end was always the same. In the aftermath of Ipsus, Ptolemy alone was content to limit his ambitions, restricting his activities to the eastern Mediterranean, particularly Cyprus and Hollow Syria to the north and Cyrene to the west. In the late 280s dynastic disturbances in the house of Lysimachus led to war with Seleucus, who had gained control of most of Alexander's Asiatic satrapies, which he administered from

Ptolemy, son of Lagus, ruler of Egypt
Ptolemy is perhaps one of the best known of Alexander's commanders to the modern reader. Nevertheless, in 323 BC he was far from being the most noble, influential or most accomplished of the king's marshals. Born in the 360s, he was older than many of the other young generals and he may not have held his first command until late 331 (at the Persian Gates); if so, he was what we would call a 'late bloomer'. During the campaigns in what are now Afghanistan and Pakistan, he came into his own as a military commander; he had also been a member of the Bodyguard since 330. When Alexander died, he received the satrapy of Egypt, which he fortified and put on a sound administrative and economic footing. Thereafter it was impossible to dislodge him, and he ruled there until 283, sharing the throne with his son, Philadelphus, in the period 285–283. At some point, he wrote a *History of Alexander*, which is now lost.

the dual capitals of Antioch on the Orontas and Seleuceia on the Tigris. Lysimachus died on the battlefield of Corupedium (282/1) and his conqueror Seleucus crossed the Hellespont to occupy Lysimacheia on the Gallipoli peninsula. He was, however, struck down by an opportunistic and ungrateful son of Ptolemy Soter known to posterity simply as Ceraunus ('The Thunderbolt'). Then it was that the Successor kingdoms came to be ruled by the offspring of the conquerors: the Hellenistic kingdoms had been formed.

The Antigonids (descendants of Antigonus the One-Eyed and Demetrius the Besieger) ruled Macedon and dominated the affairs of the south by garrisoning the so-called Fetters of Greece – Demetrias (near modern Volos), Chalcis and Acrocorinth. In 197, at Cynoscephalae, Philip V was defeated by the Romans in what is called the Second Macedonian War; a Third Macedonian War, in which Philip's son Perseus succumbed to the army of L. Aemilius Paullus, effectively brought Antigonid rule to an end.

In Egypt the Ptolemaic dynasty enjoyed a period of prosperity in the third century, especially under its 'Sun-King', Ptolemy II Philadelphus, but by the late second century it was in decline and threatening to destroy itself from within. An unpopular and weak ruler, dubbed Auletes ('the Flute-Player') by the Alexandrians, survived only with Roman aid, as did his daughter, Cleopatra VII, who linked her fortunes first to Julius Caesar, then to Mark Antony, and thus attained a measure of greatness. Ultimately, however, these associations brought her infamy and the destruction of her kingdom.

The most extensive and diverse territory, that is, the bulk of Alexander's empire, was ruled by the descendants of Seleucus Nicator. Already in his reign, the eastern satrapies were ceded to Chandragupta. In the time of his successor, Antiochus I, the Galatians entered Asia Minor and settled around modern Ankarra, posing a threat to the Hellenes of Asia Minor who gradually turned towards the dynasts of Pergamum. The third man of this line, Attalus I, gave his name to the dynasty, which sought the friendship of Rome as a means of protecting itself from the Antigonids in the west and the Seleucids in the east. There were indeed short-term advantages but, in the long run, Roman protection entailed loss of freedom in matters of foreign policy. In 133, when Attalus III died, he left his kingdom to the Romans, who converted it into the province of Asia.

The Seleucids themselves had been crippled by the War of the Brothers in the second half of the third century. A brief reassertion of Seleucid power under Antiochus III proved ephemeral; for in 189, that king met with decisive defeat at the hands of the Romans. The subsequent Peace of Apamea deprived the Seleucids of their lands west of the Taurus Mountains and imposed a huge indemnity upon them. From this point onward, it was a story of steady decline. Pressured by the Parthians in the east and threatened by a revived Ptolemaic kingdom to the south, the Seleucids embarked upon a series of civil wars between rival claimants to the throne. By the middle of the first century, they had ceased to exist, having been crushed by the competing forces of Roman imperialism, Parthian expansion and Jewish nationalism.

Glossary

agema: the elite guard of the cavalry or the hypaspists.

archon: a senior magistrate (literally, 'one who is first', 'one who leads'). Philip II and Alexander were archons of the Thessalian League.

baivarpatish: (Persian) commander of 10,000, i.e. a myriarch.

chiliarch: commander of a thousand. Also the Persian *hazarapatish*, who could be either commander of a thousand or the most powerful court official.

Delian League: A confederacy of Greek states, mainly maritime, organised by the Athenians in 478/7 (after the Persian invasion of Xerxes was repelled). The League had its headquarters on the island of Delos (hence the name) and its members paid an annual tribute called *phoros*, which was collected by officials known as *hellenotamiai* ('stewards of the Greeks'). Within a generation the League had been converted into an Athenian Empire.

Doryphoroe: (literally, 'spear-bearers') the bodyguard associated with kings and tyrants.

gazophylax: a Persian treasurer or rather guardian of the treasures.

hazarapatish: commander of a thousand. Equivalent of the Greek chiliarch.

hipparch: a cavalry commander, i.e. a commander of a hipparchy.

hoplite: heavily armed Greek infantryman. The hoplite carried a circular shield, wore a cuirass (breast-plate), a helmet which gave additional protection to nose and cheeks, and (normally, but not always) greaves. To be effective the hoplite had to fight in formation, since the overlap of the shields protected the exposed right side of the warrior. The spear became a thrusting weapon rather than a javelin.

hypaspists: (literally, 'shield-bearers') the infantry guard of the Macedonian king. Often they formed a link between the *pezhetairoi* and cavalry in the Macedonian line.

ilarches: commander of a squadron (*ile*) of cavalry.

ile: see **ilarches**.

ile basilike: the Royal Squadron. This fought in the immediate vicinity of the king as a mounted bodyguard. Cleitus the Black was its commander.

Medism: the Greek term for collaboration with the Persians. Medising was symbolised in the late sixth and early fifth centuries by the giving of 'earth and water' to the Persian King, but any form of friendly intercourse with Persia could give rise to the charge of Medism.

melophoroi: (literally, 'apple-bearers') Persian guards, distinguished by apple-shaped spearbutts.

myriarch: commander of 10,000 = Persian baivarpatish.

Oath of Plataea: according to the historian Herodotus, the Greek allies swore an oath before the battle of Plataea in 479 to punish Medisers, especially the Thebes, with destruction, enslavement and confiscation of property, with a tithe from the proceeds to be paid to the god Apollo.

Peloponnese: the southern part of European Greece, south of the Gulf and the Isthmus of Corinth.

Peloponnesian League: A league of states, mainly but not exclusively (it included the Boiotians) from the Peloponnesus, which was controlled by its military leader (*hegemon*) Sparta. Unlike the Delian League, it had no compulsory, fixed payments.

pezhetairoi: the 'foot-companions', the Macedonian heavy infantry.

proskynesis: the Persian practice of doing obeisance to their king. It involves bowing and blowing a kiss. The extent of the debasement depends on the status of the individual.

Pythia: the priestess of the god Apollo at Delphi.

Sacred Band: A Theban unit constituted in the fourth century under the leadership of Gorgidas, it comprised 150 pairs of lovers, in the belief that these would fight more valiantly for each other. It was instrumental in Thebes' major victory at Leuctra (371). The unit was destroyed at Chaeronea (338).

sarissa: (sometimes spelled 'sarisa') the Macedonian lance, normally about 15–18ft (4.5–5.5m) for infantrymen and perhaps 14ft (4.25m) for cavalry. In the post-Alexander period it seems to have become longer.

sarissophoroi: (literally 'sarissa-bearers') cavalrymen who were armed with the *sarissa*.

satrap: governor of a Persian province or satrapy. The Median name *khshathrapavan* means 'Protector of the Realm'.

satrapy: see **satrap**.

Somatophylakes: the seven Bodyguards of the Macedonian king.

taxiarch: a brigade (though some writers call the *taxis* a battalion) commander.

taxis: see **taxiarch**.

Thessalian League: a political union of the cities of Thessaly, which was normally under the leadership of one of its chief cities, either Pherae or Larisa. Its chief magistrate was originally known as a *tagus*, but later the name was changed to *archon*.

Trireme: A warship with three banks of oars (with one man per oar). The type seems to have originated in Phoenicia but was adopted and perfected by the Greeks. The normal complement of the trireme was 200 men.

xyston: the cavalryman's spear.

Further reading

Primary sources

Arrian, *The Campaigns of Alexander*, translated by A. de Sélincourt, with notes by J. R. Hamilton, Penguin Classics, Harmondsworth, 1971.

Dillon, M. and Garland, L., *Ancient Greece: Social and Historical Documents from Archaic Times to the Death of Socrates*, London, 1994.

Diodorus of Sicily, translated and edited by C. Bradford Welles, Loeb Classical Library, vol. VIII, Cambridge, Massachusetts, 1963.

Fornara, C. W. (ed.), *From Archaic Times to the End of the Peloponnesian War: Translated Documents of Greece and Rome*, vol I, Cambridge, Cambridge University Press, 1983.

Herodotus, *The Histories*, translated by George Rawlinson, Introduction by Hugh Bowden, Everyman's Library, London, 1992.

Justin, *Epitome of the Philippic History of Pompeius Trogus*, Books 11–12: *Alexander the Great*, translated by J. C. Yardley, with commentary by Waldemar Heckel, Clarendon Ancient History Series, Oxford, 1997.

The Persian Empire from Cyrus II to Artaxerxes I, translated and edited by Maria Brosius, London Association of Classical Teachers – Original Records Series LACTOR 16, 2000.

Plutarch, *The Age of Alexander*, translated by Ian Scott-Kilvert, Penguin Classics, Harmondsworth, 1973.

Plutarch, *The Rise and Fall of Athens: Nine Greek Lives*, translated by Ian Scott-Kilvert, London, 1960.

Quintus Curtius Rufus, *The History of Alexander*, translated by J. C. Yardley, with introduction and notes by Waldemar Heckel, Penguin Classics, Harmondsworth, 1984.

Thucydides, *The Peloponnesian War*, translated by Rex Warner, revised by M. I. Finley, London, Penguin, 1972.

Xenophon, *A History of My Times*, translated by Rex Warner, introduction and notes by G. Cawkwell, London, Penguin, 1979.

Secondary sources

Berve, H., *Das Alexanderreich auf prosopographischer Grundlage*, 2 vols, Munich, 1926.

Boardman, J., Hammond, N., Lewis, D., Ostwald, M. (eds), *The Cambridge Ancient History Volume 4: Persia, Greece and the Western Mediterranean c. 525 to 479 BC*, 2nd edition, Cambridge, 1988.

Borza, E. N., *In the Shadow of Macedon: The Emergence of Macedon*, Princeton, New Jersey, 1990.

Bosworth, A. B., *Conquest and Empire: The Reign of Alexander the Great*, Cambridge, 1988.

Bosworth, A. B., *Alexander and the East: The Tragedy of Triumph*, Oxford, 1996.

Bosworth, A. B. and Baynham, E. J. (eds), *Alexander the Great in Fact and Fiction*, Oxford, 2000.

Bradford, E., *Thermopylae: The Battle for the West*, Da Capo Press, 1993.

Briant, P., *L'Empire Perse de Cyre à Alexandre*, Paris, 1996.

Burn, A. R., *Persia and the Greeks. The Defence of the West c. 546–478 BC*, London, 1962; new edition with afterword by David Lewis, 1984.

Carney, E. D., *Women and Monarchy in Ancient Macedonia*, Norman, Oklahoma, 2000.

Cartledge, P., *Spartan Reflections*, London, 2000.

Cartledge, P., *The Spartans: An Epic History*, Channel 4 Books, 2002.

Cook, J. M., *The Persian Empire*, New York, 1983.

Engels, D.W., *Alexander the Great and the Logistics of the Macedonian Army*, Berkeley, California, 1978.

Errington, R. M., *A History of Macedonia*, translated by Catherine Errington, Berkeley, California, 1990.

Fuller, J. F. C., *The Generalship of Alexander the Great*, New York, 1960.

Green, P., *Armada from Athens: The Failure of the Sicilian Expedition 415–413 BC*, London, 1970.

Green, P., *Alexander of Macedon, 356–323 BC: A Historical Biography*, London, 1970; repr. Berkeley, California, 1991.

Green, P., *The Year of Salamis 480–479 BC*, London, 1970; revised edition entitled, *The Greco-Persian Wars*, Berkeley and Los Angeles, 1996.

Hammond, N. G. L., *The Genius of Alexander the Great*, Chapel Hill, North Carolina, 1997.

Hanson, V. D., *The Western Way of War: Infantry Battle in Classical Greece*, Oxford, 1989.

Hanson, V. D., *The Wars of the Ancient Greeks*, London, 1999.

Heckel, W., *The Last Days and Testament of Alexander the Great: A Prosopographic Study*, Historia Einzelschriften, Heft 56, Stuttgart, 1988.

Heckel, W., *The Marshals of Alexander's Empire*, London, 1992.

Holt, F. L., *Alexander the Great and Bactria*, Leiden, 1988.

Hornblower, S., *The Greek World 479–323 BC*, Routledge, 2001.

Kagan, D., *The Outbreak of the Peloponnesian War*, New York, 1969.

Kagan, D., *The Archidamian War*, New York, 1974.

Kagan, D., *The Peace of Nicias and the Sicilian Expedition*, New York, 1981.

Kagan, D., *The Fall of the Athenian Empire*, New York, 1987.

Kagan, D., *The Peloponnesian War: Athens and Sparta in Savage Conflict 431–404 BC*, HarperCollins, 2003.

Kuhrt, A., *The Ancient Near East c. 3000–330 BC*, Volume Two, London 1995.

Lane Fox, R., *Alexander the Great*, London, 1973.

Lazenby, J., *The Spartan Army*, Warminster, 1985.

Lazenby, J., *The Defence of Greece 490–479 BC*, Warminster, 1993.

Marsden, E. W., *The Campaign of Gaugamela*, Liverpool, 1964.

Olmstead, A. T., *History of the Persian Empire*, Chicago, 1948.

Pearson, L., *The Lost Histories of Alexander the Great*, New York, 1960.

Powell, A., *Athens and Sparta: Constructing Greek Political and Social History from 478 BC*, Routledge, 2001.

Roisman, J. (ed.), *Alexander the Great: Ancient and Modern Perspectives*, Lexington, Massachusetts, 1995.

Sealey, R., *A History of the Greek City States 700–338 BC*, Berkely, University of California Press, 1976.

Sekunda. N., and A. McBride, *The Ancient Greeks*, Elite 7, London, 1986.

Sekunda, N. and Chew, S., *The Persian Army 560–330 BC*, Elite 42, Oxford, 1992.

Spence, I., *The Cavalry of Classical Greece: A Social and Military History with Particular Reference to Athens*, Oxford, 1993.

Stainte Croix, G. de, *The Origins of the Peloponnesian War*, London, 1972.

Stein, A., *On Alexander's Track to the Indus*, London, 1929.

Stewart, A., *Faces of Power: Alexander's Image and Hellenistic Politics*, Berkeley, California, 1993.

Stoneman, R., *Alexander the Great*, Lancaster Pamphlets, London, 1997.

Todd, S. C., *Athens and Sparta*, Bristol Classical Press, 1996.

Warry, J., *Alexander 334–323 BC: Conquest of the Persian Empire*, Campaign 7, Oxford, 1991.

Wilcken, U., *Alexander the Great*, with notes and bibliography by E. N. Borza, New York, 1967.

Wood, M., *In the Footsteps of Alexander the Great*, Berkeley, California, 1997.

The Greeks at war on screen
by Lloyd Llewellyn-Jones

From its earliest conception, cinema has been fascinated with history, particularly the military achievements of classical antiquity. Even in its silent, pioneering period (1907–1928), film was able to capture massive and spectacular events in outdoor locations, as hundreds of armoured extras swarmed over gigantic sets and began to fill the screen with recreations of epic battles and great disasters.

Roman history naturally offered itself as a vehicle to filmmakers, with its narrative stories of Christian heroism and larger-than-life characters (Caligula and Nero being especially popular) who were so well known to cinema audiences, that they could fully appreciate a director's skill in adapting Roman history to an exciting new visual medium. During Hollywood's Golden Age (1930–1964), and with movies like *Quo Vadis* (1951; director Mervyn LeRoy), *The Robe* (1953; director Henry Koster) and *The Fall of the Roman Empire* (1964; director Anthony Mann), bloody battles, the fall of cities, the decimation of tribes, and the deeds of great generals became the standard fare of Hollywood big-budget filmmaking. The re-emergence of the 'sword and sandal epic' with Ridley Scott's *Gladiator* (2000) has clearly heralded a new age of epic films.

However, while Rome has most frequently featured in the cinema in historical narratives, Greece is more likely to be a setting for mythological narratives, for instance in the popular 'peplum films' of the 1950s and 1960s, featuring heroes like Hercules, Perseus and Jason, or in adaptations of ancient Athenian drama or Homeric and Hellenistic epics. While cinematic retellings of Homeric stories have been created for the screen (both big and small) – *Helen of Troy* (1956; director

Robert Wise and 2003; director John Kent Harrison), *The Odyssey* (1997; director Andrei Konchalovsky) and, most recently, *Troy* (2004; director Wolfgang Petersen) – these films fall more easily into the genre of fantasy movies than historical dramas. The battle and fight sequences of these fantasy films, often with their reliance on animated action, while containing the essence of realism, are properly regarded as fantastically heroic as is fitting for Homeric re-workings. The films of master-animator Ray Harryhausen – *Jason and the Argonauts* (1963; director John Chaffey) and *The Clash of the Titans* (1981; director Desmond Davis) – are perfect realisations of the cinematic blend of 'real' and 'fantastical'.

There are surprisingly few filmic accounts of ancient Greek military history, despite the obvious dramatic and visual potential for the subject. There are, however, two films set during the Persian invasions of Greece, 490–479 BC. One, the decidedly B-movie Italian-made peplum-film, *The Giant of Marathon* (1959; director Jacques Tourneur) sees American muscleman Steve Reeves as Pheidippides running the 26 miles from Marathon to Athens on the orders of Miltiades, as the Persian forces conquer Athens by sea and land. Of course, the story as recounted by Herodotus (*Histories* 6.105) sees Pheidippides collapse and die after his marathon feat, but in the film Steve Reeves (short of breath, admittedly) lives to get the girl – a beauty named Andromeda – and see the repulsion of enemy forces from the Greek homeland.

The film is a light confection of romance, muscles, and a bizarrely contorted version of history. Nevertheless, the naval battle sequence, with underwater photography, at the climax of the film is engaging. It shows a Persian ship with a jaw-like prow mash and pound any Greek ships that come within its grip.

Far more worthy of note is *The 300 Spartans* (1962; director Rudolph Mate), a film portraying an unforgettable battle during the Persian Wars – the heroic Spartan defence of the pass of Thermopylae and the eventual annihilation of the small Spartan force by the Persians in 480 BC. The concentration on this one heroic event – the remarkable climax of the film – enabled Mate to focus his script and his directing skills on a character-led story, which operates around three main players: Themistocles, the cunning Athenian admiral-politician (Ralph Richardson); Xerxes, the megalomaniac Persian King (David Farrar); and Leonidas, the heroic king of Sparta (Richard Egan).

The script by George St. George, draws heavily and faithfully on Herodotus' outline of events, and some character's lines are even lifted straight from the pages of the *Histories* itself. The battle scenes are thrilling: towards the beginning of the film, for instance, the Persian general Hydarnes warns Leonidas that Persian arrows will 'blot out the sun', and, indeed, this is exactly what Mate delivers for his audience. When Leonidas falls in his heroic watch over Thermopylae, his Spartan fighters are surrounded by so many Persian archers – part of antiquity's largest-ever army – that their arrows actually do blot out the sun as the red-cloaked Spartans die in droves.

The visual impact of the movie is tremendous. Filmed in CinemaScope, with a reliance on panning shots to capture the sweep of the scenery, the screen is populated by hundreds of extras, recruited in the main from the Greek National Army. Mate skilfully uses the camera to highlight the regimental and disciplined nature of the Spartan war machine: he shoots his lens at a sharp angle of the soldiers in battle formation, highlighting the line of spears and swords.

In action, Mate creates one of the most authentic battle scenes ever put on the screen. The battle comes in three parts, beginning with the Spartans encircling

the Persians with a ring of fire; next they encroach towards Xerxes' troops with a phalanx of hoplites, before finally breaking through the Persian defence.

The design contrast between the humble red-cloaked Spartans and the elaborate robes of Xerxes' 'Immortals' (his bodyguard) is particularly noticeable. The other Persian troops are less splendid, as they carry wicker shields and wear distinctive conical helmets, but their black robes create a striking contrast to the red cloaks of Leonidas and his men. Certainly, the ancient Greek contempt for Persian decadence and their love of luxury is particularly evident in the film: Xerxes is a cowardly tyrant (David Farrar's precise English accent is used to great effect to contrast with Richard Egan's wholesome American speech). Moreover, he is ill-disciplined and lascivious, and he is depicted debauching the beautiful female admiral, Artemisia of Halicarnassus (one of only a handful of female characters in the film).

Xerxes' campaign tent (later captured after Marathon) is an amazing concoction of elaborate embroidered hangings and tasselled silk swathes. Within its confines he sits on a marble throne and listens to the frantic acclamation of his rule by his troops. The king's costumes too – from his high mitra (crown) to his curled-toed boots – become symbols for Persian decadence.

Sitting on his throne, Xerxes pronounces that upon capturing his Spartan foes he will place them in cages and exhibit them all over his empire. Mate does not let the irony pass his audience by: we understands that even though the Spartans lose the battle, the Greeks ultimately win the war and that Xerxes' threats are hollow indeed. *The 300 Spartans* enables the cinema audience to revel in hindsight, knowing that the legendary Lacedaemonian sacrifice was not performed in vain.

Hollywood has twice turned its attention to the life and military career of Alexander III of Macedon, with differing degrees of critical and popular success. *Alexander the Great* (1955; director Robert Rossen) is generally regarded as one of the most historically accurate ancient-world movies. Produced, directed, and written by the Oscar-winning Rossen, *Alexander the Great* does not follow the usual sword-and-sandal treatment of ancient figures by glorifying them as individuals or romanticising their many exploits. For example, the burning of Persepolis, the Persian capital city, on Alexander's command, is seen by Rossen for what it was: an act of barbaric vandalism. But then, Rossen's Alexander (Richard Burton) is a deeply flawed individual. Over-protected by his mother Olympias (Danielle Darrieaux) and dominated by his aloof father, Philip II (Fredric March – in a brilliant portrayal), Rossen allows the family tensions between these three ambitious individuals to permeate the film at every level. Even after Philip II is killed, his memory (and March's remarkable characterisation) continues to haunt Alexander.

Yet for all its integrity (and its three years in the making), *Alexander the Great* is a dull film, made overlong by laboriously tracing Alexander's campaigns in brief battle montages which do not satisfy the viewers' thirst for engagement with the on-screen action or for the characters themselves. The Battle of Granicus, for example (actually shot by the Jarama river in Spain), is little more than a series of brief shots showing Alexander's river-charge, although some spectacle is provided by 6,000 costumed extras. More successful are the panning shots of the Macedonian sarissa-bearers, which brilliantly capture the brute force and extraordinary innovatory character of the Macedonian army.

There is a certain 1950s naiveté in the direction of *Alexander the Great*. Rossen, for instance, uses the clichéd technique of displaying an on-screen map of the ancient world onto which Alexander's campaigns are plotted with animated lines. Brief battle sequences break through this map image and then dissipate as Alexander's conquests are reconfirmed in front of the audiences' eyes: first Asia Minor, then Egypt, then Babylon and finally Persia. Even so, this does not allow the audience to engage with the battles; they sit detached from the action. Ultimately, Rossen's film has the feel of being a $4,000,000 history lecture, but not an award-winning movie.

Not so Oliver Stone's remarkable 2004 telling of the life of Alexander the Great. A veteran of both war movies (*Platoon*; 1986 and *Heaven and Earth*; 1993) and conspiracy-theory films (*JFK*; 1991 and *Nixon*; 1995), as a director Stone was perfectly in tune with Alexander's story. Working closely with the Alexander historian Robin Lane Fox, he crafted a script and a movie that completely concentrates on the exploits of Alexander (Colin Farrell) and his relationships with people who surrounded him, but particularly Olympias (Angelina Jolie), Philip II (Val Kilmer), and his Bactrian bride Roxane (Rosario Dawson). Most noticeably for a big-budget Hollywood blockbuster, *Alexander* does not shy away from the protagonist's homosexual relationships with either his lifelong companion Hephaestion (Jared Leto) or the beautiful young eunuch, Bagoas (Francisco Bosch).

Told through the viewpoint of Alexander's general, and later Egyptian pharaoh, Ptolemy (Anthony Hopkins), the story flits back and forth between Alexander's death-bed in Babylon, his childhood in Pella, his campaigns in the Middle East, and his unsuccessful military foray into India. Never losing sight of the main thrust of the narrative, nor of the characters themselves, Stone chooses to depict only two events from Alexander's complex military career, but he imbues his battle scenes with such vitality, energy and focus, that they stand as testimony to Alexander's brilliance in warfare and to the bloody nature of conflict in this period.

The film's first battle sequence is the truly epic recreation of the battle of Gaugamela. Shot over a three-week period on a vast open plain near Marrakech in Morocco, the Gaugamela battle sequence employs 2,000 extras, costumed variously as Macedonians, Persians and an assortment of mercenary forces – Bactrians, Sogdians, Ethiopians, Greeks and Babylonians. The Macedonian force is shown advancing with sarrisae as, first, the Persian archers and then the elite chariot corps attempt to break the ranks and scatter their forces. The splendidly dressed Shah, Darius III (Raz Degan), and the seven noblemen companions of his court are depicted watching the battle from afar, but later they join in hand-to-hand combat from their horses and from the royal chariot, resembling the scene depicted in the famous Alexander Mosaic from the House of the Faun in Pompeii.

As massive as this on-screen battle is, its glory is dwarfed at the climax of the film by scenes in which Alexander confronts King Porus, during his invasion of India in 325 BC.

The scenes were actually shot in Lopburi province, 70 miles north of Bangkok, Thailand, which stood in for both India and the Hindu Kush. Here Oliver Stone assembled 20 armour-clad Thai elephants, which, together with more digitally created elephants, formed the backbone of the Indian army's cavalry. The scenes show the attack on the elephants by the Macedonians, led by Antigonus (Ian Beattie). For their part, the elephants are shown running at full speed at the Macedonian battalion, grabbing spears out of soldiers' hands, knocking over trees, and causing general chaos amid the Macedonian ranks. A one point an elephant is gutted by a lance, while yet another has its trunk sliced off by a Macedonian sword, causing it to erupt in a fit of pained fury and run amok through the Indian lines. An Indian prince is shown throwing spears from atop an elephant and another elephant is depicted stomping on one unfortunate soldier's head, causing his skull to crack in half.

Such realism is unparalleled in Hollywood filmmaking and displays how audience tastes and expectations have developed. During the 1950s and early 1960s, audiences wanted sweeping stories of heroism and great courage, and films like *The 300 Spartans* and *Alexander the Great* provided them with unchallenging, if somewhat romanticised, images of the past. The battle sequences in these films, though skilfully choreographed and expertly shot, remained somewhat antiseptic visions of ancient warfare. The bloodshed and the true suffering of war is whitewashed with a more glamorous vision of a courageous world of combat, where heroic forces attempt to defeat tyranny and oppression.

Throughout the post-war period, Britain and America had to come to terms with new dangers, especially the threat of aggression from the Eastern block Communist regimes and their allies; it is no surprise, therefore, that the threats to democracy and western civilisation are represented in all the films examined here by a danger from Persia – the enemy in the East. Having lived through the horrors of World War II and the uncertainties of a post-war nuclear world, cinema-goers of the 1950s and 1960s no doubt looked for a more chivalrous take on warfare and wanted to see stories of heroism and glory in contrast to the grim realities of war and its aftermath experienced by many people at the time.

In the opening years of the 21st-century, cinema-goers have different expectations. While a new threat from the East is reputedly a cause of concern for most western audiences, they have become familiar with, or even desensitised by, television news reports of war, terrorism, and other acts of wanton carnage. Modern audiences require their cinema screens to echo the realities of violence found in today's global village. Screen images of warfare are expected to have a documentary-like candour, and are required to show battle in grim detail. The trend in depicting realistic war violence began in earnest with *Saving Private Ryan* (1998; director Steven Spielberg), but the drift has even permeated fantasy movies like *The Lord of the Rings* trilogy (2001–2003; director Peter Jackson) which, despite its make-believe storyline and characters, has elevated cinematic war brutality to an art form.

Unsurprisingly, therefore, *Alexander* and *Troy* have received much notice for the graphic battle sequences and scenes of violent death that have been employed. While some critics have condemned the bloodshed as unnecessary and overindulgent, it is fair to argue that such scenes serve a purpose: they remind us of the proper experience of war. Wars have their heroes, and they can have brilliant strategies; sometimes even the cause of war might even be justified. Yet the fact remains, in battle people die and suffer.

In the past, cinema has had a tendency to sweep the human reality of war to one side, especially when dealing with a period of ancient history so well known for its feats of heroism. But this new wave of epic realism in cinema reminds us that in antiquity warfare was a bloody business.

Index

Essential Histories Specials

The Greeks at War: From Athens to Alexander is part of Osprey Publishing's Essential Histories Specials series.

Essential Histories Specials cover the world's most significant periods of conflict, drawing together the strategic, tactical, social, political and cultural aspects of each major war in a single volume.

If you enjoyed *The Greeks at War: From Athens to Alexander*, then look out for the following Essential Histories Specials, available from all good bookstores or direct from Osprey Publishing.

Essential Histories Specials contain material from individual volumes in the Essential Histories series. See next page for more information about this series.

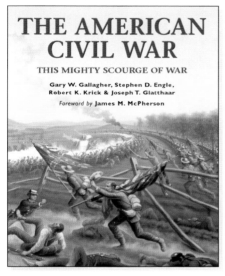

ISBN 1 84176 736 0

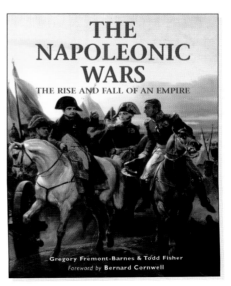

ISBN 1 84176 738 7

ISBN 1 84176 830 8

ISBN 1 84176 831 6

About Essential Histories

A multi-volume history of war seen from political, strategic, tactical, cultural and individual perspectives

- Each Essential Histories volume provides a guide to a major war or arena of war: the origins, the key players, how the war was fought, who fought it, and its lasting impact on the world around it.

- Written by leading historians from around the world and illustrated with photographs and maps.

- Each volume follows the same clear and accessible structure:

  Introduction – Chronology – Background to war – Warring sides – Outbreak – The fighting – Portrait of a soldier – The world around war – Portrait of a civilian – How the war ended – Conclusion and consequences – Index

Praise for Essential Histories

'if you want a full narrative of the high politics that led to the Norman invasion, or the details of William's campaigns in England after Hastings, then this is the place to come.' (Essential Histories: *Campaigns of the Norman Conquest*) *Times Educational Supplement*

' …these volumes provide a lucid and concise narrative of the campaigns … as well as penetrating analyses of strategies and leadership. Ideal for classroom use or fireside reading.' *James M McPherson, Pulitzer Prize winner*, commenting on the American Civil War books

'clear and concise' *History Today*

'an excellent series' *Military Illustrated*

'very useful, factual and educational' *Reference Reviews*

'accessible and well illustrated…' *Daily Express*

'they make the perfect starting point for readers of any age' *Daily Mail*

* Material from Essential Histories 27, 36 and 26 is replicated in this book.